W9-BHE-481

CAMBRIDGE STUDIES IN ECONOMIC HISTORY
PUBLISHED WITH THE AID OF THE ELLEN McARTHUR FUND

GENERAL EDITOR
M. M. POSTAN
Professor of Economic History in the University of Cambridge

INDUSTRIAL GROWTH AND
POPULATION CHANGE

INDUSTRIAL GROWTH
AND
POPULATION CHANGE

A REGIONAL STUDY OF THE
COALFIELD AREAS OF NORTH-WEST EUROPE
IN THE LATER NINETEENTH CENTURY

BY

E. A. WRIGLEY

CAMBRIDGE
AT THE UNIVERSITY PRESS
1962

PUBLISHED BY

THE SYNDICS OF THE CAMBRIDGE UNIVERSITY PRESS

Bentley House, 200 Euston Road, London, N.W. 1

American Branch: 32 East 57th Street, New York 22, N.Y.

West African Office: P.O. Box 33, Ibadan, Nigeria

©

CAMBRIDGE UNIVERSITY PRESS

1961

First printed 1961
Reprinted 1962

Printed in Great Britain
LATIMER, TREND AND CO. LTD.
Plymouth

TO MY MOTHER

CONTENTS

PREFACE

The attempt to elucidate economic change and growth has drawn economic historians into a very wide range of studies. There are histories of invention and technological change; there are studies of credit and banking;
attempts to make use of economic models to explain cyclical fluctuation
and secular change; accounts of the fortunes of individual industries, firms
and businessmen; discussions of the relation between sociological changes
in society and changes in the forms or climate of economic activity; and,
of course, innumerable studies which either do not fit into any of these
categories or stretch across several of them. Some attack the problems of
economic change and growth directly; others by implication; others
again are content with autonomous studies of more modest scope. This
book is about industrial growth, population changes, and demographic
history.

These subjects have received extensive historical and theoretical treatment in the past and are again popular at the present time. They connote,
however, a wide range of subject matter and types of analysis, and it
seems useful, therefore, to begin by sketching in the form and content of
this study, in order to make its inclusions and omissions intelligible.

The form of the book has been governed by one prime consideration: a
belief in the fruitfulness of regional analysis of economic and demographic
material. It is, indeed, essentially an essay in technique, arising from a
conviction that the tendency, deep-seated in most students of society, and
perhaps especially in historians, to think in terms of national areas as the
natural units for study, may be a severe handicap to the understanding of
some aspects of economic growth and demographic conditions. Neither
the similarities across national frontiers, nor the dissimilarities within them
are always given sufficient attention. The study of them helps to put out of
court arguments which it is otherwise difficult to disprove, and to establish
others easily overlooked.

Within this context the two chief subjects studied are the relationship
between industrial development and the growth of population, and the
demographic history which was associated with the population growth.
The area and period covered were both chosen to make possible extensive
use of regional analysis.

During the second half of the nineteenth century the introduction of
the new industrial techniques developed earlier in England transformed
the economic life of the coalfield belt which stretches almost without

interruption from Pas-de-Calais in the west to the Ruhr in the east. Since the area extends into three countries with very different national economic histories, it is a good test of the usefulness of regional analysis. If it can be shown that some of the developments which took place in each part of the coalfield area can better be understood in relation to the common experience of the coalfield area as a whole than in relation to the individual national economies, then the aim of one part of the study is realized. The place and period are also appropriate for the study of demographic history in a regional context. After about 1850 sufficient demographic material is available from the periodic censuses and annual vital statistics published to permit a fairly detailed study of the demography of the rapidly growing industrial areas, and the contrasts they afford with other areas.

The content of the study is largely drawn from the industrial and population censuses and the periodic industrial and demographic statistics published by the three countries. They constitute an enormous mine of material relatively little used except as a source of information about global, national, economic or demographic trends. They are not, of course, uniformly reliable, especially in the earlier decades; and changes in methods of collection and in categories of division often complicate the study of secular trends. Furthermore, there are national differences in definitions which make it difficult to compare many production series. Yet, by selecting certain series where national differences of definition are slight, and which are available for small regions as well as for the nation, it is possible to build up a clear picture both of industrial growth and of demographic change in the coalfield industrial areas in the three countries.

The book falls into two parts. The first part deals with the circumstances which encouraged more rapid industrial growth in some areas while inhibiting it in others; and with the relationship between regional economic growth and the increase of industrial population. The second part deals with the demographic history of the coalfield industrial areas; their relation to the sociology of those areas; and the sources of the population growth which took place in them. In both parts the discussion centres on the contrast between the coalfield industrial areas and the three national units on the one hand; and on the other on the contrasts which existed within the coalfield industrial areas themselves.

In attempting to explore and exploit the possibilities of regional analysis I have strayed across the conventional boundaries of several branches of the study of societies and their development, and have tried to deal with changes over a long span of years in a large and complex area. Others with greater specialist knowledge will be able to recognize quickly the shortcomings of my discussion, and will, perhaps, successfully dispute my conclusions. This is to be welcomed, since it seems the proper fate of a work which is intended to be provocative rather than definitive. Conventional boundaries are not crossed without danger, but crossing them may once in a while bring new understanding to old problems.

The work which has developed into this book was begun in 1953–4 when I was a William Volker Fellow of the University of Chicago. I owe much to the help and advice at that period of Professor J. U. Nef and Professor F. A. Hayek. At a later date I learnt a great deal from Professor D. V. Glass at the London School of Economics, who was kind enough to give me guidance in matters of which I knew very little. And it is a great pleasure, lastly, to acknowledge the tremendous stimulus which everyone experiences who has the benefit of the critical comment and help of Professor M. M. Postan. This book owes a great deal to him.

An earlier draft of the first part of this book was awarded an Ellen McArthur Prize in 1958 and the book is published with the aid of the Ellen McArthur Fund.

PETERHOUSE, CAMBRIDGE   E. A. W.

July 1959

NOTE ON THE SECOND IMPRESSION

In reprinting, the opportunity has been taken to correct a number of minor errors of spelling and punctuation and to amend a figure on page 20, previously mistranscribed.

E. A. W.

PART I

INDUSTRIAL GROWTH AND POPULATION CHANGE

I. THE ARGUMENT

It is a commonplace that coal was the basis of the industrial economies of Europe and North America during the later nineteenth century. It was the common nexus connecting the various aspects of industrial change at that time. Almost every industry which was transformed by the Industrial Revolution became a consumer of coal, both directly as a fuel, and indirectly because coal was used in the manufacture of its equipment and the transport of its raw materials and end products. In particular, coal was indispensable in the use of the two most important of all the technological inventions of the new age: the steam-engine and the coke-fired blast furnace. These were the two developments which more than any other made possible the unprecedented expansion of industrial production which took place during the second half of the nineteenth century; and both were enormous consumers of coal.

It is further a commonplace that as an industrial raw material coal was exceptional in two ways. It was exceptional in the quantity which was consumed—no other industrial raw material was used in comparable amounts; and in that it is the classic example of what Weber called a 'gross' material: a material which is consumed as it is used. Because of the weight of coal required by industry, and because of its 'grossness', any industry in which coal was a major item in factor cost of production was strongly pressed to seek a coalfield location. Every mile away from the source of coal meant added costs of production for such industries. There was, therefore, a very rapid growth of industry and of industrial population in the coalfield areas in the early decades of the new era.

The broad outlines of the changes which took place are not in doubt. They follow from an elementary knowledge of the nature of the changes, and from the first principles of economics: but the rigorousness with which any abstract theory of the nature of the changes was obeyed in the hurly-burly of economic life; the nature of the influence of local conditions on the size, type, and speed of growth of industry; the importance of national differences in influencing rates of growth in similar areas in two neighbouring countries; and the effect of the growth of industry on the size of local industrial populations, have not often been carefully examined, perhaps for the very reason that the general shape of the relationships is widely accepted. The first part of this study is taken up with questions of this nature.

The belt of coalfield industrial areas stretching in a shallow arc from Pas-de-Calais in the west to the Ruhr in the east provides a good subject for the study of these questions. Within it was to be found most of the Belgian heavy industry, more than half the German, and a substantial share of the French. At the end of the nineteenth century these coalfields (which throughout will collectively be termed the Austrasian coalfield since they lack a general title[1]) provided the entire Belgian output of coal, and more than half the output of both France and Germany. This was by far the most important industrial region in continental Europe. In heavy industrial production only England and the north-eastern United States were of comparable importance.

The period covered is the half-century between *c.* 1850 and 1914. The general introduction of the coke-fired blast furnace and the steam-engine into industrial life suggests a beginning for the period. By the middle of the century both were known and used in all parts of the Austrasian field. Coal was rapidly changing in its industrial character from being a useful adjunct to some forms of industrial production to being the *sine qua non* of most modern industrial establishments.

The importance of the steam-engine lay in its provision of power on a scale far greater than any which had previously been available for industrial purposes. Before its introduction most of the power needed to work the machinery and tools of industry came still from the worker's hands, wielding the hammer at the forge, cutting the metal sheet, thrusting the shuttle across the loom, hauling the rope. In a few industries water power was important (for example, in the new cotton spinning mills, and in some sectors of the iron industry). Occasionally either wind or animal power was used: but, in general, industrial power meant man power. There were strict limits to the possible expansion of industrial production when this was the case: with the steam-engine there was almost no limit to possible growth. One man might have the power of ten, a hundred, even a thousand at his touch; and his productivity moved into a different dimension from that of his forebears. Steam power greatly magnified the productive power of changes of technique already sketched in miniature. It brought to a new fruition the ideas embodied in inventions of several centuries past in the *haut-fourneau*, the forge-hammer, and pumping and haulage in mines; or of more recent times in the mule, the jenny and the mechanical loom. The steam-engine spread from industry to industry as machines were invented to simulate the movements of the human hand in a hundred trades and crafts. Wherever there were wheels to turn, holes to punch, regular or eccentric movements to be performed; wherever the

---

[1] The name is suggested, of course, by the old division of the Carolingian Empire.

application of a great pressure was required, the steam-engine could be harnessed to do the job more quickly, more accurately, and on a vastly greater scale than had previously been possible. Many operations which were not feasible before became possible when such power was available. Levasseur expressed the new situation in France forcefully and picturesquely. He wrote, 'En effet, si, conformément à l'évaluation de l'administration des mines, on estime le travail d'un cheval-vapeur comme équivalent à celui de 21 manœuvres, on voit d'une part, qu'en 1840 l'industrie et le commerce disposaient de 1,185,000 manœuvres de cette espèce dont le travail ne coûtait que de la houille—qui étaient de véritables esclaves, les plus sobres, les plus dociles, les plus infatigables que l'imagination puisse rêver; d'autre part, qu'en 1885–7 leur nombre s'était élevé à près de 98 millions: deux esclaves et demi par habitant de la France.'[1] In almost all industries coal consumption grew rapidly. In the lighter industries this might not in itself be sufficiently important to enforce a coalfield site for the successful development of the industry; but a firm with an abundance of cheap coal at hand was clearly at an advantage, and might be encouraged to install modern machinery because of the cheapness of the fuel.

The introduction of coke firing into blast furnace practice was of equal significance, permitting for the first time the cheap production of iron on a very large scale. By 1850 this method was known in all parts of the Austrasian field, though in the less advanced areas in the east it had not by then supplanted the charcoal furnace as the chief source of iron supply. Iron was essential to modern industrial growth because of its physical properties: it could be very accurately worked, was rigid and durable. For most of the requirements of the new mechanical industries it was a much more suitable material than its predecessor, wood. It was as vital to the development of modern transport as to industry. 'Sans fonte, ni fer, ni rails, ni locomotives, ni steamers: c'était l'isolement des marchés, l'impossibilité de développer les échanges.'[2] Iron had long been in demand for many industrial uses; but as long as furnaces were charged with charcoal it could never become plentiful or cheap. To produce iron with charcoal on a scale to meet the needs of the later nineteenth century would have denuded the forests of western Europe within a few decades.

Together with the steam-engine, the coke-fired blast furnace helped to liberate industrial production from the bounds set by the techniques of the past, and raise it into a new realm of high production. Iron was the skeleton of modern industry, just as the steam-engine formed the muscles

[1] E. Levasseur, *La Population française* (Paris, 1889), vol. III, p. 74.
[2] G. de Leener, L. Wodon and E. Waxweiler, *Le Charbon dans le nord de la Belgique* (Brussels, 1904), p. 5.

B

of the new giant. Both required coal in large quantities: each emphasized the advantages to be gained from a coalfield site.

Between the middle of the century and 1914 industrial growth was rapid throughout the Austrasian field industrial area; population grew swiftly; it was the classical period of coalfield growth, unbroken by any prolonged war, and unmarked by any technological innovation which seriously threatened the industrial supremacy of the coalfield area. Towards the end of the period there were signs of changing circumstances. The generation of thermal electricity made power almost as cheap at a distance from the coalfields as within the older industrial areas. Hydro-electric power and oil, though not absolutely of much importance, showed that in future coal would have rivals as source of industrial power. Transport costs had fallen very substantially since the early days of coalfield industrial growth, and coal was used much more efficiently, a combination of trends which reduced the saving in production costs attending a coalfield location. For example, a point was reached about 1890 when it became cheaper to carry coke to the Lorraine iron ore fields than to carry the ore to the Ruhr, because blast furnaces had grown much more economical in their use of coke than in the early days of the coke-fired furnace, and the lean ores of Lorraine were unusually costly to transport. None of these new developments, except perhaps the last, had made serious inroads into the economic strength of the coalfield areas, or undermined their unique advantages before 1914: but they, and a host of changes arising out of the dislocation of economic life during the war, combined to produce a very different European economy in the inter-war period. The outbreak of the First World War, therefore, makes a convenient end to the period within which the characteristic features of the regional growth of coalfield industry and the relation between industrial growth and population changes can best be explored.

Although the close links between coalfields and industrial growth are well known, some aspects of the tie deserve a closer review as background to later discussion.

The concentration of new industrial development in the coalfield areas has frequently been remarked, and the reason for it is generally understood: that coal is perhaps the most *transportempfindlich* of all industrial raw materials. The fact that coal is bulky, heavy, and used in very large quantities necessarily means heavy expense if it is transported over any distance to the point of consumption; but this is less important than its nature as a raw material. If the full weight of the raw material is embodied in the product there is no saving in the total cost of transport when the source of the raw material is also the point of manufacture: but if a part or the whole of the weight disappears during manufacture, the saving in transport costs which follows from manufacture at the source of the raw material may be considerable. Two very simple examples in the primary processing of raw materials may serve to illustrate the point. The milling of grain into flour is an example of the first case: the product is almost as bulky and heavy as the raw material, less amenable to bulk handling, and more likely to deteriorate or be damaged in transit. Processing at the point of origin is, in consequence, not usually desirable when economic considerations govern policy. On the other hand, in the treatment of non-ferrous metal ores, such as copper, there is a great saving in transport costs if the concentrating is done near the mine, for the metal content may be only one or two per cent of the ore body. Coal is a still more extreme example than copper ore since its whole weight disappears when it is used as a fuel:[1] but it is far from being as simple a case as corn and flour, or copper ores and concentrates because it is the source, not of a substance to be further processed or sold, but of power and heat: and power and heat were needed by almost all industries in some degree.

All industries were not, of course, equally dependent on coal. Some were large absolute consumers and yet not closely tied to coalfield areas because coal was not an important element in factor cost of production. The textile industry of the period is an example of this. A small percentage saving in labour costs (which were a much more considerable element in factor cost) obtained by establishing a factory a hundred miles from a coalfield might reduce total production costs, even though hundreds of tons of coal were used each year and coal prices were doubled by its distance from the field. At the other end of the scale, in the iron industry, coal was usually more than a quarter of the factor cost of production. Other things being equal, to erect a blast furnace a hundred miles from the nearest source of coking coal would greatly increase the cost of production: things were seldom so unequal as to justify this. The great majority of the new blast furnaces were, therefore, erected in the coalfield industrial areas. In this connexion the absolute level of transport charges is very important. At one extreme, if there were no charges for the transport of coal, its nature as a 'gross' material would be irrelevant, and there would be no especial advantage in a coalfield site. At the other extreme, exceedingly high transport charges would make it very difficult for any coal-consuming industry to establish itself away from the coalfields. In the mid-nineteenth century the new railway networks, over which most of the coal moved, were only just taking shape on the Continent, and charges per

[1] Economically, if not chemically.

ton-kilometre were several times higher than at the end of the century. These were the formative years of the coalfield era, and the scale of transport charges was a strong reason for seeking a coalfield site.

Although the advantages of coalfield location were less pronounced in the case of the lighter industries, indirectly such industries might benefit greatly. As a large, experienced industrial population grew up on the Austrasian field and a wide range of service industries developed, many types of industry shared in the dramatic upsurge of production in which the heavier industries led the way. A close transport net, good water supply, developed banking and commercial services, and a large local market proved a strong attraction. The rapid growth of all industries in the coalfield areas is an excellent example of the well-known 'snowball' effect of marked and sustained prosperity and expansion in one group of industries upon all other economic activities in the area.

The presence of coal was of cardinal importance to rapid industrial expansion. Where it was cheap and abundant the portents for swift growth were encouraging. If such a condition were fed into an economic model reflecting the salient economic characteristics of the period, the result would be vigorous expansion.

Not all coalfields, however, were equally stimulating to industrial growth. Within the Austrasian field there were half a dozen major coal-producing areas; some well endowed, others with poor or inaccessible resources. Coal was everywhere a cheap raw material, costing usually between five and fifteen shillings a ton during the half-century 1850–1914: but it was much more expensive in the poorer areas than in the richer ones. Pithead coal prices in the Belgian part of the field, for example, were often more than half as much again as in the Ruhr: but coal did not move from the cheaper to the dearer areas, because the cost of transporting a ton of coal from the one to the other much more than wiped out the price differential. Each division of the Austrasian field, therefore, in so far as coal influenced its economic life, followed a separate destiny. This is a point of the first importance. In areas where coal was plentiful, of good quality, and easily mined, production might be rapidly and cheaply expanded as demand grew; whereas the reverse was true of the more poorly endowed areas. The low-cost coal-producing areas could not gain a foothold directly in their rivals' territories by winning markets for their coal within their rivals' boundaries. Their advantage told indirectly through the more rapid growth of industry in areas which flourished on cheap coal. It was to be expected that the better-endowed parts of the Austrasian field would grow more quickly. If it can be established that the pace of industrial growth in the major divisions of the Austrasian field varied in direct accord with the abundance or poverty of their endowment of coal, then an analytic tool of some power lies to hand. New light is shed upon the reasons for rapid growth in some parts of the field and comparative stagnation in others. Furthermore, the part played by national or other influences upon their economies may be inferred from the extent to which the development of the several divisions of the field diverges from what might be expected on theoretical grounds.

The argument used in the last paragraph is essentially the same as that used by W. S. Jevons in his book *The Coal Question* published almost a century ago. Jevons's fear for Britain's industrial future arose from his belief that coal production tended to grow by geometrical progression parallel with general industrial growth. He considered British coal reserves too slight to sustain this type of growth much longer without an enormous increase in costs of production; and discussed the prospects of her chief rivals in terms of their coal resources. He thought it likely that those best endowed with coal would prove the most formidable rivals. His argument depended upon a high degree of mobility in the factors of production other than raw material resources. Only when capital and labour are willing and able to move to exploit superior resources in raw materials, and when markets are equally accessible after such a move, can the potential advantages of the superior raw materials be realized. Since the Austrasian field areas were close together geographically and had a long history of interchange of men and money, this is a less rash assumption in the present context than in the context of Jevons's discussion; but it is still an assumption. An effort will be made to justify it in the later chapters of this section.

The connexion between conditions of coal mining, the rate at which coal production expanded, and general industrial growth forms one main theme of this section. The other is the link between industrial activity and population growth; for, just as the whole range of industrial activity on the Austrasian coalfield had a nexus in coal on the one hand, so on the other it was reflected in the size and rate of growth of industrial populations. These two are the most convenient tools available for the type of regional analysis which is the main concern of both parts of this book. Together they make possible both the comparison of different parts of the Austrasian field, and the comparison of each national section of the field with the national whole of which it is a part.

An example drawn from Blanchard's study of the Nord department will serve to illustrate the intimate connexion between industrial activity and population growth.[1] The population of the group of *communes* near Armentières, which was the heart of the French linen manufacture, rose slowly during the first forty-five years of the nineteenth century, increased sharply in the next thirty years, and then reverted to a more sedate rate of increase in the last decades of the century. The period of most rapid growth coincides with the period when the Belgian linen industry was in full decline after a crisis in the 1840s as a cottage industry. The decay of the cottage industry of Belgian Flanders was the opportunity of the factory production of the Armentières entrepreneurs. Their success is clearly reflected in the record of population growth of the area (as a complement to the spurt of population in and near Armentières, the populations of East and West Flanders grew slowly, or, in the worst years, declined in the crisis period). In contrast to the history of the Armentières group of *communes*, the rate of increase in the nearby wool manufacturing *communes* of Roubaix-Tourcoing showed no such time of unusually strong advance, but instead pursued a steady, even course throughout the century. In other words, the mid-century burst of the Armentières area was not simply a part of a similar acceleration of growth throughout the whole Lille textile area, but can be attributed to its successful rivalry with the Flanders linen manufacture.

The sensitivity of populations dependent upon industry to the changing industrial fortunes of an area, of which the above is a crude example, is of the first importance to the argument of the first part of this study. One of its main objects will be to attempt to relate the size and rate of increase of coal production to the total industrial production of an area and its rate of increase, as a basis for the discussion of regional differences. The most direct approach to this task would be to measure the total physical volume of production and/or its total value in each separate major division of the Austrasian field, and to set the results against the coal production material. Though desirable, this is not practicable. Production series for such small areas do not exist for all classes of production. Such series as do exist are seldom uniform throughout the period, for the constant tension between the desire to perfect the bases of each series and regret at introducing a break into it, which is the bane of the statistician, led to frequent changes during the half-century. In addition there is the difficulty of equating differing national statistical definitions.

The problem, therefore, has to be tackled indirectly through the measurement of industrial populations. If it can be shown that industrial populations grew in an intelligible relationship to increases in industrial

[1] R. Blanchard, *La Densité de population du département du Nord au XIXe siècle* (Lille, 1906).

production, then they may be used as substitutes for it for certain purposes, and it becomes possible to examine the problems touched on above, in a framework of regional rather than national analysis. Population returns for each of the three countries during the half-century after 1850 were regular, and fairly accurate: and unlike most statistical series it is possible to compare returns from one country with those from another without so many problems of definition as bedevil the comparison of industrial statistics. The counting of heads is a simpler affair than, say, the definition of an employee in the textile industry. Coal and population series are the warp and weft of the tapestry upon which the picture of coalfield industrial growth will be woven in the next four chapters. They form the two great nexus of industrial growth on the Austrasian field. Their use permits some interesting possibilities of regional analysis to be explored.

The Austrasian field may be divided up in several ways for the purposes of a regional analysis. The simplest is to separate only those areas which are geographically discontinuous. In this case there would probably be five divisions—the Ruhr, Aachen, Liège, the Hainaut fields, and the French group serving the Lille textile area and the Valenciennes metal *communes* (the last might perhaps be sub-divided). This system of division has much to commend it, especially as it is easy to obtain the necessary statistical information about each of the five divisions. Yet for the purposes of this essay, a division into eight areas has been preferred because the wider range of examples provides a better test for the techniques used, and illustrates more fully the characteristics of coalfield industry during this half-century. One limiting factor upon the choice of units is that they must be areas for which information about coal production and population growth is available throughout the period, or at least for all but the earliest years. With this limitation in mind, the Ruhr has been divided into three; *Regierungs-bezirke* Arnsberg, Düsseldorf and Münster (in effect *Kreis* Recklinghausen): and the French area into two; Nord and Pas-de-Calais, making eight divisions in all. These eight divisions provide a fair sample of the several different ways in which coalfield industrial areas developed.

In the mid-century the Austrasian coalfield belt was already an industrial area of importance, though not as yet specifically a coal-based industrial area. There were textile industries of long standing in the Lille area, at Verviers, at Aachen and in the Rhineland; and a scatter of iron industries throughout its length. But whereas some areas had been quick to adopt modern methods, others were notably slow. It is necessary to have this contemporary scene clearly in mind before any discussion of the later industrial growth can profitably be undertaken.

The dominance of Belgium was the cardinal feature of the industrial life of the Austrasian coalfield in 1850. In quantity of production the Belgian heavy industries were unapproached by other areas, and the vigour of her entrepreneurs had given her a handsome technological lead over her neighbours. In 1850 Belgium was producing two tons of coal for every one produced elsewhere on the Austrasian field.

Table 1. *Coal Production in* 1850 *('000 tons)*[1]

Belgium			Other Areas		
Hainaut	4,753	(1851)	Nord†	1,000	
Liège	1,292	(1851)	Ruhr	1,666	
			Aachen	424	(1852)
TOTAL	6,234*	(1851)	TOTAL	3,090	

* The difference between the sum of Hainaut and Liège and the total Belgian production is accounted for by the small Namur output.

† Coal production in Pas-de-Calais had not yet started in 1850.

The Belgian lead in iron manufacture was still more striking. In 1851 Liège produced 77,000 tons of pig-iron; Hainaut 71,000 tons: a total of 148,000 tons. Nord and Pas-de-Calais produced just a third of this amount (49,000 tons): the Ruhr less than a twelfth (11,500 tons): and Aachen about the same. Belgium also showed to advantage in the total of steam horse-power installed in stationary engines, a more general measure of modern industrial activity. In the Belgian segment of the field in 1851 the total was 44,000 h.p. (28,000 in Hainaut; 16,000 in Liège): in the German areas in the following year 41,000 h.p. (Aachen 11,000; Düsseldorf 16,000

[1] Unless given separately in footnotes, the source of material used in all tables will be found in the Note on Statistical Sources.

Arnsberg 14,000): in the French in 1853 20,000 h.p. (Nord 17,000; Pas-de-Calais 3,000).

Belgium was also in the van technologically. The first coke-fed blast furnace was successfully operated at Seraing in 1823: Nord did not have such a plant for a further seven years (and waited seven years more for a second): the Ruhr not for another twenty-six years. In textiles the Liège woollen industry led the Continent in technical improvement and innovation throughout the first half of the century. It seems proper, therefore, to treat Belgium as the starting point for an examination of the industrial development of the Austrasian coalfield as a whole at the beginning of its era of greatest growth.

BELGIUM

When the 1846 Census of Industry was taken in Belgium, the pattern of industrial development which was to become typical of the whole Austrasian field was already largely formed in Belgium. Heavy industry had become a large employer of labour. There were 46,000 persons engaged in the coal and coke industries; 29,000 in metal industries. Between them the two accounted for more than a sixth of the total industrial employment in the country. The great majority of the blast furnace workers, the nailers, the small-arms makers, the glass workers, the woollen textile workers and, of course, the coal miners were concentrated in the two coalfield provinces, Hainaut and Liège. These two provinces housed steam-engines of a total of 31,000 h.p. in a national figure of 37,000 h.p. The concentration in heavy industry and on the coalfield was in part fortuitous, since there had been an important iron industry in the Sambre-Meuse valley before the new technology: but in part even at this early date it was a response to the changing conditions of industrial growth.

Technological progress had been proceeding steadily for several decades in coal and iron, the two key industries of the new industrial age. In the iron industry, for example, the period after 1820 saw the solution of the problem set by the difficulty of making sufficient quantities of charcoal to smelt iron ore on a large scale. For the Continental industry no less than the British shortage of charcoal had long been the chief bar to greater production. It has been estimated that the production of 10,000 tons of iron products involved the felling of 40,000 hectares of forest.[1] Clearly the iron industry had either to limit itself to a modest annual production and cut no more than the average annual growth of timber—live off the natural timber dividend, as it were: or boost production above this level over a

[1] P. Benaerts, *Les Origines de la grande industrie allemande* (Paris, 1933), p. 454.

short term of years, at the cost of encroaching on the timber capital. The solution to the dilemma lay in the successful application of coke to the smelting of iron ore (coal had long been used in the further working of the pig). In Belgium this was first done in 1823 at Seraing. Almost simultaneously another British invention of great importance made its first appearance. This occurred in 1821 when Michel Orban built the first Belgian puddling furnace at Grivegnée. Puddled iron and steel were vital to the new engineering industries. The new techniques spread rapidly. By the middle thirties there were more than twenty coke-fired blast furnaces in operation.

Their success was made easier by the fact that the Belgian coalfields, especially those of Hainaut, were already producing much more than other Continental fields, and had a long history of economic importance behind them. The outcrop areas had been in use for many centuries. In the coal industry, like the iron, technological change was rapid in the early years of the century. Perhaps the most important single advance was the harnessing of the steam-engine to raise coal from the pit bottom to the surface. This took place first at Bois-du-Luc in Hainaut in 1807: four years later Michel Orban brought the system to Liège province when he installed the new winding gear at his Plomterie colliery (in both areas steam drainage of water from the mines, initially with Newcomen engines, had long been a commonplace). The ventilation of pits was improved. Their safety was enhanced by developments such as the introduction of the Davy safety-lamp (again a result of Orban's initiative at Plomterie) in 1817. Joseph Chaudron with his *cuvelage en fer* found a better way of strengthening mining shafts with a revetment of iron. The production of coal grew rapidly. By the decade 1831–40 it was averaging 2,917,000 tons per annum; in the following decade the annual output was 4,815,000 tons.

A small group of able and determined men was rapidly transforming the economy of the country—the Orbans, the Bauwens, the Hudsons, the Lelièvres; but above all the Cockerill dynasty, whose history, as an epitome of Belgian industrial growth during the first half of the century is worth sketching.[1]

Continental industrial advance in the early decades of the nineteenth century was largely a matter of absorbing the lessons afforded by the British example. Frequently it was an Englishman who taught the lesson. It is ironical that the Englishman whose family was to do more than any other to give Belgium the lead for many decades should have been found out of work in the country which was ultimately to advance further and

---

[1] See E. Mahaim, 'Les débuts de l'établissement John Cockerill à Seraing', *Vierteljahrschrift für Social—und Wirtschaftsgeschichte*, Bd. III (Berlin, 1905), pp. 627–48.

faster along the road to industrial achievement than any other Continental state. William Cockerill, the founder of the line, was discovered by a member of the Verviers firm of Simonis et Biolley in Hamburg in 1798. Within two years he was producing textile machinery. In 1802 his two sons, James and John, built their own textile machinery factory at Liège. It was immensely successful, and a decade later in 1812 was producing spinning and carding machines at a rate of several hundreds a year. The Cockerill interests expanded rapidly. An important stage was reached in 1817 when their Seraing iron-works was built: an old episcopal palace was converted into a machine shop for the construction of steam-engines. In 1823 James retired from the firm, making over his share to his remarkable brother. This was a significant year for John in another direction also since it was then that he disproved the belief, general at the time, that Belgian coal would not coke satisfactorily. He supervised the installation of the first coke-fed blast furnace in Belgium at Seraing. This plant was capable of a daily output as high as ten tons, or more than most charcoal furnaces could manage in a week. By 1829 the Liège district was producing over 7,000 tons of pig-iron a year, chiefly at Seraing. In 1835 the first continental-built railway locomotive was constructed there. Two years later Cockerill's enthusiasm for technical excellence led him to introduce the hot-blast system into his Seraing plant, at a time when Neilson's invention was less than a decade old, and still little used in Britain outside Scotland. In 1840 shortly before the death of John Cockerill, his Seraing works alone employed 2,000 men and were reckoned the largest in Europe (eight years later Krupp, the colossus of the future, employed only 70 men). This man, described by Schnabel as the first 'truly princely businessman since the days of the Fugger',[1] travelled constantly to foster his interests, which extended over most of western Europe north of the Alps. His range of interest, knowledge and energy were invaluable to the Belgian metal, engineering and textile industries.

The new developments of coalfield industry had revolutionized the scale of production of certain industries and lowered unit costs of production; but it is easily possible to exaggerate the degree to which the country outside the coalfields had come under the sway of the new coal age. Older methods of production were not entirely replaced even in those industries which were most changed by the new conditions. This was true, for example, even of the iron industry. In 1838 sixty-six out of the eighty-nine blast furnaces in the country were still charcoal fed. It was not until the middle fifties that the Semois iron industry in the Belgian Ardennes,

---

[1] F. Schnabel, *Deutsche Geschichte im neunzehnten Jahrhundert*, Bd. III (Freiburg, 1934), p. 262.

which was entirely dependent on charcoal, fell into decline, although its annual capacity, which never much exceeded 10,000 tons, had for many years been far outdistanced by Seraing.

The implications of the new age were to be seen in Belgium not only in the positive achievements of the age—the great growth in coalfield industry and the exciting possibilities of the new and developing railways; but equally strikingly in a negative sense. In the 1840s the largest of the traditional industries of Belgium, the linen industry of Flanders, was in crisis, a fatal one as it proved, because the Flemish spinsters could not compete with the machine-made thread of the English mills. Since there were estimated to be 280,000 spinsters in the linen industry in 1840 (often, of course, only partly dependent on their spinning for a livelihood) the negative side was as keenly felt and widely recognized as the positive side represented by the work of the Cockerills and their rivals. There was a whip to goad as well as a carrot to entice.

The new pattern of industrial life which was spreading to the Continent from England affected Belgium a little earlier than other countries. Within the Austrasian field it was the two Belgian areas, Hainaut and Liège, which were first to use the two key advances of the new age extensively. The coke-fired blast furnace and the steam-engine were commonplaces there when they were still rare in Nord and almost unknown in the Ruhr. It was natural, therefore, that Belgian men and Belgian money should have taken the lead within the field even in French and German areas. Capital, technical expertise and entrepreneurs proved quite footloose within the field in its formative years, seeking employment always where the expectation of profit was greatest. Since it is important to the theme of the other chapters of this first part of the book to show that in such matters national boundaries were seldom of great consequence in the early years, it is worthwhile considering the extent of Belgian participation in the development of areas of the Austrasian field outside Belgium before considering Nord, Aachen and the Ruhr separately.

The Belgian Influence in the Nord

Between Nord and Hainaut there had long been close ties. The Mons portion of the Hainaut coalfield had been occupied by France during the War of the Spanish Succession from 1701 to 1709, and during this short time French capital gained a foothold in the coal industry of the area which proved long lasting. The industry of Nord became heavily dependent upon coal drawn from this source during the eighteenth century, and remained so to a lesser and declining extent into the nineteenth. It was recognition of the danger of this dependence combined with the high duties on Belgian coal which prompted a persistent search for a French source of coal in Nord itself (when this search culminated in a great success at Anzin in 1734, the vicomte de Desandrouin, whose tenacity under disappointment led to the discovery, imported 200 Belgian miners and their families from Charleroi to help to bring the new pits into production). In spite of the development of local production, Nord's dependence on Belgian coal remained considerable, and was a source of weakness and distress in troubled times. Towards the end of the century in the Revolutionary Wars an Austrian threat to cut off supplies of coal to Nord caused consternation among the local manufacturers. They feared to see 'their commerce and manufactures completely destroyed by competition and the interruption in the supply of Austrian coal'.[1] Nord was as dependent upon Belgium for pig-iron for her metal industries as she was for coal, even before the obsolescence of charcoal smelting. The *pays de Liège* supplied the great bulk of the needs of the Maubeuge and Valenciennes areas, the two chief groups of metal-using *communes* in the department. There were only two blast furnaces in Nord at the time of the Revolution, at Hayon and Fourmies: and it was said that these were preserved from unsuccessful competition only by the tariff on Belgian iron.

At the turn of the century, therefore, French dependence physically upon Belgian materials was very marked in the heavy industries; but Belgian men and money were of little importance, and she had no clear-cut technological lead. The new century brought no immediate change. Indeed the second period of French occupation of Belgian soil served only to accentuate the existing pattern. In 1814 the completion of the Mons-Condé canal increased the ease with which Mons coal might be sent to Nord (ten years later the opening of the Saint-Quentin canal allowed the passage of Mons coal by a cheap water route all the way to the Paris market). As the years passed, however, Belgium did more than supply coal and raw pig for the iron industry: Belgian firms took a leading part in the establishment of modern works in Nord. In 1849 the largest metal works in Nord was the Belgian S. A. Hauts-fourneaux, forges et laminoirs de Hautmont, near Maubeuge. It had been built in 1842, and employed more than 400 workers. It was only one of several Belgian metal firms which became established in the Maubeuge area in the forties and fifties to gain access to the French market, or even, as in the case of Victor Dupont at Sous-le-Bois to avoid labour difficulties at home. Maubeuge lay less than

[1] M. Rouff, *Les Mines de charbon en France au XVIIIe siècle* (Paris, 1922), p. 34. See also R. Gendarme, *La Région du Nord* (Paris, 1954), esp. pp. 99–104.

thirty miles up the valley of the Sambre from Charleroi, one of the two largest centres of the Belgian iron industry. Its metal industries were an extension across the national frontier of the industries of Charleroi: its economic life was orientated to Charleroi. The penetration of Belgian industry and entrepreneurs is therefore very understandable. Belgian influence extended further, however. There was at least one Belgian metal venture in the Valenciennes metal region—the rolling mills at Blanc-Misseron: and Belgian influence in Nord's most important industry, textiles, was important. Belgian capital and personnel were seldom directly concerned in the industry; but Belgian textile machinery found a ready market in Nord. Once again Cockerill was the great stimulus. Mahaim, after describing the early days of the Cockerill plant in Liège, added, 'Then, with an astonishing rapidity in view of the slowness of communications, the clothing centres of northern France took part in the re-equipment. Once Cockerill was established at Liège, his clientèle appeared in France.'[1]

While Belgian influence in Nord was considerable, it was less marked here than in the parts of the Austrasian field which lay to the east. Although Belgian coal and coke was indispensable to Nord; Belgian firms in the van in the metal industry; and Belgian technological leadership often apparent, even in textiles, French capital and industry could show reason for a claim to near equality. The Mons coalfield was still directed by French capital, for example, and the linen industry of Armentières was very quick to take advantage of the difficulties of the Flemish spinsters across the border and put its modern mills to their best use. In Germany, on the other hand, the superiority of Belgian methods, men and capital was almost unchallenged, unless indeed by French or English concerns.

The Belgian Influence in Aachen and the Ruhr

Of these two areas, Aachen, although incomparably the less well endowed with resources of the type useful in the new era, was the more advanced industrially in the early decades of the nineteenth century. In part this was due to the long industrial tradition of the area, whose eminence in woollen textiles and small metal trades is reminiscent of the West Riding. In part it was a legacy of the France of the Hundred Departments which had afforded a great stimulus to local industry by providing a vast and rich market and by abolishing many of the local city and guild regulations which had strait-jacketed industry. French mining law and the French industrial code persisted after 1815 on the left-bank, while on the right-bank of the Rhine the entrepreneur had still to struggle with the cumbrous local dues and

---

[1] Mahaim, *Vierteljahrschrift für Social—und Wirtschaftsgeschichte*, p. 637

economic regulations which had been inherited from the eighteenth
century. Yet a part of the advantage of Aachen over the right-bank areas
sprang simply from its physical proximity to Liège and the close business
ties which united the two cities (it was symptomatic of this that both
Cockerill brothers married Aachen women).

A brief chronological review of some Belgian enterprises in the Aachen
area gives a good idea of the scope of their participation. In 1836 Belgian
capital lay behind the formation of the Société des charbonnages de la
Wurm. In the following year Vonpier built a machine-shop at Aachen
with the assistance of John Cockerill. Michelis and Bourdoux in 1841
supplied the capital to build the first rolling-mills of the area at Eschweiler, and brought in Walloon labour to run it. In the same decade one
of the great family concerns of the Aachen area, Hoesch, built rolling-
mills in the same town under the direction of the Belgian Dacier. The
Aachener Walz- und Hammerwerk, whose capital was entirely Belgian,
built the Rote Erde rolling-mills near Aachen in 1846; an enterprise upon
a scale unknown on the right-bank at the time. A few years later the
Société Minière d'Aix-la-Chapelle was formed: once again the capital was
Belgian. In the lead and zinc industry at Stolberg, the A. G. Altenberg, the
A. G. für Bergbau, Blei- und Zinkfabrikation and the Rheinische-
Nassauische Bergwerks- und Hütten A.G. were all dominated by Belgian
capital. French capital was also active in the area. For example, in 1852 the
Saint-Gobain company built a glass-works at Stolberg. Belgium was the
source of material as well as men and money. It was not until 1853 that
the Concordia company showed that some of the local coals were suitable
for coking, and hence of use in blast furnaces. Up to that date the great
bulk of the pig-iron requirements of the rolling-mills and forges of the
Aachen area (Aachen itself, Düren, Eschweiler, Eupen, Stolberg, etc.)
were met by imports from Belgium.

In the Ruhr Belgian ventures were also important: in part for their size,
but still more because of the lead they gave in technical matters.[1] French
capital, much of it from Nord, was also actively engaged in the Ruhr.
Instances of foreign supremacy in most branches of technology and
organization are numerous: only a few of the more striking examples are
listed. The first joint-stock company to be formed in the Ruhr, the
Société des mines de Hardenburg et Duisburg was founded by a group of
Frenchmen from Lille, Anzin, Douai and Valenciennes (i.e. the French
section of the Austrasian field in Nord). It owned four of the more impor-

[1] For both the Ruhr and Aachen areas, see especially Benaerts, *Les Origines de la
grande industrie allemande*; K. Wiedenfeld, *Ein Jahrhundert rheinischer Montan-Industrie*
(Bonn, 1916); M. Baumont, *La Grosse industrie allemande et le charbon* (Paris, 1928).

tant Ruhr mines, the Petersburg, the Gabe-Gottes, the Caroline, and the August-Erbstollen. In the 1840s the first locomotives to run on the new Ruhr railway lines were made at the Cockerill works. Although the first coke-fired blast furnace, the Friedrich-Wilhelmshütte, was blown in by a German firm in 1849, it was not until 1852 that its advantage over the older charcoal smelting method was conclusively proved, and then by the Belgian firm of Ch. Detillieux et Cie at Berge-Borbeck. The Société de la Vieille Montagne, whose capital was Belgian and French, owned foundries at Mülheim and Borbeck, and rolling-mills at Oberhausen; and introduced for the first time on German soil the method for the reduction of zinc ores which had been devised by Dony. A majority of the capital in the giant Phönix concern of Ruhrort, founded in 1852, was French and Belgian (in 1861 this single concern produced more than a sixth of the total Ruhr output of pig-iron). The Société des mines de Mülheim which ran the big Altstaden mine from 1856 was created by a parent Belgian company.

The key workers in the new Ruhr firms, as well as the capital, were commonly Belgian where they were not English. The letter written from the firm of Gutehoffnung to the Espérance blast furnaces at Seraing to obtain, 'an experienced master-puddler, capable of instructing the local workers for four weeks',[1] must be typical of scores of similar import written between 1840 and 1860. Belgian technical advice, and especially that of Cockerill, was widely sought after upon the installation of new rolling-mills or puddling-furnaces. This guidance and initiative extended over the whole field of industrial enterprise. It was a Belgian firm, for example, which installed the first gas lighting in Elberfeld.

Foreign capital in the Ruhr reached a peak about 1857, when its total was estimated at 125,000,000 francs (it is perhaps indicative of the size of this sum that when the Cockerill firm was made into a joint-stock company after the death of John Cockerill, it was capitalized at 12,500,000 francs). Some of this money was British; many of the experts who directed the new works were British: but a substantial share of the men and capital which sparked the Ruhr into life came from parts of the same Austrasian field farther west. The words of the Irishman, Thomas Mulvany, who had a hand in many of the most important coal-mining and metal ventures of the fifties and sixties (he sank the great Hibernia pit near Gelsenkirchen; and his origin is reflected in the names of other Ruhr mines which he helped to sink; Erin and Shamrock, for example) characterize the attitude of himself and his Belgian and French rivals in the Ruhr. 'Those men', he

---

[1] Quoted Benaerts, *Les Origines de la grande industrie allemande*, p. 356.

remarked of the local inhabitants, 'don't realize the value of what they possess.'[1]

The evidence of the frequency with which national boundaries were crossed by men and money in search of greater returns is interesting on many counts since it is a condition which is less common in the modern world. It is of particular consequence in the present context because it lessens the number of factors to which the faster growth of certain areas can be ascribed. If men and money moved so freely from one area which was momentarily further advanced than its rivals to another which offered greater opportunities but lacked capital and expert knowledge, then one must look to some other production factor or factors which were less mobile in order to account for a rapid growth here or a slowing in the pace there in the long term. Mulvany pointed to such a factor when he wrote of the Ruhr: 'These two provinces [i.e. Rheinland and Westphalia] in every way are endowed with astonishing riches.'[2]

NORD AND PAS-DE-CALAIS

Sée wrote of the Revolution that, 'this slowing-down of economic life doubtless explains why until about 1840 it should still be in many respects of the same type as under the *Ancien Régime*'.[3] On a sufficiently broad canvas of presentation perhaps this is true: on a narrower plane the chief reason for the lack of change in Nord before 1840, and the rapid change thereafter, was the timing of the introduction on a large scale of the new industrial technology, especially the steam-engine and the coke-fired blast furnace. Upon such a reckoning also 1840 might well seem, symbolically, a watershed. The first signs of change were apparent in the early thirties: by the time of the 1847 industrial census the mark of a new industrial age was strong in Nord.

In the van of change, as so often, were the cotton-spinning mills. Even in 1832 seventeen of the fifty cotton-spinning mills in Nord were using steam-engines, and a further five were in the process of conversion. By the time of the census of 1847 a cotton-spinning mill of from one to four hundred workers using one or more steam-engines had become typical in *arr.* Lille, the heart of the Nord textile area. This *arrondissement* in 1847 contained more than 62,000 persons engaged in industry (three out of every five in the whole department), almost all of whom were engaged in the cotton, woollen and linen industries. The weaving side of these industries

---

[1] Benaerts, *Les Origines de la grande industrie allemande*, p. 354.
[2] Benaerts, *Les Origines de la grande industrie allemande*, p. 354.
[3] H. Sée, *Histoire économique de la France* (Paris, 1942), vol. II, p. 363.

was not yet normally dependent on steam power, or indeed housed in factories (Nord lagged behind the Alsatian cotton industry in this respect). In spinning, however, the factory and the steam-engine were predominant. The cotton industry was the most completely committed to steam-driven spindles: there were fifty-five steam-engines and 6,200 workers in cotton spinning at this date. But the woollen industry, following the example of Théophile Legrand at Fourmies and Paturle at Cateau in the early decades of the century, was little less developed with fifty steam-engines and 5,400 workers. Even in flax-spinning there were twenty-three steam-engines and 3,600 workers. The mill of Scrive Frères (at Lille), for example, employed more than 500 workers in 1847, and used three steam-engines (it was Antoine Scrive who had risked the severe penalties of the English law of the day to bring over to France the first effective flax-spinning machinery). Such mills as these were well placed to profit from the opportunities afforded by the contemporary troubles of the Flemish spinsters across the Belgian border.

The history of iron production in Nord is like that of the Belgian areas immediately to the east, though on a smaller scale and with a time-lag of many years. In 1801 the sole blast furnace in the whole department was at Hayon in *arr.* Avesnes. Conditions were very like those of the Semois valley in Belgium, which indeed was only some thirty or forty miles distant. Each industry was dependent upon the swift streams, heavy woods, and patches of iron ore found both in the French and Belgian Ardennes (as also in the Eifel in Germany which is a continuation of the same country to the east). In the case of Hayon the woods of the *ci-devant* duc d'Orléans were the source of fuel; and the iron ore came from the small local deposits at Couplevoie.

In the mid-century an iron industry existed in two areas in Nord. The Maubeuge area was an extension of the Belgian iron centre at Charleroi. It used Charleroi pig and coal; but the development of the area suffered from poor communications due to the fact that Mons coal-owners, who were French, saw in the Charleroi area a potential competitor in the Paris coal market. The political pressure they were able to exert, combined with the military opposition to improving the communications of the Sambre valley, which had often been used by invading armies in the past, prevented a full development of the routes along the Sambre valley. A canal was built along the Sambre in 1835, twenty-one years after the Mons-Condé canal was opened; and a rail link completed in 1853, seven years after the Lille-Valenciennes-Mons network: but it was too little and too late. Transport costs remained rather high. Largely as a result the Maubeuge area found the raw materials of a primary iron industry more expensive than the Valenciennes area, and concentrated instead on the metal-finishing trades: forges, rolling-mills, wire mills, etc.[1] The Valenciennes metal *communes*, on the other hand, with excellent communications and abundant local coal, developed a primary iron industry of importance. The first coke-fired blast furnace in the department was erected at Raismes near Valenciennes in 1830, running initially on Belgian coke. Its capacity, like that of the Seraing furnace in the previous decade was about ten tons a day. Seven years later the Société de Denain et Anzin blew in the first Nord blast furnace to run on locally produced coke. By the time of the industrial census in 1847 the Valenciennes area was an important centre of heavy industry. *Arr.* Valenciennes counted 8,000 coal-miners, and more than 3,000 metal-workers (notably concentrated at Denain, Trith-Saint-Léger, Raismes and Anzin). Some establishments were of considerable size. At Denain Serret, Lelièvre et Cie employed 300 men in making iron products, including rails, and had three steam-engines installed in their works. In addition, there was in the area a notable glass industry, a further point of similarity with Belgian Hainaut.

Reference should also be made to the large sulphuric acid plant at Loos near Lille which had been built by Charles-Frédéric Kuhlmann in 1824, and which employed 160 men in 1847: and to the great scale of the sugar-beet industry in Nord. This latter over large areas of Nord afforded the first local examples of a large-scale industry driven by steam-engines. The employment was, of course, heavily seasonal; and the 1847 census, which was based on material collected over a two-year period, does not make it clear to what part of the year its figures refer: but it records more than 10,000 persons employed in the sugar industry (almost half of them in *arr.* Valenciennes), and it must have been an important source of orders for steam-engines, and a useful market for coal. Each of the scores of factories employed at least one steam-engine, often of a large capacity for the day.

In Pas-de-Calais, Béthune, the *arrondissement* which by 1910 was producing more coal than any other coalfield area of the Austrasian field west of the Ruhr, bore no trace of the future in 1847. The largest industry was brewing, which afforded employment to 246 persons dispersed in as many as eighty-two establishments. There was only one large industrial concern, a sugar-beet factory at Carvin which employed 158 persons. The first coal was not discovered until two years later when the brothers Mathieu struck a promising seam at Courrières. By the mid-fifties there were six mines in production in Béthune.

---

[1] The Maubeuge area was not entirely without blast furnaces. For example, at Hautmont the Providence concern (Belgian) began work on three blast furnaces in 1845. The first was blown in two years later.

The history of coal production in Nord provides a vivid illustration of the lack of growth to which Sée referred. In 1830 it stood at 432,000 tons, an increase of only 42,000 tons upon the figure of 1790. By 1840 production had reached 776,000 tons; ten years later it was 1,000,000 tons; and in 1860 2,185,000 tons (including the output of the new mines in *arr.* Béthune). The tempo of industrial life had changed suddenly. With new sources of power, of metal, and of freedom of movement (Nord was linked both with Paris and with Belgium by rail in 1846) current production began to dwarf the achievements of the past.

Perhaps the most telling way of showing the difference between the old tempo and the new is to consider the percentages of increase of population in various types of department in the last thirty years before 1851 and in the succeeding thirty years.

Table 2. *Percentage Increases in Population (France)*

	Nord	Pas-de-Calais	Aisne	Finis-terre	Seine	Bouches du-Rhône	FRANCE
1821–51	27·8	10·5	21·5	27·9	73·0	36·6	24·1
1851–81	38·4	18·2	−0·4	10·3	96·9	37·2	5·3*

* French national totals were affected by the loss of territory after the Franco-Prussian war.

During the first thirty-year period the rate of growth of population in Nord was little more than that of Aisne, an adjacent department almost entirely agricultural in its economic life; was little higher than the national average; was actually less high than in Finisterre, a remote Breton department of high birth-rates and backward agricultural economy; and was noticeably less than in either Bouches-du-Rhône, which contained Marseilles, or Seine, which was chiefly Paris. Pas-de-Calais was well below any of the other six percentages. In the following thirty years the pattern changed completely. Now France as a whole increased very little; the two agricultural departments, Aisne and Finisterre, showed greatly reduced rates of growth (in the case of Aisne the rate of growth was just negative): but the pace in the industrial departments, Nord and Pas-de-Calais, had quickened significantly (though the latter was in 1881 only at the beginning of the development of coal mining on a big scale). The great city departments shared this enhanced vigour of growth. Areas of increase were becoming rare, but within them growth continued at an accelerated pace.

Before 1851 the prosperity of the textile trades in Nord, the growing metal industry, the glass, sugar-beet and other industries added something to the rate of population increase, but did not suffice to distinguish this department from other departments in France, though of a chiefly agricultural economy, in any marked fashion. After 1851 coalfield industry became a primary determining factor in population growth, bringing about a rapid increase in numbers. Absence of industry, except in the case of administrative and commercial centres, usually meant stagnation or decline in population.

THE GERMAN AREAS

A similar review of population increases in Germany reveals similar features. Arnsberg and Düsseldorf, within which the entire Ruhr area was

Table 3. *Percentage Increases in Population (Germany)*

	Arns-berg	Düssel-dorf	Aachen	Minden	Prussia	Pomer-ania	Berlin
1816–49	53·7	53·8	33·8	37·4	70·9	75·4	114·1
1849–80	84·1	75·0	27·3	8·4	34·1	28·5	164·8
	Hamburg		PRUSSIA				
1816–49	43·1		57·8				
1849–80	117·1		67·0				

Arnsberg, Düsseldorf, Minden and Aachen were *Regierungs-bezirke*; Berlin a *Stadtkreis*; Prussia and Pomerania were provinces (Prussia being the later provinces of East and West Prussia combined); and Hamburg a city-state outside Prussia.

to be found, grew a little less quickly than Prussia as a whole between the end of the Napoleonic Wars and 1850; less quickly than the capital city, Berlin; less quickly than the agricultural provinces of the east, Prussia and Pomerania. On the other hand, they grew a little more rapidly than their near neighbour Minden, an agricultural area; more rapidly than the port of Hamburg; and more rapidly than Aachen, which in spite of its industrial importance, was never an area of rapid population growth. During the next thirty years much the same happened in Germany as happened in France, taking into consideration the fact that the push of population in Germany was so much greater that rates of increase are not directly comparable. In Germany, as in France, the capital and the great port, Berlin and Hamburg, increased most rapidly of all. Agricultural areas became much less expansive: Minden's population in fact was almost stationary. The coalfield industrial areas, other than Aachen, showed a gain in the rate of increase, and became, other than the capital and great port, the most swiftly growing of the areas considered, and comfortably ahead of the national average. If the two periods are broken down into sub-periods, the effect of a gathering momentum of increase in industrial areas, and a waning vigour in agricultural areas is still more clearly visible.

The scale of industrial production in Aachen and the Ruhr before 1850 was not large, as statistics of coal output help to make clear. In the Ruhr coal production in 1830 was 571,000 tons; in 1840 990,000 tons; and in 1850 1,666,000 tons. At the last date Ruhr production was only half as large again as that of Nord (which imported much coal from Belgium to supplement its own output); only a third larger than Liège province; and barely a third of Hainaut. In Aachen production in 1828 was 150,000 tons; in 1834 200,000 tons; in 1852 424,000 tons.

The oddest feature of the German areas of the Austrasian field before 1850 is that in almost all branches of industrial activity there was a marked time-lag between the development of Aachen, which benefited from its proximity to Belgium, from a long experience in both textile and metal trades, and from twenty years of French administration; and the Ruhr, which enjoyed none of these benefits so fully, and some not at all. Its development was so belated that Schnabel remarked bluntly, 'Even in the mid-century the Ruhr remained a very remote district.'[1]

It is symptomatic of the relatively advanced state of the more westerly area that in 1815 Aachen was the most populous town of any in the German section of the Austrasian field. It had a population of 32,000 at that date; next came Düsseldorf with 22,000; then Elberfeld 21,500; Barmen 19,000; Krefeld 13,000; and finally Eupen 9,000.[2] These were chiefly textile towns and market centres; none owed its development at any previous time to its proximity to coal. Essen, Dortmund, Gelsenkirchen, Ruhrort, Witten, Hörde, etc., which were to become the centres of heavy industry in the future, were small country towns with populations of less than five thousand; or, in the case of Ruhrort and Gelsenkirchen, tiny villages.

The Aachen area gained from the abolition of restrictive economic legislation brought about by the French occupation. The economic life of the German states had long been hampered by the host of guild regulations, internal dues and local taxes which were characteristic of eighteenth-century Germany. These were either removed or regularized. In addition, the woollen manufacturers of the area had opened to them a vast new market as a result of political union with France. Thun expressed himself strongly when commenting on this period. 'When French rule came,' he

[1] Schnabel, *Deutsche Geschichte im neunzehnten Jahrhundert*, Bd. III, p. 407.
[2] B. Kuske, 'Die rheinischen Städte', in *Geschichte des Rheinlandes von der ältesten Zeit bis zur Gegenwart* (Essen, 1922), II, Bd. 2, p. 71.

wrote, 'all legal barriers fell and the long-delayed, belated development
went forward with giant strides. Knowledge and capital streamed into
the city.'[1] Aachen knew great prosperity in the Napoleonic period. Pro-
French feeling remained for some years on the left-bank a factor with
which the Prussian government was forced to reckon, and no attempt was
made to reintroduce the irksome restrictions which still hampered the
right-bank.

The leadership enjoyed by Aachen over the Ruhr during the first half
of the century may be illustrated in several ways. In technological matters
Aachen's advantage was clear-cut. The first steam-engine to be used for
drainage purposes in a pit in the Aachen area was installed at Eschweiler in
1794; it was not until 1820 that the first similar Ruhr venture took place
at Schlebusch. The proximity of Aachen to Liège, where the Cockerill
spinning machines were made, and the many close contacts between
Aachen and Belgium (many young Aacheners, for example, were sent to
Belgium for part of their education) ensured a swift absorption of the new
textile machinery in the mills of Eupen, Düren, Malmédy, Stolberg and
Aachen itself. The old iron, brass, copper and lead industries which had in
the past found ores, water-power, and charcoal in the rugged terrain of
the Eifel were dying out *in situ*, but were rejuvenated in *Kreise* Aachen
and Düren where there was coal, simpler transport, and the benefit of
Belgian and French capital and expertise. In organization no less than
technique Aachen led the Ruhr. The French mining concession system
made it easier to concentrate the ownership of many mines in the hands of a
single person. Christina Englert, a member of one of the great industrial
families of Aachen, took advantage of this fact to group a number of mines
in her own hands between 1815 and 1830. In 1834 the firm became the
Eschweiler Bergwerksverein, a joint-stock company, and the first mining
venture to escape from the old form of mining organization, the Gewerk-
schaft, which was ill-adapted to a large scale of production. This form was
almost unknown to the German manufacturers in the Ruhr until the
fifties. Another Aachen family concern, that of Hoesch, has become cele-
brated as one of the two early exponents in the Rhineland area of vertical
integration of the iron manufacturing processes from pig-iron to the
finished product. This followed the example set by Cockerill at Seraing;
and anticipated the Ruhr industrialists by many years. Because of the
French inheritance taxation sat much less heavily upon the left-bank
enterprises than upon those of the right-bank. In 1848 Lette reported to
the Assembly that mine owners on the left-bank paid 5 per cent on their

[1] A. Thun, 'Die Industrie am Niederrhein und ihre Arbeiter', Pt. I, p. 19 in *Staats-
und socialwissenschaftliche Forschungen*, Bd. II (Leipzig, 1880).

net product in taxes, whereas on the right-bank almost 14 per cent of the gross revenue was lost in *dîmes* and taxes.[1]

In the Ruhr the pace of change was much slower. A few men showed enterprise and a conviction of the future of the area. Dinnendahl at Sterkrade in the first decades of the century spent many weary years acquiring the ability to make with his own hands machines which the local smiths were not nice enough in their skills to make for him. In the year of his death, in 1826, another whose name was to be associated with a very wide range of economic activities, Harkort, built at Wetter near Hagen a puddling furnace on the English pattern to help supply the machine factory which he had built in the same town seven years before. These enterprises, however, were exceptional. Successes were few: complaints about the quality of the local labour supply many and bitter.

The real wealth and the great opportunity of the Ruhr lay in its resources of coal. Coal had long been mined along the line of outcrop in the south near the river Ruhr: but the exceptional wealth of the field was not apparent until the layer of Secondary rocks which covered the concealed part of the field to the north had been penetrated. This was first accomplished in the middle thirties. The first pit was near Essen; proved rich; and was rapidly followed by many others. The necessary foundation of industrial prosperity for a new age had been established, though it was many years before the Ruhr's natural advantages were translated into material success. It was not until 1849 that the first coke-fired blast furnace was erected at Mülheim. A year later, of the twelve blast furnaces in the Ruhr area, two only were coke-fired, eight were charcoal furnaces, and the two remaining were mixed. It was only in 1855 that so important an iron-making firm as that of Haniel abandoned charcoal in favour of coke. In other respects also the Ruhr was not as well provided with the instruments of economic expansion as were the other areas of the Austrasian field. The deficiencies of the transport network were especially important. Although the first railway line in the Ruhr, from Düsseldorf to Elberfeld, was opened in 1838, communications were still poorly developed in the Ruhr in 1851. In that year it is estimated that as much as 45 per cent of the Ruhr coal production was still moved by road; 30 per cent by river; and only 25 per cent by rail. Perhaps the most striking single indication of the mid-century backwardness of the Ruhr is the contemporary estimate of Hübner of the price of coke-made pig-iron delivered at Cologne in 1850. The prices are in *thaler* and *gros* per ton.[2]

---

[1] Benaerts, *Les Origines de la grande industrie allemande*, p. 408.
[2] Taken from Benaerts, *Les Origines de la grande industrie allemande*, p. 456.

From:

Rheinland   17·2 (including 0·8 transport costs)
Saar   15·5 (including 2·4 transport costs)
Scotland   10·9 (including 3·9 transport costs)
Seraing   11·5 (including 1·6 transport costs)

The table calls for little comment. Apart from the heavy transport charges on non-German pig, the Zollverein tariff on imports of pig-iron was some 15–20 per cent on value at that time. Thus the degree of superiority enjoyed by either Scotland or Seraing was very marked. The Ruhr still had far to go before dominating the heavy industry of the Continent.

Even so the old industrial areas in the wooded horst blocks to the south had been under increasing pressure for some time before 1850. In order to take advantage of some at least of the new industrial processes, the textile and metal industries of Sauerland, Westerwald, the Rothaar Gebirge, and the valleys of the Lahn, Sieg and Dill, were making increasing demands for coal. In 1833 it was estimated that *Kr.* Elberfeld, Barmen, Remscheid, Solingen, Lennep, Hagen, Altena and Iserlohn were consuming coal at an annual rate of 270,000 tons. Transport was becoming a serious problem. At this date *Kr.* Siegen alone produced 16,000 tons of charcoal pig annually (or more than the entire make of the Ruhr in 1850), but decline was imminent. In 1836 there were 383 small metal firms in Siegen; in 1849 the number had fallen to 259; and by the end of the fifties to 186. Only the building of the Ruhr-Sieg railway renewed prosperity in the local metal industry. Throughout the area further growth waited on good rail communications; and when it came, took the form of small metalware production and engineering. The basic iron-producing processes could not economically be carried on away from the coalfields once coke replaced charcoal in the smelting of iron ore. The long-term solution of the problem of providing iron in quantities sufficient to meet the demands of an age of railways and steam-engines could only be found in the Ruhr, where the coke-fired blast furnace produced as much pig-iron in one day as one of the small furnaces of Siegen could achieve in a fortnight. During the 1850s the rail network in the Ruhr rapidly took shape (already by the end of the 1840s there were rail links with both Berlin in the east and Aachen and Belgium in the west), emphasizing with each newly completed stretch of track the advantages enjoyed by the Ruhr over the coalless hills to the south where transport costs were high and fuel expensive.

The transformation of the Ruhr, when at last it came about, was very rapid. The production of pig-iron, which was only 11,500 tons in 1850, had grown to 139,000 tons in 1857. Coal production increased from 1,666,000 tons in 1850 to 4,366,000 tons in 1860. In 1854 the Hörder

Verein began to use on a large scale the blackband iron ores which had been discovered in the Ruhr five years earlier. The Gutehoffnungshütte, the Hörder Verein, the Phönix concern and Krupp all bought up coal mines in the fifties to ensure a supply of raw material for their blast furnaces and metal shops, and to achieve the economies possible with a large-scale integrated production. Krupp, who had employed only seventy men in 1848, employed ten times that number in 1855, and a thousand in 1857. At the same time the textile industries of Barmen, Elberfeld and Krefeld grew fast and adapted themselves to modern conditions. Mechanical power weaving, which completed the transformation of industry begun by the introduction of power spinning, made its appearance in the fifties. The slow process of cutting the ground from under the feet of the hand-loom weaver, industry by industry, grade by grade, skill by skill, began. This meant suffering for many individuals; but for industry as a whole a useful new source of labour.

By the end of the fifties Mevissen's hope of 'the transformation of industry by capital' was well on the way to fulfilment. After the revolutionary crisis of 1848, during which it was forced to close its doors, he and Oppenheimer transformed the old Schaaffhausen bank into a joint-stock concern. Thereafter progress was rapid. This bank was, in its new form, instrumental in forming the Hörder Bergwerks-und Hüttenverein, the Kölner Bergwerksverein, and the Eschweiler-Concordia company among others. And it was followed by the Darmstadt bank and the Discontogesellschaft. All were avowedly interested in promoting industrial ventures and finding the capital necessary for them. Between 1840 and 1849 only five heavy industry companies were founded in the Ruhr: between 1851 and 1856 there were twenty-five such foundations: and in the following year alone a further twenty-eight.

In 1850 the different parts of the Austrasian field were very unevenly advanced, with Belgium firmly in the lead. The basic techniques of the new age, however—the use of the steam-engine in the metal, mining and textile industries; the use of coke in the smelting of iron ore; and railway transportation—were present in all political divisions of the field from Nord in the west to Arnsberg in the east. Everywhere the older metal industries of the rugged hill country to the south, and the domestic textile industries were either under pressure or in full decline according to the degree of industrial and technical advance in the nearest coalfield area. The old order was changing, giving place to new. Even by the mid-century it was clear that the older strongholds of industry would meet a powerful challenge from other parts of the coalfield which had not previously been of much industrial importance.

III. THE COAL RESOURCES OF THE AUSTRASIAN FIELD

Industrialists in all parts of the Austrasian field had the great advantage that they had only to dig beneath their feet in order to supply themselves with a key raw material of the later nineteenth century. Yet it would be as misguided to suppose that this left them all on an equal footing as to suppose that because half a dozen properties have access to the same trout stream, the fishing must be equally good in all of them. In parts of the Austrasian field the coal was easy to mine since it occurred near the surface in rich, level seams: in other parts it lay at great depths in steep, contorted seams, where mining was often plagued by difficulties of drainage and hazard of gas. Some parts had a full range of all types of coal in successive horizons: in others only anthracitic and semi-anthracitic coals could be won. These things had a very direct bearing on the industrial fortunes of each area, for they were immediately reflected in the possible output per man-year of the coal-miners, and hence in the cost of producing coal; and at one remove in the size of the capital outlay necessary to secure a given increase in production; even in the types of industry possible in a given area. These in turn might intimately affect the general industrial life of each area, placing limits upon the pace at which industrial production could be expanded. In order to understand the varying economic fortunes of the several areas of the field, therefore, it is first necessary to understand its geology in broad outline, for the regional differences were marked and important.

The Austrasian coalfield lies at the northern foot of the Hercynian complex of central Europe, stretching in a long, narrow, shallow arc for more than 200 miles from Fléchinelle in Pas-de-Calais to Hamm in Westphalia. It is not the only coalfield of its type: there are many important related coalfields from South Wales in the west to Silesia in the east, all associated with the same mountain system and disposed along its flanks. The coalfields are remnants of the Carboniferous system, once much more widely present, but reduced through the millenia by erosion, which has bared the older rocks beneath them. Commonly the coal measures occur in pockets isolated from one another by large areas of 'barren' rocks; but between Fléchinelle and Hamm there is a very well maintained strip of coal measures lying to the north of the Ardennes, the Eifel and the Sauerland Hercynian blocks, and broken only by the Samson fault in Belgium and, perhaps, by a break in the coal measures between Aachen and the left-bank section of the Ruhr area. The latter is not certain because the coal measures may exist at a great depth. The field as a whole possesses greater coal reserves than any other on the European Continent west of Russia: greater reserves indeed than the total of the other coalfields. Within the field, however, the resources are not evenly distributed either in quantity, quality or accessibility.

There is a fundamental difference between the western and eastern wings of the field. To the west of Aachen the coal measures are confined to a narrow strip along the valley of the Sambre-Meuse with the Ardennes Massif and the pre-Devonian Brabant Massif on either side, to south and north respectively. The coal measures are trapped between older rocks, and are severely contorted and faulted. To the south the coal measures are overlain by a massive overfold of the Ardennes Massif, from which they are divided by the great Faille du Midi. Farther to the west, beyond the Couchant de Mons, the coalfield dips beneath a hidden upfold in the Secondary chalk, so that the whole coalfield area of northern France is a concealed field. The main features of the Belgian section of the field are, however, continued into France. The characteristic Faille du Midi continues to divide the field from the overthrust Ardennes Massif to the south, so that a north-south cross-section of the field here, as in Belgium, looks like a shoe whose toe is tucked under the Ardennes Massif and whose top either outcrops to the surface as in Belgium in the east or is thinly crowned by a layer of chalk as in the concealed western section in France. In the western wing of the field there are several islands of limestone in the coal measures caused by faulting, such as the Faille du Boussu between Valenciennes and Mons, or the Faille de la Tombe south of Charleroi; and one complete break just east of Namur where a neck of Carboniferous Limestone, the Samson fault, connects the Ardennes and Brabant Massifs. The Aachen area itself, at the hinge between the two wings of the field, consists of two pockets of coal, the Wurm and Inde basins, which resemble geologically the areas to the west in the Sambre-Meuse valley. The problems of coal mining in this area are similar to those in the Liège district.

East of Aachen, on the other hand, the absence of a barrier like the Brabant Massif to the northward continuation of the coal measures permits the free development of a concealed coalfield under the later Cretaceous Sandstones. This concealed field escaped the erosion to which the coal measures farther west were exposed by the older blocks to north and south. The vast bulk of the Ruhr reserves are in the concealed field, which continues to the west as the Brüggen-Erkelenz field, the Dutch Limburg field and the Campine field. In the eastern wing there is no break in the continuity of the coal measures, though there is a gap of about fifty miles between the easternmost exposed measures of the Wurm and Inde basins at Aachen and the western extremity of the exposed part of the Ruhr coalfield. Concealed coal measures may, however, link Aachen and the Ruhr, sweeping north of the lower Rhine Bay which fills the triangle of 'dead' ground Bonn-Düsseldorf-Düren.

The eastern wing possessed advantages other than the sheer size of the coal resources available, since there was in this area a much better representation of the full range of coal types than in the west, ranging from the rich gas coals with a content of volatile matter as high as 45 per cent to the anthracites and semi-anthracites whose content of volatile matter was no more than 10 to 15 per cent. The former lay nearest the surface where pressure from the weight of overlying rocks was least, and the latter at the base of the coal measures. In the concealed part of the Ruhr coalfield the full range existed, and coals of all types could be extracted either by one mine of sufficient depth in the north where the full range was present vertically underneath any surface point; or, as was much more economic, by siting mines in such a manner that they lay above the point at which the types of coal required outcropped to the overlying beds. In the west, where the coal measures were exposed, erosion had often removed all the upper coals of high volatile content and left only the anthracitic and semi-anthracitic coals. Thus in the Sambre-Meuse valley in Belgium there was no coal so high in volatile content as the Ruhr Gasflammkohle (37–45 per cent), and only in the extreme west of the field, close to the point where it dips beneath the chalk into France was there any coal as rich as the Ruhr Gaskohle or upper Fettkohle (this was in the Assise de Flénu, continued into France as the Assise de Bruay). Originally, no doubt, the exposed field contained as wide a range of coal types as any elsewhere; but, in the absence of any protective cover of younger rocks, the upper seams have been eroded away. The vital coking coals, however, which usually contain 18–28 per cent volatile matter, were present in all parts of the field.

The Ruhr area was favoured in many ways; it enjoyed a wide range of coal types, thick and level seams, relative freedom from gas and water problems, and a relatively shallow average depth of working: but its most striking advantage lay in the size of the coal reserves in this eastern wing of the field. The coal reserves of the world were reviewed at the 1913 Toronto Geological Congress, and it is the estimates arrived at on that occasion which are used here, in part because they were compiled by leading experts from each country, but primarily because they were supposed to be arrived at by a common method of estimation agreed upon beforehand. In fact the results are not given in a uniform manner, but they are yet, perhaps, better comparable than the isolated estimates of experts at other times.[1] Some of the general geological description given by each contributor is also of value.

In France the coal measures increase steadily in thickness from west to east. In the far western tip of the field, at Fléchinelle, the thickness of the coal measures is 350 metres. At Liévin this has increased to 1,300 metres, containing 51 seams of coal of a total thickness of 47 metres, with a full range of coals present including gas and coking coals in the upper seams. At Denain the thickness has grown to 1,850 metres; at Valenciennes to 2,675 metres. The coals at Valenciennes are to be found in 77 seams of 50 metres total thickness, and are chiefly semi-anthracitic and steam coals with a volatile content of 9–18 per cent. The total reserves of the French section of the field to a depth of 1,200 metres were estimated in 1913 to be 9,520 million tons, of which 3,790 were held certain; 3,010 probable; and 2,720 possible. Below 1,200 metres but above 1,800 metres possible reserves were put at a further 2,580 million tons. Mining conditions were easier in the west of the French area in Pas-de-Calais than in the east. In the west the seams were richer and less folded, although the total thickness of the coal measures was less. In Defline's words, 'Relatively rich and regular zones are to be found in the Pas-de-Calais basin, not throughout its whole extent, but over a large proportion thereof, especially to the south of the Reumaux fault. As a result the Pas-de-Calais basin is richer than that of Nord, at least to a moderate depth, and development has taken place more rapidly there.'[2]

Immediately across the border into Belgium the Mons field is similar to that of Nord, but farther to the east the coal measures decrease in thickness. The coal seams rich in volatile content, the Assise de Flénu and the Assise de Charleroi, are either found only in the west, or are much thicker there than in the east. With the anthracitic or near-anthracitic coal measures of the Assise de Châtelet and the Assise d'Andenne the reverse is true. The Assise de Flénu is found only in the westernmost section of the Belgian part of the Austrasian field near Mons. The beds of this coal are here 1,020 metres thick and contain 45 seams of a total thickness of 27 metres. Beneath them in the Mons field lie 1,200 metres of the Assise de Charleroi with 20 seams of 16 metres thickness: then comes the Assise de Châtelet of 280 metres thickness: and deepest of all the Assise d'Andenne of 120 metres.

[1] *The Coal Resources of the World, Inquiry of the Executive Committee of the XIIth International Geological Congress* (Toronto, 1913): M. Defline, *France*, in vol. II, pp. 649–711; A. Renier, *Belgium*, in vol. III, pp. 801–19; H. E. Böber and others, *Germany*, in vol. III, pp. 821–960. See also S. von Bubnoff, *Geologie von Europa* (Berlin, 1930), vol. II, ch. 5, esp. pp. 307–18.

[2] Defline, *France*, p. 660.

The two latter contain few workable seams, and these very thin. The total depth of the coal measures in Mons is 2,520 metres; almost the same as in the Valenciennes area to the west. To the east the thickness of the upper measures decreases, and the topmost measure, the Assise de Flénu, disappears. The greatest contrast with Mons is afforded by the Herve area in the east where the Assise de Charleroi is only 275 metres thick and contains only 7 workable seams. On the other hand, the Assise de Châtelet is much thicker than in Mons, 450 metres: and the Assise d'Andenne is more than twice as thick as in the west of Belgium. The total thickness of the coal measures here, however, is only 1,005 metres, less than half their thickness at Mons.

The geologist responsible for the report on Belgium to the Toronto Congress was much less ready to commit himself to an exact estimate of coal reserves of the type made for the French part of the Austrasian field. He remarked cautiously that he was inclined to put the 'workable reserves' of the basin Haine-Sambre-Meuse at about 3,000 million tons. He added that the largest reserves were in western Hainaut, a result in accord with the general geological information available about the richness of the Mons section of the field; but he did not venture upon more specific estimates. He emphasized the difficult conditions of working in the Belgian fields due to extensive faulting and folding, and drew attention to the fact that seams as thin as thirty centimetres, in beds whose dip was never less than 25 degrees, were worked commercially. Belgium was short of the rich coals used in gas making except in Mons: and had limited supplies of good coking coals.

The Aachen areas are a continuation of the Sambre-Meuse strip with very similar working conditions (they shared with the Liège area special difficulties over the drainage of pits). The Wurm basin lies to the north of Aachen and the Inde to the east. Krusch estimated the thickness of coal measures for the Aachen region as a whole at 1,130 metres, or very much the same as in the Herve area of Belgium immediately to the west. The reserves of the Inde basin are of *mager* and *fett* coals, some of which are suitable for coking: those of the Wurm are of higher volatile content ranging through the *fett* coal to the *gasflamm* coal. The total reserves were estimated to be 1,612 million tons in 1913. These were proved reserves. Both probable and possible reserves were described as 'considerable'.

The total proved reserves of the western wing of the Austrasian field on the the estimates presented to the Congress (admittedly estimates without a fully uniform base) were about 8,500 million tons (France *c.* 4,000 millions; Belgium *c.* 3,000 millions; and the Aachen area *c.* 1,500 millions). An allowance for probable and possible reserves might raise this figure to

20,000 millions, but no reasonable allowance could produce a figure of a different order of magnitude. This was the part of the Austrasian field pinched in between two hard old massifs; and it contrasts strongly with the riches to the east. In 1913 a great part of the concealed coalfield to the north of the Ruhr was not known in any detail; but the overwhelming advantage enjoyed by this area over any other part of the Austrasian field had long been clear, and the estimates presented to the Congress illustrate this well enough.

On the left-bank of the Rhine the proved reserves of the Nord-Krefeld area were 7,100 million tons, mostly of *fett* and *mager* coal: those of the Brüggen-Erkelenz area were put at 1,746 million tons. In each case the probable and possible reserves were both described as considerable. In the left-bank areas alone, therefore, the proved coal resources were about as great as in all those parts of the field from Aachen to Pas-de-Calais. It was on the right-bank, however, that the reserves were so spectacularly great. In the main Ruhr area the coal measures are between 3,000 and 3,500 metres thick. The *gasflamm* coal seams occur over a horizon of about 1,000 metres close to the surface in 23 seams of about 20 metres total thickness. Below them is a band of 300 metres between the lower limit of the *gasflamm* seams and the Katharina seam with 8 seams of gas coal, each on an average one metre thick: and below this there is a great thickness of coal measures containing seams of *mager* coals. The estimates prepared by Kukuk and Mintrop for the Toronto Congress put the proved reserves of coal to 2,000 metres (ignoring seams of less than 30 centimetres) at 56,344 million tons; the probable reserves at 68,722 millions to the same depth; and the possible reserves at 88,500 millions, making a grand total of 213,566 millions. Counting the proved and probable reserves together, the resources of *gasflamm* coal were 6,700 million tons; of gas coal 36,300 millions; of *fett* coal 48,300 millions; and of *mager* coal, 33,600 millions. The coal seams of the Ruhr were normally thicker, less faulted, and less steeply tilted than those of the French, Belgian or Aachen parts of the coalfield.

Other estimates of the Ruhr reserves have embodied more modest conclusions. For example, the Preussische Geologische Landesanstalt estimated the reserves of Ruhr-Westphalia to 1,000 metres to be only 63,950 million tons. Yet even this last estimate is many times as large as the total for the entire western wing of the Austrasian field. The tremendous difference between the two wings of the field is very clear.

At the beginning of the period 1850–1914 it was natural that production should be concentrated mainly in those parts of the field where the coal measures were exposed (Belgium, Aachen and the southern Ruhr): just as at a still earlier date mining was restricted to those areas where there was outcrop coal accessible by shallow pits or adit mining. As the techniques of drainage, ventilation and coal haulage from the pit bottom improved however, and as the richness of the reserves of the hidden part of the coalfield became apparent, mining moved into the concealed coalfield areas. By 1910 the most productive areas of the field, both in the eastern and western wings, were in the concealed coal areas—the northern Ruhr in the east and Pas-de-Calais in the west. The shift of production to the new areas was the keynote of mining development in the French and German parts of the field; and even in Belgium the first steps towards development of the concealed Campine field had been taken by the end of the period, for the reserves of the Campine field were more than twice those of the valley of the Sambre-Meuse. At the same time the first shafts in the adjacent Dutch Limburg field were being sunk.

During the second half of the nineteenth century the commercial success of coal mining depended on a restless search for new productive areas when existing reserves were insufficient or difficult to mine. This, allied to a growing geological knowledge, led to a relative decline of the older mining areas and the rise of new areas, both in the far east and the far west of the Austrasian field. The predominance of the Ruhr area within the field was foreshadowed by its enormous lead over other areas in the quantity, accessibility and range of its reserves, Given the critical importance of cheap and abundant coal between 1850 and 1914, its 'grossness' as an economic raw material, and a continuance of the mobility of capital, technical expertise and entrepreneurs observed in the last chapter, it was to be expected that this should come to be reflected in sweeping industrial gains in the Ruhr and in increasing difficulties in the less well endowed areas such as Hainaut, Liège and Aachen. The technological changes absorbed from England implied changes in the balance of regional advantage: a new regional industrial pattern was appropriate to the new technology. The areas most favoured in the past encountered great difficulties, whilst some areas without great industrial traditions were caught up in tumultuous industrial growth.

IV. THE DEVELOPMENT OF COAL PRODUCTION

In the half-century which ended in 1914 coal production grew immensely throughout the Austrasian field; but the rate of growth was not uniform in all areas. The old dominance of Hainaut rapidly disappeared as the eastern and western extremities of the field began to exploit their richer resources. By the end of the period three coal-producing divisions of the Ruhr, Düsseldorf, Arnsberg, and Münster and Minden (substantially Kr. Recklinghausen in Münster) had surpassed Hainaut; and so had one in the west, Pas-de-Calais. Hainaut remained the largest producer of the central divisions of the field, ahead of Nord, Liège and Aachen. These four latter divisions all increased their output considerably, but at a much more sedate pace than the better endowed divisions of the field.

There is an obvious general correspondence between the areas of swiftest growth and the areas best endowed with coal, but the point can be established with much greater authority by examining the figures of output per man-year in each part of the field. This was the aspect of production most directly influenced by the geology of the field; and at the same time is an important clue to differences in the rate of growth of coal production in the several divisions of the field, since production tended to grow most rapidly in those areas where it was highest. As time passed the figures of output per man-year came to reflect the geological conditions of each division of the field very closely; and to correspond very well with the rate at which production expanded.

Table 4. *Output per Man-Year (in tons)*[1]

	Pas-de-Calais	Nord		Hainaut	Liège
1853–8 and '60	90	119	1851	134	102
1861–70	142	135	1861	129	104
1871–80	167	167	1870	148	151
1881 and '88	240	216	1880	164	163
1895–7 and '99	249	232	1890	172	180
1901–10	225	206	1900	172	188

[1] Because statistical definitions and methods of collection differed from country to country comparison of these figures requires caution. Even within the same country there may be breaks in the series owing to changes in methods of collection or definition, as in Germany between 1884 and 1885.

	Aachen	Düsseldorf[1]	Arnsberg[1]	Reckling-hausen
1871–80	187*	237*	225	173*
1881–90	209†	317†	282	280
1891–1900	218	295	257	265
1901–10	216	275	239	249

     * 1872–80   † Excluding 1883 and 1884

The pattern at the beginning of the period forms an interesting contrast with that at the end. In 1850 Hainaut, where total output was much larger than anywhere else on the Austrasian field, had the highest output per man-year. At the end of the century productivity was lower in Hainaut than in any other part of the field. In 1850 the better equipment and greater expertise available in Belgian mines more than counterbalanced the physical disadvantages under which the area laboured. In the next three decades, however, output per man-year in Belgium, where resources were least and conditions of working most difficult, fell behind all other areas. The rapid growth in demand for coal caused a great volume of production to be required; and the older industrial areas experienced increasing difficulty in meeting this demand.

By 1880 the position had taken new shape. In the western wing of the field the highest figures were to be found in Pas-de-Calais (after two decades when a high proportion of the labour force was engaged in shaft-sinking and similar, unproductive development work). After 1880 productivity in Pas-de-Calais was notably higher than elsewhere in the west, and at times approached the levels reached in the Ruhr. Pas-de-Calais, of all the western areas, was the division in which folding and faulting were least, and the coal seams thickest. At the other extreme were the two Belgian divisions where mining was very difficult. Of these two Liège consistently showed the higher figures of productivity towards the end of the century, perhaps because of the relative shallowness of pits in Liège (in 1902 the average depth of working there was 336 metres: in Hainaut 477 metres). Nord and Aachen occupy intermediate positions. The geological kinship between Aachen and the areas to the west is strongly reflected in these statistics. In the eastern wing of the field conditions of working were much more favourable. Production per man-year was usually between

[1] Baumont estimated output per man-year in the Ruhr in the decade 1851–60 as 131 tons (Baumont, *La Grosse industrie allemande et le charbon*, p. 566). Oldenberg gives a figure of 116 tons for Westphalia in 1858 (the figure may refer to the whole Ruhr for the passage is not quite explicit). See K. Oldenberg, 'Studien über die rheinisch-westfälische Bergarbeiterbewegung', *Schmoller's Jahrbuch*, vol. xiv (Leipzig, 1890), p. 624.

fifty and a hundred tons higher than in the west. Of the Ruhr divisions, Düsseldorf invariably returned the highest figures, perhaps because the richest seams lie nearer the surface in the west than in the east, where the northward dip of the seams is slightly greater. So marked was the contrast between the richest and poorest parts of the Austrasian field, that there were years, especially in the late 1880s when the miner in Düsseldorf produced almost two tons of coal to every one produced by the miner in Hainaut.

It is possible to argue that the levels of output per man-year, though chancing to coincide with the levels suggested by the comparative geology of the coalfield, were governed as much or more by the amount of capital sunk into them, by the national habits of work, or by local differences in production techniques, and so on. There is no way in which such assertions can be disproved directly, since all such factors must be present where coal is produced, and have their influence upon its production. Yet there are features of the picture which tend to be anomalous on alternative explanations, such as the correspondence between the figures of Aachen and other parts of the western wing of the field, or the surprising exception which Pas-de-Calais makes to the general rule of lower productivity in the west. The very points which form anomalies in other explanations are the strength of an explanation which rests chiefly on the geology of the coalfield. If the other elements in the situation had been of prime importance they must either have produced similarities which in fact are lacking, or differences where none is to be found. On the other hand, the levels of output per man-year in 1880 and subsequently agree very well with the pattern which a knowledge of the geology of the coalfield would suggest.

In coal mining much the most important single factor in the total cost of production was the cost of labour. In France, for example, Simiand concluded that the labour employed in the mines formed 42 per cent of the total costs in the years before 1860, and that this percentage rose steadily to about 52 per cent in the last years of the century.[1] For Germany Walker's estimate for the years 1878–94 is 55 to 59 per cent; a conclusion similar to that of Baumont.[2] The areas, therefore, in which labour was most productive were always those where, other things being equal, coal could be mined most cheaply; and production expanded most economically. The connexion between the conditions of working and output per man-year

[1] F. Simiand, 'Essai sur le prix du charbon en France au XIXe siècle', *L'Année Sociologique*, tome v, 1900–1 (Paris, 1902), pp. 68–9.

[2] F. Walker, 'Monopolistic Combinations in the German Coal Industry', *Publications of the American Economic Association*, 3rd series, vol. v, 1904 (New York, 1904), p. 605; Baumont, *La Grosse industrie allemande et le charbon*, p. 601.

might consequently be expected to extend to the rate at which production expanded in each division of the field. Table 5, which shows the share of each division of the field in its total production at various dates, may help to clarify the connexion.

Table 5. *Percentage Share of each Division in Total Coal Output*

	1850	1860	1872	1880	1890	1900	1910
Hainaut	52·0	45·0	31·8	25·8	20·9	15·8	11·9
Liège	14·1	11·4	10·0	7·9	7·1	5·9	4·6
Nord	10·9	9·6	8·8	7·6	6·7	5·4	4·7
Pas-de-Calais		3·5	7·3	10·0	13·0	13·6	13·4
Aachen	4·6	4·3	2·8	2·5	2·1	1·7	2·0
Düsseldorf ⎫	18·3	26·2 ⎧	14·5	15·7	14·8	17·0	20·2
Arnsberg ⎭		⎩	24·1	28·7	30·7	32·7	30·9
Recklinghausen			0·7	1·9	4·9	8·0	12·4
Total eastern wing	18·3	26·2	39·3	46·3	50·4	57·7	63·5
TOTAL	100·0	100·0	100·0	100·0	100·0	100·0	100·0

The figures for 1850 and 1860 may not be precisely accurate since occasionally a figure for a year earlier or later has been included. The percentages have been rounded and do not in all cases add up to precisely one hundred.

The close correspondence between this table and the previous one is very clear. Among the individual divisions the most rapid proportional decline was in Hainaut where mining conditions were most difficult and productivity lowest: and the swiftest advance in Arnsberg and Düsseldorf where they were most favourable and output per man-year was highest (Recklinghausen is a special case discussed below). Areas of similar production per man-year gained or lost ground at similar rates. For example, there is a broad similarity between Nord and Aachen in both tables: output per man-year was normally about the same in both areas, and their share of the total production of the Austrasian field fell in each case by a little over a half during the sixty-year period. The two Belgian divisions, hampered by meagre resources, lost ground more rapidly than Nord and Aachen: while Pas-de-Calais, where conditions of mining were most nearly comparable to the easy working of the eastern wing, retained a stable share of the total production after an early period of rapid expansion. The share of the eastern wing of the field rose rapidly throughout the half-century. Between 1870 and 1910 the proportions produced in the eastern and western wings were almost exactly reversed; at the first date the western wing having a little over three-fifths of the total production, at the second the eastern wing. The great bulk of the production of the eastern wing came from Arnsberg and Düsseldorf. Of the two, Düsseldorf, where productivity was the higher, grew the more quickly over the period as a whole, but it was only in the last two decades that Düsseldorf became the faster-growing area. It is possible that in the early decades Arnsberg grew the faster for the same reason that Recklinghausen or Pas-de-Calais grew so swiftly—that production was expanding because new areas were being opened up for the first time, rather than because efficient production in the areas already developed was encouraging a rapid expansion *in situ*.

Table 6. *Coal Production ('000 tons)*

	Pas-de-Calais	Nord	Aachen	Düsseldorf	Arnsberg	Recklinghausen
(1) 1850		1,000	424*	1,666		
(2) 1858–62	679	1,627	713†	4,366‡		
(3) 1868–72	2,066	2,654	1,041§	5,158‖	7,318	249§
(4) 1878–82	4,775	3,533	1,175	7,480	13,874	951
(5) 1888–92	8,528¶	4,561¶	1,437	10,348	21,691	3,472
(6) 1898–1902	13,787**	5,506**	1,844	16,821	32,190	7,946
(7) 1908–12	19,120	6,589	2,636††	27,850††	43,495††	16,972††

Percentage changes

	Pas-de-Calais	Nord	Aachen	Düsseldorf	Arnsberg	Recklinghausen
(1)–(2)		38·8	68·2			
(2)–(3)	204·3	38·7	46·0			
(3)–(4)	131·1	33·1	12·9	45·0	89·6	281·9
(4)–(5)	78·6	29·1	22·3	38·3	56·3	265·0
(5)–(6)	61·7	20·7	28·3	62·6	48·4	128·9
(6)–(7)	38·7	19·7	43·0	65·6	35·1	113·6

	Hainaut	Liège			Hainaut	Liège
(1) 1851	4,753	1,292	(1)–(2)		58·0	47·0
(2) 1860	7,508	1,899	(2)–(3)		35·8	66·5
(3) 1870	10,197	3,162	(3)–(4)		23·1	20·9
(4) 1880	12,549	3,824	(4)–(5)		17·7	32·2
(5) 1890	14,769	5,056	(5)–(6)		11·9	22·4
(6) 1900	16,533	6,191	(6)–(7)		1·0	5·3
(7) 1910	16,700‡‡	6,500‡‡				

* 1852.   †1861.   ‡1860.   § 1872.   ‖ 1871 and 1872.   ¶ 1888 and 1893.
** 1897, 1899 and 1901.   †† 1908–11.   ‡‡ Approximate.

The absolute figures of coal production naturally support the same conclusion: that there was an intimate connexion between the manpower productivity and the rate at which production expanded in any given area. It is noticeable that where one division within a national area consistently shows a higher output per man-year than another, output comes to grow more quickly in the former than in the latter: in France, Pas-de-Calais more quickly than Nord; in Belgium, Liège more quickly than Hainaut; in Germany, Düsseldorf more quickly than Arnsberg. International comparisons bear out the same conclusion no less than those within a single national area. In some instances there may have been other contributory factors at work (for example, the move of the Ruhr iron and steel industry to the Rhine increased the local demand for coal in Düsseldorf in the nineties and later); yet there is an impressive correspondence between high rates of expansion and a high manpower productivity. Anomalies are few and slight.

The interpretation of Table 6 presents two difficulties. In the first place, the information is too elaborate and diffuse to be easily assimilated. Secondly, the rates of increase in Recklinghausen and Pas-de-Calais are misleadingly high. They were new producing areas and attained enormous percentage increases because the absolute amounts involved were initially very small. Therefore the following short table is included. It is designed to summarize the chief lesson of this section, and to be used in conjunction with Table 6 as a key to it.

Table 7. *Rates of Increase of Coal Production*[1]

	A	B	
Hainaut	12·8	164·0	A is the average decennial rate of increase in coal
Liège	19·1	170·5	production between 1870 and 1910 (except for
Nord	25·5	205·3	Pas-de-Calais where the period is 1890–1910 for
Aachen	26·1	207·6	reasons shown above). The rates are obtained by
Pas-de-Calais	44·9	220·3	considering lines (3) and (7) of Table 6 only. They
Arnsberg	51·8	250·8	are not the result of averaging the four separate
Düsseldorf	52·4	281·0	percentage changes between 1870 and 1910.

B is the average output per man-year in tons in the coal mines 1870–1910.

The importance of manpower productivity appears in another, related sphere of coalfield economics. It was a major, even a decisive, influence on the course of coal prices. In an industry in which labour was so great a

[1] Recklinghausen has been omitted from the table because it remained a pioneer area of new pit sinking until the outbreak of the Great War.

proportion of all production costs, such a relationship is, of course, to be expected.

In most areas of the field output per man-year rose steadily in the early decades of the period to reach a peak in the eighties, and then declined somewhat in the last quarter-century of the period. The improved productivity of mining kept down, and even gradually reduced, the price of coal until the 1880s. Thereafter the impact of higher wages and capital costs could no longer be counterbalanced by increased productivity, and prices rose persistently.

Table 8. *The Price of Coal per Ton (in marks). Annual averages*

	Pas-de-Calais	Nord	Belgium	Aachen	Düsseldorf	Arnsberg	Recklinghausen
1860	12 06	11 32	8 92	—	—	—	—
1865	9 62	9 50	8 36	—	—	—	—
1870	10 03	9 34	8 73	—	—	—	—
1876–80	11 11	9 87	8 63	6 17	4 72	4 90	—
1881–5	9 13	8 56	7 72	5 79*	4 57	4 61*	—
1886–90	7 78†	7 03†	7 57	5 93	5 30	5 55	5 56
1891–5	8 24‡	7 73‡	8 16	6 31	6 93	7 03	7 35
1896–1900	8 40§	8 25§	9 70	8 03	7 52	7 48	7 35
1901–5	11 11	10 38	10 58	9 05	8 42	8 43	8 43
1906–10	11 86	11 43	12 32	11 22	9 73	9 56	9 60

    * 1881, 1882 and 1885 only.   † 1886, 1887 and 1888 only.
    ‡ 1893, 1894 and 1895 only.   § 1896, 1897 and 1899 only.

The bases on which each national price series were calculated were more various than those of output per man-year, so that the direct comparison of price levels between one country and its neighbours cannot be pushed very far. Moreover, the balance of types of coal produced was important. Gas coal frequently cost between a third and a half more than coal of low volatile content. Nevertheless many of the characteristics which were noted in connexion with the statistics of output per man-year are also visible in the coal prices. The advantage of the Ruhr areas over other parts of the field is apparent: and the rapidly increasing difficulty of working the Belgian parts of the field appears in the rise of coal prices in Belgium to levels higher than in Nord, after being substantially less than Nord in the early decades when output per man-year in Nord was lower than in Belgium. In general, the inverse correlation between prices and the rate of expansion of production is close, though not so good as the direct correlation with the manpower productivity figures. There is nothing in the price series, for example, to suggest why output should have risen so much more quickly in Pas-de-Calais than in Nord since prices were normally lower in the latter area. In this case the explanation may lie in the fact that each served one chief market, the Lille industrial complex; and this was actually closer to the main Pas-de-Calais producing areas than to those of Nord, which would tend to keep the prices quoted *sur les lieux de production* lower in the more distant area. Producers in Pas-de-Calais in these circumstances might well make the larger profits as a result. It is not surprising, however, that coal prices should be rather less sensitively in agreement than manpower productivity statistics with rates of growth of production because of the play of other influences on prices. There were, for example, frequently price agreements within each country among producers anxious to avoid the exhaustion of bitter price wars.

The argument up to this point has shown the congruity between the geology of the coalfield and the amount of coal which a miner dug in the course of a working year: and between his productivity, in turn, and the rapidity with which production grew in the several divisions of the field. It has also become clear that prices were very closely linked to this chain of circumstances, though the congruity is less complete in this case. The next important step will be the examination of the intimate interdependence regionally between coal production and general industrial production, especially in regard to rates of growth.

Before taking this step, however, it seems well to discuss two preliminary points. The first is to show by a very brief discussion of another group of coalfields that the characteristics of the Austrasian field during this period were not peculiar to it alone. Otherwise there is a strong temptation to believe that an unusual series of coincidences produced the congruities of geology, productivity and rates of expansion which are apparent throughout the Austrasian field. The second point is to establish the autarky in coal of each of the divisions of the field. If the differences in production costs between the areas of best and worst coal-working conditions had been sufficiently great, coal from the former might well have been imported into the latter to supplement local production. In that case the momentum of general industrial development would have ceased to be directly connected to the growth of local coal production, since industrial production might have increased while coal output remained stationary or declined. Such a situation would make it pointless to attempt the next step in the argument. A discussion of price differentials, the cost of coal transport and the volume of coal movement within the Austrasian field is a necessary preliminary to the consideration of the relationship between the growth of coal production and general industrial growth.

The great barrier to an understanding of the changing fortunes of the several divisions of the Austrasian field is the temptation to think of the growth of the Ruhr as something *sui generis*, which may by coincidence fit a general scheme, but which was in essence apart from other, parallel instances because of its immense scale of production and rapid rate of growth. The mind will accept arguments about congruities readily when size is much the same for all units, but is wary of accepting the same arguments when there are great differences in size. Therefore it is helpful to introduce an analogy with another, very different group of coal-producing areas. Differences in scale fall into perspective and the essential similarity of type becomes clearer.

In his essay on prices in the French coal industry, Simiand remarked that, in a period of expanding demand for coal, French producing areas did one of two things: either they increased output and reduced unit costs of production as in Nord and Pas-de-Calais; or limited output to keep up prices and relied on the natural shielding effects of transport costs to preserve the local market for local producers, as happened in all the other producing areas of France (between 1865 and 1910 output in Nord and Pas-de-Calais increased from $3\frac{1}{2}$ million tons to $25\frac{1}{2}$ millions: elsewhere in France output rose only from 8 to 12 millions). Simiand supposed that it was the geographical position of the Valenciennes coalfield, exposed to fierce Belgian and English competition that explained its great expansion.[1] But this is a partial and doubtful explanation only. Once more the economic geology of the coalfields seems the most important single cause of the striking contrast between the Valenciennes field and the rest of France, for the Valenciennes field was incomparably the richest in France, containing about 65 per cent of the total coal resources of the country. As on the Austrasian field the relative advantages of the several producing areas were quite slow to appear, and were reflected accurately in the levels of output per man-year and in prices. In 1850 the cost of coal in Nord was as high as in the other producing areas, and output per man-year was rather lower than the average (in 1853, for example, 125 tons per annum, compared with 154 tons in the rest of France). As the century drew on, however, output per man-year rose much higher in Nord and Pas-de-Calais (in 1901 206 t.p.a. in Nord; 239 t.p.a. in Pas-de-Calais; only 162 t.p.a. in the rest of France), and prices were lower than elsewhere. During the second half of the century, in short, the northern coalfield established within the French national production a position commensurate with its greater resources and easier conditions of working. It stood to the rest of France as the Ruhr did to the rest of the Austrasian field. It is true, of course,

[1] Simiand, *L'Année Sociologique* (1900–1), esp. pp. 62–3.

that the changes in productivity and price in Nord are consistent with Simiand's explanation, but since not only the changes in Nord and the rest of France, but also the developments in Nord and the rest of the Austrasian field, appear to conform with what would be expected on the ground of their relative resources of coal, one must assume a series of unusual coincidences not to accept the prime importance of coal resources.

There are further parallels between the relation of Nord to the rest of France and that of the Ruhr to the other parts of the Austrasian field. The first area of France to develop a modern iron industry was the coalfield area near St Etienne, which may be compared to the early industrial growth on the Austrasian field at Seraing, Liège and Verviers, or to that near Charleroi in Hainaut. Both St Etienne and the Belgian areas were growing rapidly before the mid-century, and were quick to adopt the latest metal-working and coal-mining methods from England. There were, for example, already several coke-fired blast furnaces in the St Etienne area by 1830. The relative advance of the St Etienne coalfield was so marked in 1850 that the area even held a substantial share of the Paris coal market, in spite of the difficulties of moving coal over the transport system between St Etienne and Paris. The St Etienne coal-owners showed no desire at this date to restrict their enterprise to the local market. Their subsequent inability to maintain an early lead lay largely in the inadequacy of local coal reserves. Heavy industry gave place steadily to the lighter metal finishing trades which required less coal and were less sensitive to its price. St Etienne was to France what Belgium was to the Austrasian field industrial areas. If the coal-owners of Nord and Pas-de-Calais displayed greater initiative as Simiand suggests, they were at least greatly aided by the comparative richness of their local coal resources; just as the greater enterprise and better technical achievement of the Ruhr was closely related to the opportunities afforded to entrepreneurs by its greater richness of endowment.

The second preliminary point to be considered is the question of transport costs and the movement of coal. With the building of railways the cost of transporting goods overland dropped very substantially. Before their advent the price of coal had risen precipitously away from the pit-head unless water carriage was available. In the Ruhr, for example, the cost of carting coal with horse and wagon had been about 40 pf. per ton-kilometre in the 1840s; a figure which meant that the price of coal doubled within fifteen kilometres of the pit-head if taken overland (as was often inevitable). When the first railways were built the cost dropped immediately by two-thirds to about 14 pf. per ton-kilometre; and ultimately to 2 pf. 2 (even less over very long distances where taper rates could take effect).

It is little wonder that it was a matter of the first moment to each new mining venture to secure a rail spur either to the main rail network or to a canal or navigable river. Some mines built rail links for themselves. Several companies in Pas-de-Calais in the 1850s, for example, obtained concessions for this purpose; just as many years before this the Anzin company had built the Valenciennes canal to solve the same problem. Rail transport grew rapidly in importance. Between 1851 and 1860 the proportion of Ruhr coal taken by rail rose from 25 per cent to 55 per cent. Even with the railways, however, the price of coal continued to be seriously affected by distance from the coalfield if taken overland. Very few commodities were as cheap as coal per unit-weight; and few, therefore, so sensitive to transport costs. An interesting illustration of this is to be found in the following figures of the cost of transporting one ton of coal from Essen (in marks).

Table 9. *Cost of Coal Transport (in marks)*[1]

	1879		1907	
Ruhrort	1	20	1	10
Cologne	3	20	2	40
Bremen	6	90	6	30
Mannheim	9	00	7	80
Hamburg	9	30	8	50
Berlin	11	50	10	60
Stettin	15	60	12	30
Munich	18	70	13	10

In 1879 the price of coal in the Essen area (*Reg.-bez.* Düsseldorf) was 4 m. 2 pf. per ton: in 1907 it was 9 m. 62 pf. Assuming the absence of dues and tariffs the price of coal in 1879 was doubled by a journey of about 75 miles, and in 1907 by a journey of about 240 miles. The relative importance of transport costs, therefore, declined considerably: but the absolute cost of transporting coal did not fall significantly except over the longer distances (the big falls in railway freight rates had already taken place by 1879). Unless the difference in price between coal produced in two separate mining areas was greater than the cost of transporting coal from the low to the high-cost producer, coal would not normally move from the former to the latter.

Clearly the great threat to other producing areas came from the Ruhr, since this was the lowest-cost producer. In 1879 the cost of locally produced

[1] Adapted from a table in Baumont, *La Grosse industrie allemande et le charbon*, p. 416.

coal at Essen was 4 m. 2 pf. a ton, compared with the Aachen price of 5m. 69 pf.; but Aachen coal was in no danger of successful local Ruhr competition since the cost of transporting coal by rail (there was no water link) must have been, from the evidence of the table, about 5 m. per ton, making a total cost of Essen coal at Aachen of about 9 m. altogether. So far was the Aachen area from succumbing to Ruhr competition that it competed effectively with Ruhr coal in München-Gladbach, a city roughly equidistant from the main Ruhr and Aachen producing areas.[1] Liège, the next nearest division to the Ruhr, enjoyed the same immunity in 1879 even supposing that there was no break in taper rail rates at the frontier. In that year the local price was 7 m. 52 pf. a ton. Ruhr coal would have cost about two marks more than this at such a distance from the Ruhr. In Hainaut and the French coalfield areas the disadvantage of the Ruhr coal was still more strongly marked. In 1907 transport costs had fallen slightly, but so, perhaps in sympathy with them, had the price differentials between the various Austrasian field divisions; so that even at this late date, and ignoring the added costs which invariably attended the crossing of a frontier (break in taper rates, handling charges, and, in the case of France, a tariff of 1 fr. 20 c., plus 15 c. *frais de statistique*), Ruhr coals were not directly competitive with the coals in any other area of the field in their local markets. The effects of the pressure of Ruhr competition were immense but were experienced indirectly.

Where water transport was available it was usually cheaper than rail.

Table 10. *Coal Prices in France in 1850*[2]
(in francs per ton)

Nord	14	50
Pas-de-Calais	24	33
Aisne	19	02
Somme	20	00
Oise	21	34
Ardennes	33	40

---

[1] This is not so say, of course, that the effect of the low Ruhr prices was not felt in Aachen and elsewhere. The 'Jahresberichten des Handelskammern, kaufmännischen Corporationen u.s.w.', published in the *Preussische Statistik* sometimes carry complaints about the pressure which Ruhr prices exerted on producers in the Aachen area. The Stolberg report of 1868, for example (vol. xxII, p. 143), complained that 'the competition of the pits on the right-bank of the Rhine made necessary further price cuts'. Profit margins were no doubt cut by Ruhr pressure, and expansion made more difficult (note the parallel with the French fields other than Valenciennes in another setting): but the pressure of the Ruhr was indirect, in the sense that Ruhr coal did not appear in the local markets unless in exceptional circumstances.

[2] Simiand, *L'Année sociologique* (1900–1), pp. 49–50.

Canal transport was a strong competitor of the railway in areas served by both. Extensive use of it was made, for example, in northern France. Yet even where canal transport was used coal prices still rose quickly away from the pit-head. The experience of northern France during the half-century clearly shows this. In 1850 the price of coal (*sur les lieux de consommation*) in departments near Nord varied as shown in Table 10 above.

Somme, Aisne and Oise were fed by the St Quentin canal and its lateral offshoots; and all three drew a substantial proportion of their consumption from Nord, or from the Mons area just across the Belgian frontier. They give a clue to the effect of water transport on prices. Prices were lowest in Aisne, which was best served by water routes from Nord, and nearest the producing areas: yet, even with the benefit of good canal communications and at a relatively short distance from the mines (certainly on an average under fifty miles), the price in Aisne was between 35 and 40 per cent higher than in Nord. In Somme and Oise, which lay at a greater distance away from the coalfield, the price of coal was still higher. In Ardennes, which was not well served by canal, the price was more than double that of Nord, although the two departments are adjacent to one another (in fact transport between the two was so expensive that Ardennes drew most of its coal from Belgium). Coal mining in Pas-de-Calais had still to reach the production stage in 1850, which explains the high level of prices there.

Half a century later in 1895 the picture was not much altered except in Ardennes and Pas-de-Calais. In Pas-de-Calais the development of local

Table 11. *Coal Prices in France in 1895*
(*in francs per ton*)

Nord	12	46
Pas-de-Calais	13	22
Aisne	20	40
Somme	18	05
Oise	21	88
Ardennes	18	27

production on a very large scale is the reason for the fall in prices to a level like that of Nord: in Ardennes the development of the extremely important Metz-Valenciennes rail link, which was a major carrier of coke and iron ore, helped to bring down prices to a level similar to those found in other departments adjoining Nord. The swift rise of coal prices away from the coalfield was still very marked. Indeed the gap between Nord and Aisne, Somme and Oise had widened slightly.

A very brief survey of the movement of coal from one part of the Austrasian field to another shows that it was as slight in practice as the consideration of transport costs would lead one to expect. Although the Ruhr became the greatest source of coal in the Austrasian field during the half-century; produced most cheaply; and exported more than all other areas combined, at no time did Ruhr coal command a large market in other parts of the field. Indeed it was not until the last decade of the period that German coal (in contrast with the sea-borne British coal) entered in large quantities into the general markets of Belgium and France.

Until the end of the nineteenth century German coal exports to Belgium were small in absolute amount and showed little tendency to expand. In the decade 1881–90 they averaged 622,000 tons per annum: in the next decade the average was 755,000 tons.[1] In each case they formed only a very small fraction of domestic consumption (less than a twentieth). 1897 was the first year in which German coal exports to Belgium topped one million tons (if occasional freak years such as 1878 and 1879 are excepted). Thereafter the change was dramatic. Total imports of coal and coke grew rapidly: in 1906 their combined total exceeded that of coke and coal exports for the first time, and thereafter until the outbreak of war the gap widened steadily. For the first time German exports of coal were able to win a substantial share of the Belgian market, though probably not of the market in the immediate vicinity of the coalfields. The annual average of German coal exports to Belgium in the decade 1901–10 jumped to 2,902,000 tons; four times the average of the previous decade. In 1913 the total was 5,728,000 tons. German coke exports also increased quickly from between 100,000 and 200,000 tons per annum before the end of the century to almost 1,000,000 tons in 1913.

During this last decade before the war the gap between German and Belgian coal prices was not great, less indeed than it had been in earlier decades when Belgian coal had held its own comfortably at home, so that it seems that the pressure of Ruhr competition was now acutely felt. The increasing physical difficulties of mining were making it very difficult for coal-owners in the Sambre-Meuse valley to maintain profit margins without increasing prices and so losing markets: hence the sudden success of German coals. The rate of increase of domestic coal production had, in fact, fallen steadily for many decades: between 1900 and 1913 production did not increase at all.

German entry into the French market in strength is again of late date. In the decade 1881–90 exports of coal to France were on an average 1,063,000

[1] The German coal and coke export figures are taken from *Statistisches Jahrbuch für das Deutsche Reich*, 'Auswärtiger Handel'.

tons per annum: in the following decade the figure had sunk to 622,000 tons. The first decade of the new century saw a marked increase to a yearly average of 1,430,000 tons and a generally upward trend. In 1913 the total reached a peak of 3,243,000 tons. Coke exports also grew steadily from the nineties, reaching one million tons for the first time in 1904, and 2,377,000 tons in 1913. As in Belgium, the German share of the coal market was marginal until the new century began. In France statistics of the origins and quantities of coal consumed are available for the department as well as for the nation as a whole. It is clear from these that although German coals were of the first importance in a few departments, notably in Meurthe-et-Moselle where they fed the new iron and steel industries, they were never of any importance in Nord or Pas-de-Calais. In Nord the consumption of German coal exceeded 100,000 tons for the first time in 1909. In 1911, the last year for which this breakdown is published, it was 159,000 tons. Even then this formed less than a fiftieth of total Nord consumption.

It would seem that the radii of the circles within which Belgian and French fields were able successfully to compete with the Ruhr were shrinking steadily after the middle nineties, because it was unprofitable to expand production at existing prices and the price level in the Ruhr set a ceiling to the price rises possible without losing markets. The absence of provincial figures in Belgium makes it difficult to know just what was happening there in the last fifteen years before the outbreak of war, but, by analogy with France, it is probable that Hainaut and Liège continued to draw their coal from local sources but were no longer able to control Belgian markets at a distance from the Sambre-Meuse valley. Much of what Simiand had said of the French coalfields other than Nord—that they were defending local markets and relying on the shielding effect of transport costs—could now be said of the entire western wing of the Austrasian field *vis-à-vis* the eastern.

There was one apparent exception to the general rule that each division of the field supplied its own local market. This was Nord. Throughout the period there was a considerable import of coal from the Mons coalfield in Belgium along the Mons-Condé canal:[1] and in the later decades a great weight of coal came into Nord from Pas-de-Calais. The reason for this anomaly lies in the Lille market, which was the largest in the French part of the Austrasian field. Lille lies in Nord but well away from the Nord coal-producing area near Valenciennes. It is actually nearer the main pro-

[1] This exceeded one million tons already in the 1850s and remained at about the same level with very little variation until 1914. In the 1850s it was more than half the total local consumption, but had fallen to less than an eighth by the war.

ducing areas of Pas-de-Calais than those of Nord: and is also close to the Mons field across the border (owned by French capital). It was the centre of a lively competition from all three directions. The political divisions which have been used perforce as the units of coal production and consumption are not, of course, ideal because economic activity seldom conforms with political units. The Lille industrial area is an excellent illustration of this point and it accounts for Nord's apparently anomalous position.

In so far as the industrial *élan* of an area depended upon the price which it had to pay for its fuel, it is clear that some divisions of the field were much better favoured than others. Industry, especially industry in which coal formed a large fraction of total cost of production, might be expected to grow more quickly in the areas of cheap and abundant coal production than elsewhere. The extent to which the cost of fuel entered into the total cost of production, however, varied very greatly from industry to industry; often much more violently than other production costs. Because of this wide variation the less fortunate areas of the Austrasian field were better able to hold their own against the Ruhr in such industries as textiles and light engineering than in the heavy industries. In a French government publication of the early 1860s there appears a table which points the contrast in importance of coal prices for heavy and light industry.[1] An extract from the table, which shows how the cost of each 100 francs of finished product was apportioned under five main heads of expenditure is reproduced as Table 12.

Table 12. *Relative Importance of Several Factors of Production*

	A	B	C	D	E
Metallurgy	2·47	12·65	45·26	23·29	16·33
Ceramics	2·73	31·01	23·09	16·98	26·19
Chemicals	1·90	5·41	62·46	4·39	25·84
Metal-working industries	1·91	19·61	45·16	3·39	29·93
Food	1·20	2·82	75·87	2·64	17·47
Textiles	1·46	12·01	68·46	1·34	16·73
Leather	1·16	6·17	75·86	0·78	16·03

A interest on capital
B labour costs
C raw materials
D fuel costs
E general expenses calculated simply by subtracting the first four items from the cost of the finished product

[1] *Statistique de la France*, deuxième série, tome xix, Industrie: 'Résultats généraux de l'Enquête effectuée dans les années 1861–5', p. xxviii.

E

At difference places and times during the half-century between 1850 and 1914 these proportions varied considerably, but the magnitude of the difference between the proportion which fuel formed of the total cost of, say, textiles and steel was always and everywhere great. The German section of the field provides evidence of the practical effects of this contrast. The manufacture of primary iron and steel in the Aachen area, for example, was inhibited by the proximity of the Ruhr; but the textile and engineering industries, with their lesser dependence on cheap coal, remained economically viable. Indeed some Ruhr firms with branches at Aachen sent pig-iron or raw steel to Aachen for further processing. The Phönix concern, for example, made rails and heavy metal goods at Ruhrort, but railway wheels, tin sheets and fine metalwares at Eschweiler near Aachen. The pressure exerted by Ruhr competition upon Belgian and French areas of the field was similar in kind, though the existence of substantial tariffs on the entry of iron and steel products combined with the cushioning effect of greater distance from the Ruhr enabled French and Belgian heavy industry to keep control over national markets. In textile and light engineering products the necessary disadvantage of the western wing of the field was much less pronounced, since these industries used relatively little coal. Even in the lighter industries, however, both contemporaries and historians agree in emphasizing the advantage of a coalfield location.[1]

As the quantity of coal consumed in industry rose, and its cost became a matter of moment to an increasing range of industries, the natural advantages of the eastern wing of the Austrasian field were steadily translated into industrial achievement. The general connexion between large coal reserves, favourable mining conditions, cheap coal and rapid industrial growth can hardly be questioned, given the circumstances of economic life which prevailed in the late nineteenth century. It has often been remarked in the past. Jevons believed that a ready abundance of cheap coal, combined with good communications, would enable an area to overcome the handicap of late entry into modern industrial practice and ensure a swift, subsequent growth. He also believed the converse of this: that no matter what the advantages of an old-established industrial area might be,

---

[1] An example of this is the Lille textile area, of which Sée wrote, 'Lille, Roubaix and Tourcoing owe their prosperity above all to the nearness of the Nord coalfield' (Sée, *Histoire économique de la France*, vol. II, p. 168). Fohlen says of the Nord textile industry that, 'The decisive stimulus was the opening between 1840 and 1850 of new coal mines in the departments of Nord and Pas-de-Calais' (C. Fohlen, *L'Industrie textile au temps du second empire* (Paris, 1956), p. 224). Such remarks might be paralleled many times over. The absence of a local source of coal was not fatal to textile industries as universally as it was to iron industries, but its presence was usually a great stimulus.

if it lacked coal, it lacked the source of continued success so long as the existing conditions of industry persisted: that abundant, local coal, in short, was the *sine qua non* of industrial growth and prosperity.

It is interesting to try to establish how far the implications of the general connexion postulated by Jevons can be traced in the economic history of important industrial areas over a period of several decades: to examine in detail the utility of the general statement as a tool of regional analysis which may throw light on the circumstances of coalfield economic growth and show the usefulness in detail of reasonable general assumptions. Three steps have now been taken. They have shown that within the Austrasian field area, even though it is broken up into three national sections, the distribution and accessibility of coal reserves appears to have controlled the growth of coal production uniformly throughout the field through the middle term of manpower productivity, with which the rates of growth of production can be closely correlated. Where geological conditions were favourable the output resulting from the investment of each unit of capital was high, prices were low, growth rapid, and productivity high. If Jevons's general assumptions hold true in the rough-and-tumble of practical economic affairs, a fourth step is possible: to show a close agreement between the rate at which coal production expanded and the rate of general industrial growth in each division of the Austrasian field.

V. REGIONAL INDUSTRIAL GROWTH AND ITS RELATION TO POPULATION CHANGES

In the introductory chapter the difficulty of constructing an adequate measure of total regional industrial production was touched upon, and the suggestion advanced that an acceptable substitute for a direct measure of the physical volume or total value of production might be found in the population growth of each industrial area since this could be shown to reflect delicately changes in rates of industrial growth. The illustration then used related the growth of the total population in one textile area to its fluctuating industrial fortunes. The general correspondence was good: but this is a clumsy method. The total population of any industrial area is likely to include large numbers of people whose livelihood does not depend upon industry, and whose numbers cannot, therefore, be expected to change in accordance with industrial development in the area. If an accurate way of measuring the population dependent on industry can be found, however, a much subtler instrument becomes available. With it it is possible to trace the growth of local industry; and it will serve, with certain reservations, as an index of total industial production.

Other things being equal, it is reasonable to assume that a doubling in industrial population will be associated with a proportionate increase in industrial production. There are, of course, many circumstances in which this assumption would be false. For example, if the expansion of local industry were chiefly in the more capital-intensive among the local industries, a doubling of total industrial production would mean a less than proportionate increase in industrial population. The same effect would result from a general rise in productivity even when the balance of industries in the area remained unchanged. These and other cognate problems will be considered in more detail later in the argument. This method can only be approximate:[1] but used in conjunction with the statistics of coal production it throws light on the question of the connexion between rates of growth of coal production and total industrial production; and

[1] This drawback is less serious than might appear, because alternative methods of measuring trends in total industrial production over a long period also involve inaccuracies and margins of error, even where statistical information is sufficient for them to be attempted. See, for example, the recent article of W. A. Cole, 'The Measurement of Industrial Growth', *Economic History Review*, 2nd series, vol. XI, no. 2 (1958), pp. 309–15. In this article several of the difficulties of obtaining meaningful measures of the physical volume of production are discussed.

between this in turn and population growth: and, as will become clear, some check upon its accuracy is inherent in the method used.

There are eight main divisions of the Austrasian field for which both output of coal and growth of population can be traced throughout the period. They are Nord and Pas-de-Calais in France; Hainaut and Liège in Belgium; and Aachen, Düsseldorf, Arnsberg and Recklinghausen in Germany. The dominant types of industry varied greatly from area to area: and some areas were much more successful than others in fostering rapid expansion. It is possible, therefore, to study the relationship between coal production and industrial expansion in a wide range of circumstances.

The simplest cases are Pas-de-Calais and Recklinghausen, where coal production began for the first time during the half-century. Here one may consider the coalfield industrial population as beginning only with the first coal mining ventures. From this point forward all increase of population can be related directly to the increasing coal production.[1] In all areas other than Pas-de-Calais and Recklinghausen there was already a considerable production of coal before the beginning of the period. It follows that there was already a population dependent upon this production whose size must be estimated before the growth of coal production and industrial population can be compared. The solution to this problem must be arbitrary, but need not be unrealistic. The figures of the total increase of coal production and population during the first decade for which they are both available may be taken, and the former divided by the latter to give a unit population/coal ratio. This ratio shows how much increase of coal production (in tons) was associated with a unit increase of population in the ten-year period. This in turn suggests how many people were dependent upon coal-based industry at the first date—the figures being the total given by dividing the total coal output at that date by the unit population/coal ratio. Thereafter, all non-industrial population being treated as stationary, any increase of population taking place within the coalfield industrial area can be added to the base figures of industrial population.

As an illustration of the method, let us suppose that in a given area in 1860 the population was 500,000 and coal production was at a rate of 1,000,000 tons per annum; and that by 1870 the population had risen to 600,000 while coal production advanced to 1,800,000 tons per annum. By subtraction an 800,000 tons increase of coal production had been associated with a rise of 100,000 in population; or each eight tons of increase in coal output was accompanied by the addition of one person to the

---

[1] The justification for treating all non-industrial population as stationary and therefore all increase as increase in industrial population is explained below, pp. 60–1 and 67–8.

population, giving a unit population/coal ratio of eight. Further it would follow that in 1860 the population dependent upon coal was 1,000,000 divided by eight, or 125,000. The hypothesis assumes that the rest of the population is almost stationary in number, and that the relationship between coal production and population growth is a constant one. In the example the proportion of eight tons of coal to one person is the assumed constant. A simple test of the two doubtful elements in the hypothesis is possible: to calculate the base figure of population, assume that all increase of population is increase of industrial population, and discover how nearly at subsequent census dates the rates of increase of coal production and industrial population are similar to one another. If either the unit population/coal ratio changes significantly, or the non-industrial population grows (or declines), or the base figure is unrealistic, then there must be a divergence between the two growth rates which will show up when the two series are plotted semi-logarithmically (unless indeed in the very unlikely case that the variables altered in such a manner as to cancel each other out).

A pertinent objection to the proposed method is that the argument of the first chapter demands rather that population growth be compared with the growth of coal consumption, not that of coal production, because there might well be a considerable export of coal from an area or import into it which would modify the total used by local industry, which last is the amount which should be related to the trend of industrial population growth. There can be no question that this is the better procedure. Unfortunately only France published figures of coal consumption throughout the period for the same areas as the figures of coal production. These have been used for Nord, where there was a large net import of coal from the adjacent Belgian and Pas-de-Calais fields, which might have distorted calculations. For Pas-de-Calais, the other French area, the coal production figures have been preferred. In this department coal miners formed the vast bulk of the total industrial labour force, and so industrial population was peculiarly closely associated with coal production. Coal consumption figures were very different, since so much coal, latterly three-quarters of the annual output, was exported from the department. In Nord, on the other hand, coal miners contributed only a small fraction to the total of industrial employment. General industry, especially textiles, was dominant; and coal consumption is therefore the more suitable series. For other areas only figures of coal production are available. To use them does some violence to principle since no area consumed all its production locally; but as long as the proportion used locally was high and constant, this is not a grave drawback. An accurate measure of consumption would mean only a slight lowering of the unit population/coal ratio. Thus, if the ratio were eight when coal production figures are taken, and the amount exported from the area were constant at one-quarter of the total production, a substitution of coal consumption figures would simply mean that the ratio fell to six. It would not affect the validity of the ratio for most purposes.

Throughout, of course, industrial population does not refer just to those working in the mines, mills and factories of the coalfield area, but also to all employed in the service, distributive and transport industries dependent upon them: and to the wives and families of them all.

Before it is possible to discuss the growth of industrial population and its relation to coal production, it is first necessary to decide what shall be held to constitute a coalfield industrial area, and then to determine the size of the total populations of each division of the field at successive census dates. Only then can the form of analysis suggested above be applied.

THE DEFINITION OF THE COALFIELD INDUSTRIAL AREAS

Any population which is dependent for its livelihood upon the industries of a coalfield area, though it may not be for census purposes an urban area, is properly a part of the coalfield industrial area. For example, the census of industry and occupation taken in Germany in 1895 showed that the vast majority of people living in *Landkreis* Hagen were dependent upon the same industrial employments as were those living in *Stadtkreis* Hagen. The population of *Ldkr.* Hagen was larger than that of the *Stkr.* (78,000 compared with 51,000 in 1900), but it covered an area seven times as great (227 sq. kms. and 33 sq. kms. respectively). To exclude the former from the coalfield industrial area as a whole on the grounds that it was not a densely built-up urban area like the latter would defeat the purpose of this study, which demands a general view of the agglomeration of industry and people which developed with the growth in coal production.[1] In Belgium and Germany cheaper housing and more attractive surroundings, combined with the very low price of period returns on the railways, made it possible for large numbers of people to live in the small towns and country areas surrounding the big industrial centres, and yet left them as completely dependent on the factory or mine as if they lived in the shadow of the factory chimneys. Where the occupational censuses show that an

---

[1] In each 1,000 persons engaged in a profession or occupation in 1895, 641 were engaged in mining and industry in *Stkr.* Hagen compared with 664 in the same category in *Ldkr.* Hagen (*Statistik des Deutschen Reichs*, Neue Folge, Bd. 111, vol. III, Anhang, Ubersicht 43, 'Die berufliche Gliederung der Bevölkerung nach Berufsabtheilungen und-Gruppen in den kleineren Verwaltungsbezirken', p. 358).

area termed rural for census purposes was in fact largely a dormitory for industrial workers, it has been included in the coalfield industrial areas.[1]

During the half-century preceding the Great War the coalfield industrial area in all three countries increased considerably, so that places which at the beginning of the period were entirely agricultural became either sites of industrial development, or dormitories for people who made their living from industry. There are only two possible solutions to the problem of accommodating these changes in area. Either new areas are added to the original core as their occupational structure changes: or any area which ultimately became a part of the coalfield industrial area is included from the start. In the first alternative the addition of a new area greatly exaggerates the rise in total population since it means adding also the agricultural population of the area. This, in such an area, is sure to be a large fraction of the total since otherwise the area would have been included at a previous census date. The 'step' effect which such a method involves makes all plotting of population series very difficult. The second alternative means that in the early part of the period areas which were still mainly agricultural are included with the industrial districts. At first sight this might seem an equally grave drawback; but it involves very little distortion in the measurement of industrial populations because agricultural populations were almost at a standstill throughout the period. If it is possible to measure the size of the original industrial population in the manner suggested above and if the agricultural population remains stationary, then the rate of increase of the industrial population is easy to calculate, and this is the vital statistic.

Even in the remote parts of Germany, Belgium and France it was rare for an agricultural population to grow by as much as a quarter in the half-century.[2] In the immediate vicinity of the Austrasian field, where industry provided alternative sources of employment, agricultural populations changed little. In Westphalia and Rheinland, for example, the numbers dependent on farming and forestry fell slightly over a twenty-five year period:[3]

---

[1] See, in this connexion, the remarkable study by Mahaim of the effect of very cheap period returns on the Belgian railways towards the end of the century: E. Mahaim, *Les Abonnements d'ouvriers sur les lignes des chemins de fer belges et leurs effets sociaux* (Brussels-Leipzig, 1910).

[2] In East Prussia, for example, population grew only from 1,934,000 in 1880 to 2,064,000 in 1910; in province Luxembourg in Belgium the increase between 1856 and 1910 was only nineteen per cent (from 194,000 to 231,000); in France agricultural departments in which any increase of population took place were a rarity, except in Brittany.

[3] From *Statistik des Deutschen Reichs*, Bd. 211, Anhang, Übersicht 10, 'Die Berufsgliederung der Gesamtbevölkerung der einzelnen Bundesstaaten und Landesteile', p. 38*

	WESTPHALIA	RHEINLAND
1882	727,000	1,286,000
1895	698,000	1,233,000
1907	680,000	1,175,000

The same pattern appears in the neighbourhood of the French industrial area. The total population of the agricultural *arrondissement* of Hazebrouck in Nord increased by only seven per cent between 1851 and 1901. In Pas-de-Calais for the same period the population of *arr*. Montreuil was stationary; that of *arr*. St-Omer increased by six per cent; that of *arr*. St-Pol declined by ten per cent. The evidence strongly suggests that when the coalfield industrial area has been defined it is possible to consider all increases of population within it as increases in *industrial* population, even where there subsists a large group of people not industrially employed. The changes in the size of non-industrial populations were not sufficiently great to do more than affect this marginally.

The next step is to establish the limits of each of the eight divisions of the Austrasian field, and to trace the growth of population in them.

Population information in Germany, France and Belgium was collected at four levels beneath the full national unit. In descending order of size these were:

GERMANY	FRANCE	BELGIUM
Provinz	*département*	*province*
Regierungs-bezirk	*arrondissement*	*arrondissement*
Kreis	*canton*	*canton*
Gemeinde	*commune*	*commune*

The best unit for defining the size of the coalfield industrial areas and measuring their rate of growth is the third in rank, the *canton* in France and Belgium and the *Kreis* in Germany. The vast number of *communes* and *Gemeinden*, the smallest units, and the absence of statistics for many purposes for such tiny areas, excludes them; while the *arrondissement* and the *Regierungs-bezirk*, which were the census units next larger in size, covered such an area as to invite inaccuracy. They are used only where the absence of more detailed statistical information enforces their use.

The size of the *cantons* in Belgium and France in the coalfield areas was normally between 80 and 130 sq. kms., although the great urban areas, such as Charleroi and Lille, were sub-divided into much smaller *cantons*. The German *Kreis* in agricultural areas was a larger unit, usually between 100 and 700 sq. kms., but sub-division in industrial areas was much more common than with *cantons* in the Belgian and French industrial areas, giving an average size near that of the *canton*, though the range of size remained greater.[1]

In 1870 the Belgian *canton* with the smallest population of any in the industrial coalfield area was Dour with 28,500: and the largest Liège with 134,000. At the 1872 census in France Norrent-Fontes with 19,300 was at one extreme, and Lille (sud-ouest) 76,300, at the other. A year previously the German census showed that *Stkr.* Bochum, 21,000, was the smallest of the coalfield area *Kreise;* its fellow, *Ldkr.* Bochum, was the largest with a population of 128,000. At this period the range of size of population of the basic units was almost identical in all three countries. Later both *cantons* and *Kreise* grew in average population: one German giant (*Stkr.* Düsseldorf) reached a population of 359,000 in 1910, but the tendency to divide the largest units kept most *Kreise* and *cantons* in the same order of magnitude. Division was most common where the population increase was most rapid: for example, the number of *Kreise* in the industrial coal-field area of *Reg.-bez.* Arnsberg increased from twenty-three in 1861 to forty-five in 1910. The *cantons* and *Kreise*, in short, are sufficiently uniform both in area and population to make them very suitable units for the purposes of this study.

It is a relatively straightforward matter to decide which *cantons* and *Kreise* are to be included in the coalfield industrial area. An examination of the occupational censuses or similar material gives the necessary informa-tion. Any *Kreis* or *canton* in which by the end of the half-century coalfield industry was strongly represented in the returns is included: others, which had remained primarily agricultural, are excluded.

In Germany the two exhaustive industrial and occupational censuses of 1895 and 1907 provide an excellent source. In both censuses the *Berufs-statistik* divides the active population into its major occupational types—agriculture and forestry, mining and industry, trade and transport, etc.: and the *Gewerbliche Betriebsstatistik* provides a breakdown into the chief industrial employments—mining and smelting, metal-working, machines, chemicals, textiles, paper, wood, food, clothing, etc. The former is suffi-cient to decide in many cases whether an area is primarily agricultural or industrial in type, but in borderline cases reference to the latter, giving an insight into the chief forms of industrial development, decides the issue.

In all areas, no matter how remote from the main industrial centres,

[1] 100 sq. kms. is approximately 6¼ miles square: 250 sq. kms. approximately 10 miles square.

there were large numbers employed in occupations which the census defined as industrial, but which were closely tied to agriculture; such industries as food, wood, clothing, building and some small metalwares contained many essentially rural workers. *Kr.* Rees in *Reg.-Bez.* Düsseldorf is an extreme instance of this. In 1895 there were more people in industrial employment than in agricultural in Rees, yet an examination of the *Gewerbliche Betriebsstatistik* leaves no doubt that Rees was an agricultural *Kreis.* An area's employment structure might change very swiftly between the census dates. In *Kr.* Mörs in 1895 the tone of the economy was clearly agricultural. At that date there were 1,520 persons engaged in mining and smelting: twelve years later there were 13,848, mostly coal miners. Mörs has been included in the coalfield industrial area, therefore, even though if the survey had stopped in 1900 it must have been excluded.

The German coalfield industrial area occupied parts of four *Regierungsbezirke*, Münster, Aachen, Arnsberg and Düsseldorf. In Münster only *Kr.* Recklinghausen is a part of the industrial area; it was the scene of a very rapid and important growth in coal production from about 1880. By 1907 there were more than 51,000 coal miners in Recklinghausen. Like Münster, Aachen was chiefly agricultural, though here there were three industrial *Kreise*: *Stkr.* Aachen, *Ldkr.* Aachen, and *Kr.* Düren. The woollen industry was of importance in all three, but most notably in *Stkr.* Aachen; coal mining in *Ldkr.* Aachen and Düren; iron, steel and glass industries in *Ldkr.* Aachen. In contrast to Münster and Aachen, the other two *Regierungs-bezirke*, Arnsberg and Düsseldorf, were primarily industrial for they contained the Ruhr. In the former all but seven *Kreise*, Meschede, Brilon, Lippstadt, Soest, Olpe, Siegen and Wittgenstein, were industrial (in each of the seven there were many industrial workers, but few engaged in industry of the coalfield industrial type). The latter contained six nonindustrial *Kreise*. These were Kleve, Rees, Geldern, Neuss, Grevenbroich, and *Ldkr.* Krefeld.

The following are the coalfield industrial *Kreise* in each area. The list is taken from the industrial and occupational census in 1895. The area which they covered is the unit for the population tables, and is constant; their number and names, on the other hand, changed from census to census as the original *Kreise* were sub-divided (or occasionally reunited). The choice of 1895 is quite arbitrary. At an earlier date a shorter list of *Kreise* would have been given; at a later date a longer list, but the area is the same at all census dates.

The German Coalfield Industrial Kreise in 1895[1]

In *Reg.-bez.* Münster
   Recklinghausen

In *Reg-.bez.* Aachen
   Stkr. Aachen   Düren
   Ldkr. Aachen

In *Reg.-bez.* Arnsberg
   Arnsberg   *Ldkr.* Gelsenkirchen
   Hamm   Hattingen
   Stkr. Dortmund   *Stkr.* Hagen
   Ldkr. Dortmund   *Ldkr.* Hagen
   Hörde   Schwelm
   Stkr. Bochum   Iserlohn
   Ldkr. Bochum   Altena
   Stkr. Gelsenkirchen

In *Reg.-bez.* Düsseldorf
   Stkr. Krefeld   *Stkr.* Elberfeld
   Stkr. Duisburg   *Stkr.* Barmen
   Mülheim-am-Ruhr   Mettmann
   Ruhrort   *Stkr.* Remscheid
   Stkr. Essen   Lennep
   Ldkr. Essen   *Stkr.* Solingen
   Mörs   *Ldkr.* Solingen
   Kempen-in-Rheinland   *Stkr.* München-Gladbach
   Stkr. Düsseldorf   Gladbach
   Ldkr. Düsseldorf

Table 13. *Growth of Total Population in Industrial Kreise*
(to nearest '000)

	1861	1871	1880	1890	1900	1910
In Düsseldorf	799	978	1,213	1,573	2,164	2,944
In Arnsberg	447	600	780	1,036	1,516	2,014
In Aachen	199	232	262	305	353	410
In Münster	50	53	65	94	189	375

    In Belgium the *cantons de justice de paix*, which are the basis for population calculations, were not used in industrial censuses. In the 1896 and 1910 industrial censuses information is either for the province, a much larger unit, or for the *commune*, which is much smaller than the *canton*. This makes a direct comparison of the total population and the numbers engaged in industry, or of the numbers engaged in individual industries in

[1] See maps at end of book.

each *canton* impossible: but it is not impossible to separate the industrial *cantons* from the others satisfactorily. A preliminary list reveals some *cantons* which were fast-growing throughout the period, and are clearly influenced by the presence of industry; some where the population remains almost stationary; and a number where the increase is moderate, and which might fall into either category. Since the 1896 census of industry gives the total industrial employment in any *commune* where more than 500 persons were industrially employed, it is possible to discover how many *communes* in the doubtful *cantons* were of industrial importance, and so to determine the status of the *cantons*. If all or almost all the industrial *communes* are to be found either in these *cantons*, or in the *cantons* originally assumed to be industrial, it follows that the coverage of the coalfield in-industrial area by the *cantons* is tolerably complete. The 1910 census of industry, which carries a more detailed record of the total and type of in-dustrial employment in each *commune*, affords a second check.

The Belgian Coalfield Industrial Cantons in 1900[1]

In Province Hainaut

Charleroi (sud)	Mons
Charleroi (nord)	Boussu
Châtelet	Dour
Binche	Pâturages
Fontaine-l'Evêque	Roeulx
Gosselies	La Louvière
Seneffe	

In Province Liège

Liège	Grivegnée
Fléron	Hollogne-aux-Pierres
Herstal	Seraing
St Nicolas	Verviers
Spa	

Table 14. *Growth of Total Population in Industrial Cantons*
(*to nearest* '000)

	1846	1856	1870	1880	1890	1900	1910
In Hainaut	321	384	489	569	633	688	763
In Liège	228	265	323	375	449	508	554

[1] The list of *cantons* covering the same area might be slightly different at an earlier or later date, just as in the German industrial areas.

The French Coalfield Industrial Cantons in 1901

In *arrondissement* Avesnes
    Mauberge   Trélon

In *arrondissement* Valenciennes
    Bouchain   Valenciennes (est)
    Denain   Valenciennes (nord)
    St Amand (rive droite)   Valenciennes (sud)
    Condé

In *arrondissement* Douai
    Douai (nord)   Douai (sud)
    Douai (ouest)

In *arrondissement* Lille
    Armentières   Tourcoing (nord-est)
    Haubourdin   Lille (centre)
    Lannoy   Lille (nord-est)
    Quesnoy-sur-Deule   Lille (ouest)
    Roubaix (est)   Lille (sud-est)
    Roubaix (ouest)   Lille (sud-ouest)
    Roubaix (nord)   Lille (est)
    Tourcoing (nord)   Lille (nord)
    Tourcoing (sud)   Lille (sud)
    Seclin

In *arrondissement* Béthune
    Béthune   Houdain
    Cambrin   Lens
    Carvin   Norrent-Fontes

In *arrondissement* Arras
    Vimy

French industrial and occupational censuses were much less ambitious than those of Belgium and Germany: yet, even so, the remarks of their authors cast doubt upon their reliability. The census of 1847, for example, was first begun in 1839, but work on it was suspended until 1845 because it became evident, as the introduction to the census made clear, 'that if the undertaking were obstinately continued, it would be liable to collect defective material, or even to have to do without a part of what was necessary'.[1] Fifty years later, in 1896, a limited occupational census was carried out as a part of the population census of that year. Again the introduction was apologetic: it recognized the force of the argument that a modern industrial country needed information about wages, prices, production and the physical equipment of industry, and that this information

[1] *Statistique de la France, Industrie*, 4 vols. (Paris, 1847), vol. i, p. xxv.

should be both detailed and reliable. But the author concluded, 'It does not seem that in France a general census, referring to so large an area, has any chance of success'.[1] After 1847 the only ambitious undertaking was the *Enquête effectuée dans les années* 1861–5. Other than this there were the rather perfunctory attempts of the population censuses to provide occupational statistics, and the annual publications of the *Statistique de l'industrie minérale* and other rather specialized series. None of these gives any information for political divisions smaller than the *arrondissement*; which leaves much concerning the occupational type of each *canton* to be deduced from the rapidity of its population growth. There is ample evidence that the population of agricultural areas was stationary throughout the period. Therefore in *arrondissements* where there is evidence of industrial activity, *cantons* whose population is stationary can be discounted. A few, such as Seclin in *arr.* Lille or Trélon in *arr.* Avesnes, are borderline cases; but their size is not sufficient to make a large difference to the totals of population; and makes almost no difference, because of their very doubtfulness, to the size of the increase of population between census periods: and this, for reasons explained in the first part of the chapter, is the important point for purposes of analysis.

Table 15. *Growth of Total Population in Industrial Cantons*
(*to nearest* '000)

	1846	1872	1881	1891	1901
In Nord	532	791	933	1,050	1,172
In Pas-de-Calais	123*	159	193	237	317

* Approximately.

Unfortunately, population totals for the *cantons* are not to hand at all census periods, so that a parallel table for the much larger and clumsier *arrondissements* is included. It is significant that in the years for which both series are available, although the totals of population for the two are very different, the increase between any two census periods is almost identical. In the first table, for example, the increase in Nord between 1872 and 1901 is 381,000: in the second table the increase is 386,000. In Pas-de-Calais the increases over the same period were 158,000 and 149,000 respectively. This seems to clinch the claim that agricultural populations were almost at a standstill. Any important growth of non-industrial population must have been reflected in a larger gross increase in the clumsier method of measurement by *arrondissement*. If the same were done for the larger political units containing the Belgian and German parts of

[1] *Recensement général de la population* 1896, vol. IV, p. cxxii.

the Austrasian field, the same result would appear. Everywhere agricultural population was at a stand while industrial population raced ahead.

Table 16. *Growth of Total Population in Industrial Arrondissements*
(*to nearest '000*)

	1851	1861	1872	1881	1891	1901	1911
Lille	371	458	555	636	733	812	856
Avesnes	145	158	172	200	208	211	216
Douai	101	112	116	128	133	146	164
Valenciennes	157	171	180	204	214	240	262
TOTAL (Nord)	774	899	1,023	1,168	1,288	1,409	1,498
Béthune	136	153	172	205	245	313	403
Arras	169	171	173	174	175	181	179
TOTAL (Pas-de-Calais)	305	324	345	379	420	494	582

THE GROWTH OF INDUSTRIAL PRODUCTION AND POPULATION

It is now possible to bring together the threads of the argument of earlier chapters in the hope of understanding more fully the circumstances of regional industrial growth on the Austrasian field. An effort has been made to show the intimacy of connexion between the coal resources and conditions of working of each division of the field; its level of output per man-year; and the rate at which production expanded. The state of industrial activity in each part of the field at the beginning of the half-century has been sketched in in order to emphasize the revolution in industrial fortunes involved in the emerging congruity of these three aspects of economic life, so that areas which had been most advanced found their prosperity checked and their early promise blighted, while the backward and neglected Ruhr rode to success on the back of capital and skills imported initially to a considerable extent from other areas of the field to the west. The next step is the use of population material as a crude measure of rates of regional industrial growth in order to extend the analysis a stage further.

The following table embodies the principles suggested in the opening paragraphs of this chapter. The first two lines of figures for each area are its coal production and total production at various census dates. The third line represents the putative industrial populations. These were calculated, as in the example at the beginning of the chapter, by obtaining unit population/coal ratios for the first decade of the period and using them to arrive at an estimate of the industrial population when the period opened. From this date onwards the putative industrial population has been found simply by adding the total increase of population within the industrial areas to the original figures. The coal production figures and those of putative industrial population have also been plotted on semi-logarithmic graphs. The results appear in Table 17 and on pp. 72–3.

Table 17. *Growth of Coal Production and Putative Industrial Populations*

    A Coal production ('000 tons)
    B Total population of industrial *cantons* or *Kreise* ('000s)
    C Putative industrial population ('000s)

Pas-de-Calais		1861	1872	1881	1891	1901	1911
A		809	2,248‡	5,290	8,528§	13,913‖	19,770
B		324	345	379	420	494	582
C		12	33	67	108	182	270

Unit population/coal ratio 68 in first decade

Nord*	1851	1861	1872	1881	1891	1901	1911
A	1,620	2,487	3,734‡	5,002	5,737§	6,866	8,888¶
B	774	899	1,023	1,168	1,288	1,409	1,498
C	231	356	480	625	745	866	955

Unit population/coal ratio 7 in first decade

Hainaut	1851	1860	1870	1880	1890	1900	1910
A	4,753	7,508	10,197	12,549	14,769	16,533	16,700†
B	352†	415†	489	568	633	688	763
C	108	171	245	324	389	444	519

Unit population/coal ratio 44 in first decade

Liège	1851	1860	1870	1880	1890	1900	1910
A	1,292	1,899	3,162	3,824	5,056	6,191	6,500†
B	246†	281†	323	375	449	508	554
C	76	111	153	205	279	338	384

Unit population/coal ratio 17 in first decade

    * Coal consumption figures in Nord, for reasons given above.
    † Approximately.
    ‡ Average 1870–2.
    § Average of 1888 and 1893.
    ‖ Average of 1899, 1901 and 1902.
    ¶ Average 1909–11.

F

Table 17—*continued*

Aachen	1871	1880	1890	1900	1910
A	970	1,176	1,461	1,810	2,720
B	232	262	305	353	410
C	139	169	212	260	317

Unit population/coal ratio 7 in first decade

Düsseldorf	1871	1880	1890	1900	1910
A	5,200†	7,430	10,498	17,214	28,272
B	978	1,213	1,573	2,164	2,944
C	577	812	1,172	1,763	2,543

Unit population/coal ratio 9 in first decade

Arnsberg	1861	1871	1880	1890	1900	1910
A	2,900†	7,759	13,779	21,780	32,873	43,716
B	447	600	780	1,036	1,516	2,014
C	91	244	424	680	1,160	1,658

Unit population/coal ratio 32 in first decade

Recklinghausen	1871	1880	1890	1900	1910
A	220†	951	3,460	8,132	17,421
B	53	65	94	189	375
C	4	16	45	140	326

Unit population/coal ratio 61 in first decade

† Approximately.

Coal production figures are three-year averages centred on the year quoted, except in Belgium where they are for one year only.

Study of the eight graphs shows how remarkably good is the fit between the two growth curves. The steepness of the curves reflects the rates of growth: gentle in the central section of the field, comprising Hainaut, Liège, Nord and Aachen; much steeper in Arnsberg and Düsseldorf, reflecting the vast growth of industry in an area extremely rich in coal; steepest of all in the eastern and western extremities of the field, Recklinghausen and Pas-de-Calais, the newest coal-producing areas, which were characterized by a very steep rise during the early decades of production, becoming more moderate in the last decades (Pas-de-Calais was more mature than Recklinghausen in this respect). In all divisions except one as the size of the industrial populations grew and the volume of output rose, the rate of increase fell. The exception, however, was the most important division of all, Düsseldorf, the heart of the Ruhr, which was growing as quickly in the last decade as in the first, although five times larger in both coal production and population.

That the curves are in all cases so nearly parallel suggests a close relationship between the two phenomena. It is scarcely conceivable in areas with such diverse industrial economies, where rates of growth were so various, that this is coincidental. Clearly the circumstances in which a coalfield industrial area developed in the second half of the nineteenth century demanded a very close tie between coal, the foundation of the system, and every ramification of industrial activity, so that the rate at which local industrial populations grew was intimately linked with the growth in the production of coal. Regional presentation of these trends suggests great homogeneity of experience in all parts of the field.

The unit population/coal ratios of the eight divisions of the field fall into three main types. At one extreme are Pas-de-Calais and Recklinghausen, in each of which an increase of one person in the population was associated with a rise of 60-70 tons in coal output; next come Hainaut and Arnsberg (44 and 32); at the other extreme lie Liège (17), Düsseldorf (9), Nord (7) and Aachen (7). This agrees well with what might be suggested by an *a priori* scheme. The newest mining areas with little industry other than the mines themselves make little use locally of the coal they mine, so that the demand for labour is not greatly increased when the production of coal rises, except by the direct requirements of the mine owners. In other areas, like Hainaut and Arnsberg, where important heavy industry had established itself locally, much of the coal produced was used in blast furnaces, coke ovens, rolling mills, forges and the like, thus multiplying the employment which accompanied any increase of coal production, and involving a greater increase of population per unit increase of coal production than in the coal mining areas pure and simple. Thirdly, coalfield regions might be the scene of general industry—textiles, small metal wares, pottery, glass, food processing, woodworking, machine making, etc. In such places there were many industries where the consumption of coal was not large, though a necessary part of efficient production. Here comparatively small increases of coal production were associated with considerable gains in employment. It is interesting that in this third group Liège and Düsseldorf, where there was heavy industrial development of iron and steel as well as a number of light industies, had higher unit population/coal ratios than the other two. In Liège the Cockerill plant at Seraing made an important contribution to Belgian iron and steel output, while in Düsseldorf there was a large iron industry. In Nord and Aachen, on the other hand, where textile and the attendant chemical and engineering industries were predominant and the production of iron and steel less important, the ratio was lower. The ratios reflect the types of industrial development quite delicately. This point is further illustrated when the unit population/coal

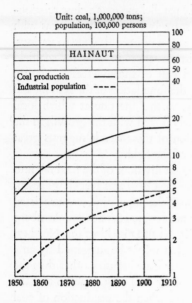

Unit: coal, 1,000,000 tons;
population, 100,000 persons

HAINAUT

Coal production ———
Industrial population - - - -

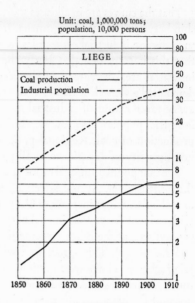

Unit: coal, 1,000,000 tons;
population, 10,000 persons

LIEGE

Coal production ———
Industrial population - - - -

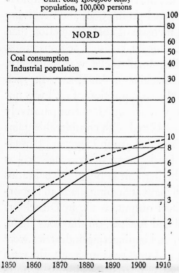

Unit: coal, 1,000,000 tons;
population, 100,000 persons

NORD

Coal consumption ———
Industrial population - - - -

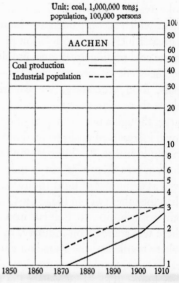

Unit: coal, 1,000,000 tons;
population, 100,000 persons

AACHEN

Coal production ———
Industrial population - - - -

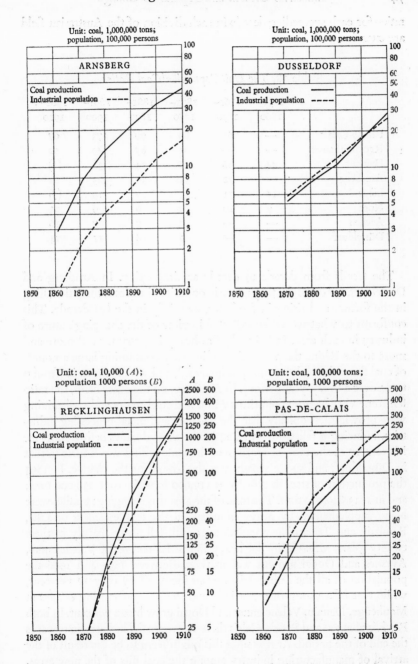

Unit: coal, 1,000,000 tons; population, 100,000 persons

ARNSBERG

Coal production ————
Industrial population — — — —

Unit: coal, 1,000,000 tons; population, 100,000 persons

DUSSELDORF

Coal production ————
Industrial population — — — —

Unit: coal, 10,000 (*A*); population 1000 persons (*B*)

RECKLINGHAUSEN

Coal production ————
Industrial population — — — —

Unit: coal, 100,000 tons; population, 1000 persons

PAS-DE-CALAIS

Coal production ————
Industrial population — — — —

ratios for each succeeding decade in each division of the Austrasian field are examined.

Table 18. *The Unit Population/Coal Ratios*

	1851– 1860	1861– 1870	1871– 1880	1881– 1890	1891– 1900	1901– 1910
Pas-de-Calais	—	68	89	79	73	67
Recklinghausen	—	—	61	87	49	50
Hainaut	44	36	30	34	32	(2)
Arnsberg	—	32	33	31	23	22
Liège	17	31	13	17	19	(7)
Nord	7	10	9	6	9	23
Aachen	—	—	7	7	7	16
Düsseldorf	—	—	9	8	11	14

The trends from decade to decade are interesting. In Arnsberg and Düsseldorf, for example, they move in opposite directions, the ratio falling in the former and rising in the latter, especially in the last decade. This conforms to what would be expected in view of the changing nature of industry in each area. In Düsseldorf as heavy industry moved more and more to the Rhine the proportion of industry consuming large amounts of coal for each worker employed increased, and with it the ratio (from 9 to 14 over a thirty-year period). In Arnsberg, on the other hand, the ratio fell somewhat because the primary iron and steel trades and coal mining were growing less quickly than the machine and metal processing industries, inducing a fall from 33 to 22 in the three decades before 1901–10. Movement of the ratio in Nord over the same period was similar to that in Düsseldorf: and so apparently was the reason for the change. In 1893 the production of steel in Nord was 117,000 tons; in 1901 239,000 tons; and in 1913 849,000 tons. The tone of the area was changing: textiles were being supplemented by heavy industry. In the textile *cantons* of Lille, Roubaix and Tourcoing population growth fell away sharply in these twenty years, whereas in the heavy industrial *cantons* of Valenciennes, Avesnes and Douai growth was marked. Between 1891 and 1906 the population of all the Lille textile *cantons* increased by only 12 per cent, while that of a group of seven iron and steel manufacturing *cantons* at Maubeuge, Denain, Valenciennes and Douai grew by 22 per cent. In both Recklinghausen and Pas-de-Calais there was some fall in the ratio towards the end of the period. At first sight this might seem to be the result of the arrival of manufacturing industry among the coal pits of the new areas.

Occupational censuses (see below, pp. 81-2) do not bear this out. More important may have been the fall in output per man-year from the 1880s onwards. This suggests that for any given increase of coal production more men were needed in the mines, which in areas so dependent upon the coal industry for industrial employment could only mean a fall in the unit population/coal ratio (this may also account in part for the trend in Arnsberg). In Aachen the relative decline of the textile industry and the advance of metal working and machine industries probably accounts for the rise in the ratio at the end of the period. In general the intelligibility of the ratio is as marked as the good general fit of the population and coal production curves on the graphs, though there is one striking anomaly: the sudden, isolated rise in the ratio for Liège to 31 in the decade 1861-71. In an area where apart from this decade the ratio was remarkably steady, this is difficult to explain. The two figures in brackets for Hainaut and Liège in the last decade, though a complete change from earlier trends, are intelligible enough. At this time these two areas virtually ceased to increase their production of coal. This was the period when Belgium changed from being a net coal exporter to being a very large net importer. Although most of the coal used in the coalfield area continued to be dug locally, the proportion left over for export to other parts of Belgium or overseas fell rapidly, so that the increase in consumption is not reflected in higher production figures. If the consumption figures were available and were used, there would probably be no great change in the ratio. Consumption figures are, of course, to be preferred to those for production, not merely for Belgium in this decade, but generally, and would add greatly to the accuracy of analysis if they were available.

The level of the ratio shows no correspondence with the rate of growth of the industrial areas: in other words, there seems no clear evidence that heavy industrial areas normally grew more swiftly than others. Düsseldorf with a low ratio grew very quickly; while Hainaut where the ratio was high was a slow-growing area.

The fact that the unit population/coal ratios either remained nearly constant, or varied in accordance with the changing industrial structure of each area has other implications. It implies that the two halves of technological change; on the one hand the immense saving of fuel achieved by improved steam-engines, blast furnaces, coke ovens and boilers, and on the other the provision of more power for each worker and more machines to aid him in his work, kept in rough balance. Each time the efficiency of the steam-engine doubled, the provision of power to the average worker also doubled; each time an advance in blast furnace technique permitted a saving in coal, the growing productivity of the steel worker meant that his 'consumption' of coal did not greatly alter: or at least it must be true that the total effect of thousands of slight gains in fuel economy per unit of output were counterbalanced by countless small improvements of productivity each requiring a little more power for the individual worker. The fall in input of coal per unit of finished product was equalled by an offsetting rise in manpower productivity. The one cancelled the other out. If this were not so, a general rise or fall in the ratio might be expected in all areas: a rise if the amount of power per worker were rising more quickly than gains in fuel efficiency, and a fall if the reverse were the case. Since there is no general movement visible from area to area, and since the variations in the ratio are for the most part so well explained on other grounds, it is reasonable to assume that the two trends did nullify one another.

Another apparent corollary of the intelligibility of the unit population/ coal ratios is that the totals of industrial population must have limitations as substitute measures of total industrial production. In the short term they might serve as useful guides to trends in total industrial output, but over a period as long as half a century the rise in manpower productivity must introduce a distorting element. If an industrial population X produced P industrial goods in 1860, it would seem certain that an industrial population $2X$ in 1900 must produce more than $2P$ goods. The relationship of the one to the other must change all the while as productivity slowly increases. The graph of the growth in total industrial production then becomes the graph of the growth of coal production seen through the magnifying glass of manpower productivity; a glass of slowly increasing power.

To go deeply into the question of the extent of the rise in productivity during the period is outside the scope of this inquiry, but, in order to form an idea of the degree by which the series of putative industrial population understates the rise in total industrial production when used as a substitute for it, some general considerations must be borne in mind. The degree of understatement is perhaps less than might at first sight be supposed. In the first place, the total of putative industrial population embraces all those dependent upon industrial activity, including the train of service industries. As average income levels rose it is reasonable to suppose that the proportion of those engaged in the service industries would also rise. This must tend to reduce the understatement involved in the measure used. The importance of this aspect of the question is suggested by Tables 19 and 20 which show that the increase in putative industrial population both in Belgium and Germany was distinctly greater than the increase of numbers directly employed in manufacturing industry.[1] Secondly, there were few important technological innovations during the period to increase indus- trial productivity at the pace which was possible during the preceding half-century. Many industries acquired new types of power-driven machinery, so that total national industrial productivity rose substantially, but industries on the coalfields were already usually in this stage. A large part of the general national rise in productivity was simply the movement of more and more industries to the coalfields and steam-driven machinery, which might affect national figures considerably while changing regional figures much less. Thirdly, although productivity in some coalfield in- dustries undoubtedly rose (tor example in the primary iron and steel trades and most branches of textiles), in one major industry which em- ployed many men, coal mining, productivity tended to fall in most areas from the middle 1880s onwards; and in others, for example building and some branches of the small metal trades, it probably showed little change. All these considerations tend to reinforce the belief that the putative industrial totals of industrial population are fair approximate measures of the growth of total industrial production. The difficulties involved in constructing national series of total industrial production, whether based on physical production series or on value, are considerable (one has only to refer to the difficulties experienced in this country in producing such indices for the first half of this century to appreciate this). Where prob- lems of international and regional comparison arise the difficulties are so much greater that a first approximation to total industrial production trends such as that used above may be quite useful. Its virtue is that it sets the argument on its feet and allows it to progress in some interesting ways where otherwise it must be at a stand. To wait on perfection may prevent all action.

In discussing the significance of the unit population/coal ratios many assertions were made about the types of industry to be found in each division of the field. No proof was offered that these assertions were justi- fied. Moreover, the evidence for the accuracy of the putative industrial populations themselves has been little discussed. It remains, therefore, to

[1] For example in Germany between 1895 and 1907 the putative industrial popula- tions of Arnsberg, Düsseldorf, Aachen and Recklinghausen increased by 84, 76, 36 and 292 per cent respectively, while the corresponding percentage increases for totals employed in manufacturing industry were 64, 57, 27 and 177. In Belgium between 1890 and 1900 Hainaut constitutes an exception to this rule since the p.i.p. increased only 14 per cent while the total numbers employed in industry rose 23 per cent: but Liège conformed to the pattern with 21 and 16 per cent respectively. Between 1900 and 1910 both provinces conformed to the rule (Hainaut, p.i.p. up 17 per cent, total in industry up 14 per cent: Liège 14 and 12 per cent respectively).

show that the totals of industrial population attributed to each area are congruous with the occupational censuses taken during the half-century; to show that the balance of industry which has been attributed to each of the eight divisions was to be found there; and to show that the results of the censuses conform to the trends suggested by the unit population/coal ratios.

EMPLOYMENT IN INDUSTRY

The German occupational censuses of 1895 and 1907 present much information for the *Kreise* as well as for the larger political divisions. This makes possible a direct comparison of the numbers engaged in industry with the putative totals of industrial population. Since the former includes only those working in each industry, while the latter includes their families and dependents and those working in the service industries which met their needs, the totals will clearly be very different. If, however, the ratio between the two figures proves much the same for each group of *Kreise*, then the method used in assessing the industrial populations is given a powerful empirical support, since it suggests that it is an accurate measure, though an indirect one. For example, if in three areas the numbers directly employed in industry were 50,000; 100,000 and 150,000 respectively; and if the putative industrial populations were, say, 200,000; 410,000 and 590,000, then it is clear that the method used in calculating the putative industrial populations is largely justified for that period, the ratio between the two sets of figures being very similar for all three pairs. If this proves true of both census dates, it is at least strong presumptive evidence that the putative industrial populations calculated for years in which there were no occupational censuses are also reliable. The result of the comparison for Germany appears below (the total of those engaged in industry is the sum of employment in twelve major industries: details of each are found in Table 21 below).

Table 19. *Numbers Engaged in Industry and Putative Industrial Populations* (*to nearest '000*)

		A Putative industrial population		B Numbers engaged in industry	
1895		Arnsberg	Düsseldorf	Aachen	Recklinghausen
	A	900	1,447	234	83
	B	280	435	79	26
1907					
	A	1,658	2,547	317	326
	B	458	681	93	66

The p.i.p. totals for 1895 are estimated from the 1890 and 1900 figures. Those for 1907 are the 1910 figures. Precise accuracy is pointless in this table.

The critical figures for the present purpose are the ratios between the two sets of statistics. For Arnsberg, Düsseldorf, Aachen and Recklinghausen respectively in 1895 the ratios were: 3·2: 3·3: 3·0 and 3·2. In 1907 they were 3·6: 3·7: 3·4 and 4·9. The general similarity of the ratios in all four areas encourages a belief that the putative totals were accurate. The lower figures of Aachen at the two dates probably reflects the importance of textiles in the area. In Aachen there was wide opportunity for female employment: hence the higher proportion employed in relation to putative industrial population. The two great Ruhr areas, Arnsberg and Düsseldorf, returned virtually identical ratios at both censuses, but Recklinghausen moved erratically. It was a very rapidly expanding area in which coal mining was the predominant occupation. A rather high ratio might therefore be expected, but hardly such violent fluctuation. It is possible that the change from a population of young miners to a more balanced population with many more miners' dependants may have something to do with the increase in the ratio.

In Belgium the population censuses of 1890, 1900 and 1910 provide useful occupational statistics, but not for administrative areas smaller than the *arrondissement*. *Faute de mieux* these have been used.[1] They include, of course, some workers outside the coalfield industrial areas. Since it is impossible to tell how much distortion is involved, no detailed conclusions can be drawn from the figures; but it is clear that the two sets of figures are congruous, and support the estimates of industrial population made above.

Table 20. *Numbers Engaged in Industry and Putative Industrial Populations*
(to nearest '000)

A   Putative industrial population   B   Numbers engaged in industry

1890		Hainaut	Liège
	A	389	279
	B	146	110
1900	A	444	338
	B	179	128
1910	A	519	384
	B	216	148

For B Hainaut is the sum of *arr.* Charleroi, Mons and Soignies: Liège is sum of *arr.* Liège and Verviers.

[1] The industrial and occupational censuses of 1896 and 1910 are invaluable sources of information, but for this purpose are not so good as the population censuses.

The ratio between the two series was 2·5 for Liège in 1890, and 2·6 in 1900 and 1910. For Hainaut the figures were 2·7, 2·5, and 2·4. Once again the results are encouraging, especially as so many of the industries were specifically coalfield industries where employment was chiefly in the coalfield area *cantons*.

Any conclusion drawn from French occupational material must be tentative for reasons discussed above: such as they are, however, they appear to confirm the p.i.p. estimates. This is true, for example, of the occupational statistics of the 1896 population census. For lack of comparable data at other periods, however, they are hardly worth reproducing in detail. The most, perhaps, which can be learned from French occupational censuses is the negative conclusion that they do not invalidate the p.i.p. totals.

The occupational censuses are a useful independent check upon the putative totals of industrial population, but it was only in the last years of the century that they were available in a form to permit a close check to be made. In earlier decades occupational censuses were either missing altogether, or published material in an unwieldy form. Often nothing was published for administrative areas smaller than the province or department. It is not possible, therefore, to check earlier p.i.p. totals in the same way, but a general discussion can at least consider their plausibility.

The most important problem is the level of the p.i.p. at the earliest date of the series. For Pas-de-Calais and Recklinghausen there is no problem since the p.i.p. estimates begin from scratch with the sinking of the first pits. This means a firm base even if later totals are arbitrarily calculated. For other areas, however, there is an immense spread in base figures, ranging from 76,000 in Liège in 1851 to 577,000 in Düsseldorf in 1871. The proportion of the total population of the industrial area included in the first p.i.p. estimate varied from one-fifth in Arnsberg in 1861 to three-fifths in Düsseldorf in 1871. The explanation of this wide variation is simple. The coalfield divisions fall into two groups: those in which in the early years textiles was the great industry, and those in which metal trades were dominant. To the first group belong Nord, Aachen and Düsseldorf; to the second, Hainaut and Arnsberg, with Liège in between the two groups. Initially the new coalfield heavy industries, typified by the iron industry and engineering, were not large-scale employers of labour. In areas in which these industries predominated, therefore, it was natural that the p.i.p. should be a small fraction of the total population. Textile industries, on the other hand, employed very large numbers, even in the early decades when only a part of the industry was organized in factories or based on steam power. The p.i.p. figures were necessarily a much higher proportion of the total in old-established textile areas such as Nord, Aachen and Düsseldorf. It is no mere coincidence that these are also the areas of low unit population/coal ratios. In each case the fact that they were 'labour-intensive' as opposed to 'coal-intensive' in industrial production caused common features. As time passed the p.i.p. figure became a high proportion of the total population in all divisions. By the end of the century other checks upon its accuracy can be used for Belgium and Germany. In the early years, however, for which such checks are not possible, it is reassuring to know that the wide differences from area to area are in accord with the general economic history of the time.

Just as the occupational censuses may be used to check p.i.p. estimates,

Table 21. *Numbers Engaged in Certain Industries in the Industrial Kreise*

1895	Aachen	Arnsberg	Düsseldorf	Reckling-hausen
Mining and Smelting	14,342	115,725	59,424	17,192
Stone and Earth	4,336	10,477	14,395	418
Metal-working	7,576	52,089	57,913	541
Machines	4,644	14,869	31,175	258
Chemicals	1,344	1,709	4,617	89
Textiles	19,914	7,523	121,182	172
Paper	3,003	2,494	6,481	75
Leather	770	2,385	5,310	127
Wood	2,473	8,240	20,318	1,194
Food	7,256	14,946	27,806	1,039
Clothing	7,830	21,509	43,693	1,688
Building	5,820	28,381	42,646	3,509
TOTAL	79,308	280,347	434,960	26,302

Same expressed as percentages

	Aachen	Arnsberg	Düsseldorf	Reckling-hausen
Mining and Smelting	18·1	41·3	13·7	65·4
Stone and Earth	5·5	3·7	3·3	1·6
Metal-working	9·6	18·6	13·3	2·1
Machines	5·9	5·3	7·2	1·0
Chemicals	1·7	0·6	1·1	0·3
Textiles	25·1	2·7	27·9	0·7
Paper	3·8	0·9	1·5	0·3
Leather	1·0	0·9	1·2	0·5
Wood	3·1	2·9	4·7	4·5
Food	9·1	5·3	6·4	4·0
Clothing	9·9	7·7	10·0	6·4
Building	7·3	10·1	9·8	13·3

Table 21—*continued*

1907	Aachen	Arnsberg	Düsseldorf	Reckling-hausen
Mining and Smelting	16,022	178,736	134,474	47,559
Stone and Earth	6,452	18,649	26,397	1,658
Metal-working	10,111	85,519	101,409	923
Machines	7,385	36,542	66,927	715
Chemicals	1,611	4,019	12,635	357
Textiles	19,230	8,470	127,964	543
Paper	4,583	3,578	10,018	211
Leather	916	2,366	6,402	171
Wood	2,961	11,842	26,097	1,541
Food	8,590	22,829	41,071	2,201
Clothing	6,947	21,483	44,354	2,377
Building	8,239	53,979	83,594	7,749
TOTAL	93,047	458,012	681,342	66,005
Same expressed as percentages				
Mining and Smelting	17·2	39·0	19·7	74·4
Stone and Earth	6·9	4·1	3·9	2·3
Metal-working	10·9	18·7	14·9	1·3
Machines	7·9	8·0	9·8	1·0
Chemicals	1·7	0·9	1·9	0·5
Textiles	20·7	1·8	18·8	0·8
Paper	4·9	0·8	1·5	0·3
Leather	1·0	0·5	0·9	0·2
Wood	3·2	2·6	3·8	2·1
Food	9·2	5·0	6·0	3·1
Clothing	7·5	4·7	6·5	3·3
Building	8·9	11·8	12·3	10·8

so they may be used to check remarks made about the structure of employment in each division of the Austrasian field and its changes during the
later years of the half-century. The tables above give the shares of some
major industries in the total industrial employment in several divisions.
The first table shows the structure of the four German areas in 1895 and
1907.

The relative importance of heavy and light industry in the four areas
agrees well with the unit population/coal ratios. In 1895 Arnsberg was far
more dependent upon coal mining and the iron and steel industry than
Düsseldorf: Recklinghausen still more so. Aachen was very like Düsseldorf both in the proportion employed in heavy industry and in the importance of the textile industry (the ratios were 87 in Recklinghausen, 31 in

Arnsberg, 8 in Düsseldorf and 7 in Aachen in the decade 1881–90). Furthermore, the implications of the changes in the ratios in the last two decades before 1910, discussed above, are borne out by the occupational censuses. In Arnsberg where the ratio fell from 31 in the decade ending in 1890 to 22 in the decade ending in 1910 the proportion of the working population engaged in mining and smelting (industries conducive to a high ratio) fell from 41 to 39 per cent between 1895 and 1907. In Düsseldorf, on the other hand, where the ratio rose from 8 to 14 in the same period, the proportion engaged in textiles fell between the two dates from 28 to 19 per cent. Since little coal is used in textile manufacture and much in iron and steel industries, this change also is in harmony with the unit population/coal ratio. In Aachen, where the ratio rose, the percentage employed in textiles also fell sharply in the twelve years from 1895 to

Table 22. *Numbers Engaged in Certain Industries in Belgian Provinces*

1890	Hainaut	Liège	Percentages Hainaut	Liège
Extractive industries	84,562	29,118	58·0	26·4
Iron and steel	9,634	9,975	6·6	9·1
Ceramics and glass	20,339	5,945	13·8	5·5
Textiles	1,341	22,596	0·9	20·9
Vegetable food	4,908	4,223	3·4	3·8
Small metal-ware	11,368	9,580	7·8	8·7
Machines and tools	5,761	5,940	4·0	5·4
Arms and explosives	44	14,342	0·1	13·0
Construction	7,726	8,351	5·3	7·6
TOTAL	145,683	110,070	100·0	100·0
1900				
Extractive industries	97,337	37,178	54·4	29·3
Iron and steel	13,680	15,072	7·6	11·9
Ceramics and glass	28,066	7,292	15·7	5·8
Textiles	958	19,003	0·5	15·0
Vegetable food	5,726	4,850	3·2	3·8
Small metal-ware	12,556	9,535	7·0	7·5
Machines and tools	9,776	9,022	5·5	7·1
Arms and explosives	86	14,319	0·1	11·3
Construction	10,775	10,476	6·0	8·3
TOTAL	178,970	126,747	100·0	100·0

Table 22—*continued*

1910	Hainaut	Liège	Percentages Hainaut	Liège
Mining and quarries	120,878	46,904	53·5	29·7
Crude metal production	14,026	15,094	6·9	10·5
Metal-working	35,975	43,458	17·6	30·2
Ceramics (inc. bricks)	6,522	707	3·2	0·5
Glass	18,816	4,266	9·2	3·0
Chemicals	2,141	2,468	1·1	1·7
Textiles	2,281	20,998	1·1	14·6
Construction	15,182	14,412	7·4	10·0
TOTAL	215,821	148,297	100·0	100·0

The Hainaut figure is the sum of *arr.* Charleroi, Mons and Soignies: that for Liège the sum of *arr.* Liège and Verviers.

The 1910 totals are not directly comparable with those of 1890 and 1900 because the census categories were revised.

The percentages have been rounded and do not in all cases add up to precisely one hundred.

1907 (from 25 to 21), while the percentage in the metal-working, machine and smelting industries combined rose slightly.

The congruity of the occupational censuses with the unit population/coal ratios holds good not only inside a national area, but also between similar areas in different countries, as comparison of the Belgian with the German occupational censuses clearly shows.

The Belgian censuses refer to the *arrondissements*, and not simply to the industrial *cantons* within each province. For this reason, and also because census definitions of occupation are never uniform in two different countries, it is perhaps unwise to press too strongly the marked similarity between Hainaut and Arnsberg, and between Liège and Düsseldorf in occupational structure. Yet the temptation is too strong to ignore entirely. When the unit population/coal ratios were calculated it was seen that these two pairs were very similar to one another, Hainaut and Arnsberg having high ratios, usually about 30, and a marked dependence upon coal mining and heavy iron and steel trades; while Liège and Düsseldorf enjoyed a more diversified industrial economy, including important textile industries, and small metal shops (in Liège there was the world-famous small-arms industry). The census material, therefore, agrees well with what was expected from the consideration of the variations in the ratios. Even the differences of detail conform to this pattern. For example, the ratio in

Liège was consistently higher than in Düsseldorf, and so was the percentage of total employment to be found in coal mining, metal-working and machines (in 1895 in Düsseldorf the percentage engaged in these three industries was 34; in Liège in 1890 it was 50).

In France the statistics are much less satisfactory, but the deficiency is the less serious in that the general nature of the industries of Nord and Pas-de-Calais is not in doubt. Textiles were overwhelmingly important in Nord as a whole, even though the Valenciennes and Maubeuge areas were centres of an important iron and steel industry. Coal mining stood almost alone in Pas-de-Calais just as in Recklinghausen.

In the eight divisions of the Austrasian field there were to be found during the period a very wide range of rates of increase of coal production; absolute amounts of coal production ranging from one to fifty million tons per annum; many different types of industrial economy; and industrial populations which also varied widely in number and type. Yet the uniformity of development in all parts of the field was remarkable. The same close congruity between coal production and the growth in p.i.p. totals is to be seen in all divisions; the unit population/coal ratios vary in an intelligible fashion from area to area and period to period; and there are other uniformities in the circumstances of industrial growth, examined in earlier chapters. The interest of the correlations and symmetry described in this and preceding chapters does not lie, however, solely or even primarily in the working of the model of economic development postulated by Jevons, although it is interesting to see his theory supported over a long period of time by the history of an important belt of industrial areas. The confirmation of his model is useful because by establishing some general features of industrial growth, and relating to them specific information about detail, the outlines of the economic development of each area may be etched in firmly. Often fragmentary material which is 'indigestible' on its own can be fitted into the pattern intelligibly to provide both a support for the system and a check upon it (as with the Belgian and German occupational censuses). But of equal or greater importance is the illumination which comes from the regional presentation of material. Jevons wrote about nations rather than economic regions, but coalfield industry was essentially a very localized phenomenon in the nineteenth century and some features of industrial growth can hardly be understood aright apart from their regional setting. The great weakness of many orthodox explanations of, say, the relative retardation of industrial growth in France compared with Germany has been that they have tried to explain the contrast in terms of national characteristics, when a better under-

G

standing can be gained from regional analysis. There is little evidence that
national influences created special circumstances distinguishing, say, the
development in the French part of the Austrasian field from that of the
German. In this connexion the experience of Aachen is of crucial importance since Aachen, although in Germany, belongs to the western wing of
the field in terms of the criteria used in this study, being very like its
neighbour in Belgium, Liège. The fact that Aachen experienced a typically
'western' development, both in the pace of industrial growth and in the
structural changes in industry which occurred, lends strong support to the
view that the industrial development of the Austrasian field can best be
understood by a regional treatment, rather than by considering each
national section separately.

The tendency to adduce general features of national life to explain
differences between countries which spring ultimately from differences in
the balance of types of economic region is deep-seated in historical writing.
A brief consideration of the work of two men who addressed themselves
to the question of the divergent economic experience of France and
Germany in the later nineteenth century will help to bring out the weaknesses of such work.

Veblen held strong and clear-cut views on the subject of German
success. He attributed Germany's superiority to its being a 'dynastic' staet
in the modern economic world; that is a state in which the political
organization and aims of the controlling class had not changed from those
of the eighteenth-century Enlightenment, but which had yet succeeded
in imposing the habits of mind natural to such a state upon an economic
system which had been brought abreast of any rivals in Europe. He wrote,
for example, that 'Imperial Germany does not depart sensibly from the
pattern of Prussia under Frederick the Great in respect of its national
policies or the aims and methods of government control, nor do the pre-
conceptions of its statesmen differ at all widely from those prevalent
among the dynastic jobbers of that predaceous era of state-making'.[1] This
state had borrowed from England the latest in industrial techniques without changing its inner nature so that, 'the German people have been
enabled to take up the technological heritage of the English without having
paid for it in the habits of thought, the use and wont, induced in the
English community by the experience involved in achieving it. Modern
technology has come to the Germans ready made, without the cultural
consequences which its gradual development and continued use has en-
tailed among the people whose experience initiated it and determined the

[1] T. Veblen, *Imperial Germany and the Industrial Revolution* (new ed. London, 1939),
p. 84.

course of its development'.[1] Veblen maintained that the very development of advanced industry in England had produced sociological and economic consequences which militated against its efficient working. Germany had grafted the advanced technology on to an older social system and had thereby avoided the friction and inefficiencies which were so noticeable in England. The resultant comparative advantage of the German economic system was reflected in its exceptional rate of expansion. Very similar arguments covered German superiority over her other rivals, France, Belgium and Holland. Each was hampered by some of the disadvantages of the new era which Germany had happily escaped. Veblen's argument, in short, rested upon general, national, sociological grounds.

In the course of his argument, Veblen dealt with some possible alternative explanations of German success. For example, he noted that the banking and credit facilities necessary to industrial expansion were quite generally available in western Europe, and dismissed the argument that there was special virtue in the German system whereby the banks undertook the launching of industrial companies and provided credit facilities for new enterprises, an argument which has become a key point in the mystique of German industrial expansion to many writers.[2] In this case Veblen's attitude is perhaps correct, but his tendency to dismiss explanations other than his sociological one was not always well advised. When emphasizing the absence of other factors distinguishing Germany from her neighbours, for example, he wrote, 'its natural resources available for modern industrial use are of the same kind and range as those found in the neighbouring countries; there is substantially nothing to distinguish the German lands from those of north Europe at large, unless it be that the resources of the country are slightly under grade in quality and slightly scant in quantity, at least as compared with the most fortunate of the neighbouring countries'[3]. At another point he mentioned coal specifically, saying, 'As is well known, the Fatherland is not at all specially fortunate in natural resources of the class that count toward modern industry. As regards mineral resources Germany has a decided advantage in the one item of potash alone. The iron and coal deposits are well enough, but can by no means be counted as better than second best, in point of quality, location or abundance'[4]. This is an astonishing lack of information upon a point of great importance to the conclusions which Veblen sought to establish. He laboured under a very real handicap in making his analysis, however, as will be seen shortly, and from his standpoint the error was not of great importance.

[1] Veblen, *Imperial Germany*, p. 86. [2] Veblen, *Imperial Germany*, p. 186 n.
[3] Veblen, *Imperial Germany*, pp. 63–4. [4] Veblen, *Imperial Germany*, p. 180.

Another viewpoint worth mentioning to illustrate the weaknesses of monolithic 'national' explanations is that of Blondel.[1] After reviewing the many spheres in which France had fallen behind Germany (technical education, for example), he returned in his final survey to the point which had concerned him most: the low level of the French birth-rate. 'Germany's economic growth is due above all to the '*poussée d'hommes*' which has taken place in the last twenty-five years in that country', he wrote.[2] This '*poussée d'hommes*' stimulated the economy directly by providing a rapidly expanding home market and a growing supply of labour; and indirectly in that a large family could not adopt the same 'safety-first' attitude which in Blondel's opinion had become typical of France. In a large family most of the sons cannot plan their lives round the expectation of succeeding to their fathers' lands and properties. They must be up and doing for themselves. From amongst such men were recruited those who would go to any country in the world, master the intricacies of the local market, advise manufacturers how best to exploit them, and display energy in pushing sales. Or they would enter in large numbers into industry after a sound, and often technical, education, and impart that type of informed direction which turns a conservative and stagnant trade into an expanding industry. Blondel considered, in short, that the difference between the French and German economic ethos was the result of the high German rate of natural increase of population.[3]

It is no part of this argument to discuss in detail the disagreement between Veblen and Blondel. The fact that they disagreed is not important. What is significant is that in spite of their very different and rather extreme conclusions, they share common difficulties in their work, difficulties which appear in many writers, though unusually prominent in Veblen and Blondel because of their rather simple schemes of explanation.

The most intransigent problem in the question of German success and French failure when tackled in the manner of Veblen and Blondel is that it is hard to imagine ways in which the causal weighting of the factors which they examine can accurately be checked. It is not difficult to list

[1] G. Blondel, *L'Essor industriel et commercial du peuple allemand* (3rd ed. Paris, 1900).
[2] Blondel, *L'Essor industriel et commercial du peuple allemand*, p. 394.
[3] This, like natural resources and banking systems, was a point which Veblen considered. His conclusion was radically different. 'It is safe to say', he wrote, 'that the prime mover among these factors of the nation's unfolding power has been its increased industrial efficiency rather than either of the other two [i.e. population growth or military strength]. While their increasing efficiency has doubtless been conditioned by the growth in population, the initiative, as between these two, has doubtless vested in the former rather than the latter. In the correlation between industrial advance and population the primacy belongs to the former. The like is true, of course, as regards the growth in military strength' (*Imperial Germany*, p. 62).

most of the salient differences between French and German economic and social life, during the period: and with a little care each of these features, or any combination of them, can be presented as the truly significant differentiating factor. A case can be made out for political, demographic, sociological, banking and commercial, educational or other factors as of paramount importance; or for any selection among them. Any point of difference will give a purchase from which the whole may be surveyed. Perhaps, therefore, the general methodology of this approach to the problem is misguided. But related to the first difficulty there is a second, which it is easier to resolve, for the difficulties of Veblen and Blondel spring in part also from their treating as units national areas within which the most wide-ranging and important differences are to be found: and the resolution of the second difficulty can help with the first.

The so-called 'national' characteristics of economic life are often not omnipresent features of Germany or France as a whole, but at best general observations about an average condition; whether upon the whole a high or low birth-rate prevails; whether a large or small proportion of the population is engaged in industry; whether the country in general has good transport facilities; and so on. Sometimes such general observations are legitimate because conditions are nearly uniform throughout the country, as would be true probably of an educational or banking system: but, equally, the general observation may cloak differences between different parts of the country which are more important in those areas than the average national condition. There may be areas of very high birth-rates in a country whose average rate is low: there may be areas of intensive industrial development within a country which people are accustomed to call a land of small farmers; or of deep, rural calm and conservatism in a country which is 'in the van of the race for industrial supremacy'; and so on. Where 'national' features are of this second type they may not properly be said to cause or follow from other 'national' features, but reflect mainly local conditions. It is always possible, therefore, that it is misguided to seek 'national' features to explain Germany's industrial growth, or France's relative stagnation, since these are observations about average conditions whose origins may lie in regional differences affecting comparatively small areas of each country.

The work of Veblen and Blondel illustrates two aspects of the dangers of the 'national' approach. The problem in Veblen is the more subtle of the two. His sociological explanation had the strength that it rested upon a feature of German life that was truly national; but the weakness that, having based his argument upon this feature, he was prevented by the nature of his approach from paying sufficient attention to regional differences within Germany, or between Germany and France. It was not merely that he was misinformed about German mineral wealth, but that even a fuller knowledge could not have altered his standpoint except in small details. Blondel may be taken as representing the other danger (though he shared Veblen's difficulty also). He described as a 'blanket' feature of French life something which varied quite substantially from area to area;[1] and the same is true of his treatment of Germany. His was a correct observation of an average, but it is doubtful whether it will sustain the argument he based upon it. These are the constant dangers of all mono-lithic, 'national' explanations.

It is idle to speculate upon what might have happened if France had en-joyed the same excellence of technical and scientific education as that pro-vided in Germany: or to wonder how much the speed of German growth might have been slowed and that of France accelerated if in the later nineteenth century it had been France which had enjoyed the high birth-rates, while Germany had the 'baby-famine'. It is not idle, however, to claim that local conditions were a highly significant, even a decisive, influence upon the rate of regional industrial growth on the Austrasian field, because within this group of industrial areas there is a German area with a 'French' type of coalfield geology which behaved in a 'French' way in its industrial development: and in the one area of the field outside the Ruhr where conditions of working and output per man-year approached those obtaining in the Ruhr, coal production grew at a 'German' speed.

At the turn of the century the Belgian statistician Jacquart, emphasizing the importance of regional analysis, wrote, 'It seems to me that in the future statistics will owe to this differentiation of material the ability to refine its assertions and to reduce the extent of the arbitrary and the *a priori* in the theories and the deductions which one undertakes to establish with the aid of the data which it collects.'[2] Jacquart's expectation that this method of analysis would become commoner has not been fulfilled: but it remains a true and fruitful observation.

By taking as the subject for investigation the rate of growth of a number of industrial areas, close to one another geographically, and sharing a common basic resource, coal, something can be done to throw new light on national economic growth: something done, in short, to 'reduce the extent of the arbitrary and the *a priori*'. When such a regional study re-lated to local circumstances provides a satisfactory framework of explana-

[1] See below, chapter VII.

[2] C. Jacquart, 'Mouvement de l'état civil et de la population en Belgique pendant les années 1876-1900', *Bulletin de la Commission Centrale de Statistique*, tome xix, p. 421.

tion of the differences of speed of development, there seems good reason to distrust 'national' explanations, especially as a high proportion of the total industrial potential of the three countries concerned was concentrated on the Austrasian field. An over-all explanation of the type of Veblen's sociological treatment, which distinguished Germany as a whole from other countries in western Europe would suggest that all German areas should have benefited from the peculiarities of Germany's 'use and wont'. This would not necessarily mean that all areas would benefit equally. It leaves ample room for explaining the outstanding importance of the Ruhr area compared to other industrial areas of Germany, such as Aachen: but it makes it difficult to explain why an area like Aachen should not have grown more quickly than, say, Liège which is similar in other respects. In the same way the demographic explanation might be so modified to take cognizance of differences of resource as to explain why certain areas of Germany benefited industrially from her '*poussée d'hommes*' more than others, but not why areas of Germany which were as well endowed in other respects as Belgian and French industrial areas should have been unable to show swifter growth. If it had always seemed natural to compare all parts of the Austrasian field with one another because all were in the same national area, no doubt much of the existing misunderstanding would not have arisen.

Jevons's line of approach avoids most of the pitfalls of the monolithic type of explanation. Coal resources are essentially local advantages, and, bearing in mind the peculiarities of coal as an economic raw material, are likely to affect directly only local industrial growth.[1] This form of explanation does accurately account for both the differences in the rate of growth between industrial areas within the same national section of the Austrasian field, and for the similarities between the rates of growth experienced in areas of similar natural endowment in different national areas. Alternatives of the monolithic type prove troublesome when their implications are followed out. The allegedly greater dynamism of the German areas, and the complementary conservatism and lack of the adventuring spirit which are supposed to characterize French and Belgian industry, form an attractive way of explaining the course of events in the latter half of the nineteenth century. Yet it is interesting that just those qualities of enterprise which are said to distinguish the Ruhr from an area

---

[1] Jevons himself appears to have been ignorant of the size of the Ruhr coal reserves, and this led him to underestimate Germany's threat to British industrial supremacy. There were, however, estimates available at the time which might have led him to a truer appreciation of the situation. Jakob in 1846 estimated the total Ruhr reserves at 35 thousand million tons: Dechen gave the same figure in 1858. In 1860 Küper thought 39 thousand millions.

such as Nord in France, have been supposed by Simiand to be the root difference between Nord and other French coalfields, with Nord playing the part of the Ruhr. The belief in the exceptional quality of the German labour force and its willingness to work long hours is open to the same objection as other monolithic, 'national' explanations of German success. Moreover the German manufacturers complained bitterly of the quality of the men they employed in the early years of industrial growth in the Ruhr, frequently comparing them unfavourably with English or Belgian workmen. The list of explanations of the same general nature might be greatly extended, but to detail them would serve no useful purpose since objection to them is based on the nature of the argument used and not on its particular form.

The use of a regional treatment of material to explain differences in the rates of growth of industrial areas is not, of course, an explanation of the nature of industrial growth itself. The cost of labour, the standards of training and experience of the workers, national habits of work, the state of technological knowledge, the supply of raw materials, the abundance or scarcity of capital, the attitude of the government, tariff barriers, and many things else, all enter into and influence industrial production in one form or another in all areas of Europe in the nineteenth century. They or their equivalents must do so in any industrial production. Economic, sociological and political factors of this sort, grouped for convenience by classical economics into capital, labour and resources, are the very stuff of which industrial life and growth are made. They account in combination for the industrial growth, as it were, *in se*. But though capital and labour must enter into any understanding of economic growth *in se* they were too uniformly present over the Austrasian field as a whole to explain regional differences in rates of growth. Capital was mobile within the field in the vital early stages, seeking always that area in which it could most profitably be invested. Entrepreneurs from Belgium and, to a lesser extent, from France were as footloose as capital. Many prominent Aachen and Ruhr businesses were started by such men, and native German industrialists frequently consulted Belgian experts. Even labour, at least in the skilled grades, moved with some freedom between one area and another when called upon to help in establishing plants in a less advanced area. Capital and labour, in brief, were not tied to places; but raw material sources were. Coal was much the most important industrial raw material in these areas, and, as has been shown, it was uneconomic to move it from one industrial area to another. Where other things were roughly equal, or at least mobile, while resources of coal were not, it was natural that the pattern of industrial development should be formed about the relative abundance and cheapness of coal, giving swift expansion where it was plentiful and cheap whatever the previous lack of experience in advanced industrial methods, and serving to inhibit such growth in poorly endowed areas no matter how much better supplied initially with experienced men and rich industrial traditions. This was the triumph of nature over art. If the mountain would not go to Mahomet, Mahomet had perforce to seek the mountain.

There were, of course, parts of the world during this period, even parts of Europe, where men or money were absent or immobile, and where the richest of coal resources could not spark off a sudden growth of industry. The Austrasian field, however, was a test bed of the behaviour of industrial growth where two of the three classical requirements of economic life and growth were evenly available. In such circumstances the third must become the determinant of differential rates of growth.

It is perhaps true that this pattern was necessarily short-lived. It was inconceivable that the situation should continue approximately equal in all respects except for coal resources for an indefinite period. Sooner or later other factors would cease to be equal. The very scale and swiftness of the Ruhr's advance towards the end of the period began to alter some of the other ingredients of economic life, and so broaden the differences between the Ruhr and other parts of the Austrasian field. It is arguable that the advantages of the very large scale of production in the Ruhr were creating benefits of their own, by providing general facilities more cheaply than elsewhere. The extent of the external economies of industrial agglomeration may well have become greater in the Ruhr than in other parts of the field. The large size and profitability of Ruhr concerns may have encouraged them to spend more on research and so enhance their advantages. Certainly the Ruhr was very quick to enter into the new field of fine chemical, electrical and electrical engineering industries made possible by scientific discoveries. Perhaps the virtually uninterrupted expansion at a hectic pace created a more dynamic and expansionist frame of mind among the Ruhr community of businessmen, while conversely in Belgium and France a quieter pace of growth and greater difficulties in competition with other areas induced a more cautious habit of mind. During the last decade of the period, indeed, there are signs that economic life was ceasing to move in such close conformity with the model suggested for explaining differential rates of regional industrial growth. Yet, with these reservations, it may be said that if a model of economic growth in the coalfield areas were constructed, in which it were assumed that all factors were equal except that of the local abundance of coal and the difficulty of its extraction, then the relative pace of development of each area of the field would be reflected accurately in the different results which would be obtained for each separate division. Within the Austrasian field the other elements necessary to economic growth were so evenly distributed, or else so mobile, that for a time the local circumstances of coal production were the determining element in deciding where growth would be most rapid, though not necessarily the type of industry which grew up there. If it cannot positively be shown that other factors did not cause the advance of some divisions of the field and the retardation of others, it can at least be shown that such factors did not upset the pattern which was to be expected from an understanding of regional variations alone.

PART II

REGIONAL DEMOGRAPHIC PATTERNS AND CHANGES

The main theme of this part of the book, no less than in the first part, is the examination of the usefulness of a regional treatment of material. In the first part the attempt was made to show that the relationships which are found in any one part of the Austrasian field between coal resources, the growth of coal production, the rise in industrial output and the rate of growth of industrial population, are found in all parts. The implication of this is, of course, that a better understanding of some aspects of the growth of coal-field industry can be had from studying Austrasian field industry as a whole (at least in the circumstances obtaining in the later nineteenth century) than from treating the industry of each section in relation to the industrial growth of the country of which it is a part. In this second part of the book the same general form of analysis is applied to a closely related topic; the demographic history of the Austrasian coalfield. In Part I the size and rate of population growth was discussed in relation to the industrial growth of each area: in this section the mechanism of the growth forms the subject matter. This is a more searching test of the usefulness of, say, considering the Austrasian field areas together since there were important demographic differences between different parts of the field produced by national, religious and occupational differences in the several areas. Here there is much less uniformity of experience over the whole field than in the case of the main features of economic growth, but the method still produces interesting results.

VI. MORTALITY

The demographic 'take-off' during the period of the Industrial Revolution in England and western Europe is almost as striking a phenomenon as the 'take-off' in industrial production. The rates of growth of population were not so high as in some countries which are today being drawn into the network of modern economic activities, but they were higher than any of which Europe had previous experience. National population commonly doubled in from fifty to seventy years, while the populations of the large new industrial areas frequently doubled in little more than a quarter of a century. The global size of the population increases in the several countries and industrial areas is well known; it is a part of all economic histories. The rate of increase of population must enter into any model of the economic growth of industrial countries during the nineteenth century. But the demographic mechanism which made possible such large increases of population has not been so fully explored as the size and significance of the increases themselves; nor are the sociological changes which accompanied them well understood. Some aspects at least of these questions are well suited to regional analysis. This chapter and the next are devoted to the application of the same type of analysis used in earlier chapters to the different, if related, subject of the mechanism of population growth and its relation to local sociological conditions.

The possibility of advancing the understanding of the demographic mechanism behind the increases of population depends very largely upon the availability of detailed and accurate statistical information. Where no regular and accurate censuses are taken, and no vital statistics collected, only a very general understanding of demographic mechanisms is possible. In western Europe information of a type which permits close analysis began to be collected only about the middle of the nineteenth century. This is true also of England, and means that no detailed knowledge of the demographic mechanisms in operation during the early stages of the Industrial Revolution in England can be obtained. By the time such knowledge is possible each of the chief English industrial areas already had a considerable experience of modern industrial conditions behind it. In western Europe, on the other hand, the impact of technological change came much later. In some parts of the Austrasian coalfield area the impact of industrial change can be traced in some detail from a very early stage in development. The picture which emerges is not only of interest in itself, but also for comparison with what is known or suspected about conditions in England at an earlier date.

To appreciate fully the significance of demographic features of any one area, it is useful to have parallel information about other areas in the same country, and about the country as a whole. Only when the contrast between, say, a region of heavy industry and coal mining and the surrounding rural area is apparent, can a discussion of the sociological peculiarities of the former have anything to bite on. Therefore, in addition to the coalfield industrial areas of the Austrasian field in France and Germany, areas with contrasting sociological and economic features are needed as controls. Three types of area have been chosen: agricultural areas close to the Austrasian field industrial areas (in France, Somme and Aisne: in Germany, Minden and Hannover): agricultural areas remote from the coalfield industrial areas (in France, Finisterre: in Germany, Pomerania and East Prussia); and great administrative and trading centres (in France, Seine and Bouches-du-Rhône—effectively Paris and Marseilles: in Germany, Berlin and Hamburg). The units for which demographic information is most readily available are seldom ideal for this purpose, but the inclusion of groups of people who earn a living from agriculture in a census area in which the great majority live in a city, or of small industrial towns in a rural area only reduces the statistical extremes which might otherwise occur, without obscuring them altogether. On the whole the demographic patterns in comparable areas of the two countries are similar, though there are important exceptions to this rule.[1] The absolute levels of fertility were markedly different, of course, in the two countries, and in some respects French and German mortality showed different characteristics (for example, French male mortality in early middle life was far above the German level), but, measured by deviation from national averages, the similarity of, say, Düsseldorf and Nord, Berlin and Paris, or Hannover and Aisne is strongly marked.

---

[1] The patterns in Belgium also appear to conform, but there are special difficulties in producing parallel statistics of mortality and fertility for Belgium. The chief difficulty is that the smallest unit for which detailed demographic information is readily available is usually the province. This makes it very difficult to produce a clear picture of conditions in industrial Hainaut and Liège since the industrial areas in these two provinces are only a fraction of the whole in population. Moreover, some types of information needed for the calculation of mortality and fertility tables similar to those calculated for French and German areas are not available. Finally, the demographic revolution which occurred in Walloon Belgium about 1860 and which led to a very wide divergence between fertility rates in Walloon and Flemish Belgium greatly complicates the picture, although a feature of great interest in itself, and well worth a much more detailed investigation than any it has received.

The rise in the average expectation of life in both France and Prussia was very marked during the second half of the nineteenth century.[1] In Prussia

Table 23. *Average Expectation of Life at Birth (in years)*[2]

FRANCE		Men	Women		Men	Women
Bouches-du-	1861	32·4	33·4	Somme	41·1	43·1
Rhône	1881	33·5	35·8		40·5	44·1
	1901	39·0	42·3		45·2	49·3
Seine	1861	33·4	33·9	Nord	40·8	41·1
	1881	33·2	36·2		41·1	43·0
	1901	40·6	45·2		44·6	48·1
Finisterre	1861	35·4	37·3	Pas-de-Calais	42·6	43·8
	1881	28·5	30·8		39·6	43·3
	1901	42·5	45·6		45·4	48·8
Aisne	1861	41·6	44·6	FRANCE	40·1	41·3
	1881	42·6	47·5		41·5	43·9
	1901	46·6	50·8		45·4	48·9

[1] Prussian figures have been used because it is not possible to obtain mortality and fertility series for the whole of Germany before the formation of the German Empire in 1871, and because even after this date fuller information is available for Prussia from Prussian sources, than for the whole of Germany from imperial statistical publications.

[2] The method used in calculating expectation of life and survivors, tables is that described in R. R. Kuczynski, *The Measurement of Population Growth* (London, 1935), pp. 177–82. Five-year age-groups were used except for age-groups 0–1 and 1–4. Except for infantile mortality the deaths occurring in the census year only have been related to the numbers in the corresponding age-group. Infantile mortality, however, fluctuated more widely than mortality at other ages, and it seemed better in calculating it to relate deaths under one to births over a three-year period centring on the census year (e.g. the deaths under one in 1879, 1880 and 1881 to three-tenths of the births in 1878, the births in 1879 and 1880 and seven-tenths of the births in 1881, both births and deaths being summed into single global figures). It was assumed that those dying in the first year of life lived for an average of three months. It is possible to apply these methods without modification in most cases: only in the Prussian figures for 1861 is approximation necessary. The Prussian census of 1861 on which the tables are based did not divide the population uniformly into five-year age-groups. Above the age of thirty the unit was a ten-year age-group: below it the division was irregular (10–13; 14–15; 16–18; 19–23; 24–29). In this case below the age of twenty population was regrouped on the assumption that the number in any one year was the same throughout each census age-group. Above the age of twenty ten-year age-groups were used (with an appropriate adjustment in the formula for calculating survivors to each successive age level). The distortion involved is very slight except at a very advanced age.

It is probable that both the vital statistics and census figures became more accurate as time passed. No allowance has been made for possible under-registration, misstatement of age, or other causes of inaccuracy. Further, more detailed work may suggest modification of these results, but not, in all probability, of the general outline suggested. The dangers involved in basing the tables on a single year's mortality experience are considerable, and are discussed below in the text.

Table 23—*continued*

PRUSSIA		Men	Women		Men	Women
East Prussia	1861	34·3	37·0	Münster	42·3	41·7
	1880	35·1	39·6		40·9	40·7
	1900	38·8	42·1		42·2	45·0
	1910	45·4	50·0		48·1	50·5
Pomerania	1861	40·1	42·4	Arnsberg	38·9	39·4
	1880	40·6	43·3		37·6	40·3
	1900	40·0	43·5		41·7	46·5
	1910	47·3	50·8		48·7	52·5
Berlin	1861	33·4	36·5	Düsseldorf	39·8	40·8
	1880	29·9	34·6		37·6	41·0
	1900	38·9	45·0		41·8	46·1
	1910	46·2	51·2		49·5	52·7
Hannover	1861	—	—	Aachen	38·8	39·3
	1880	43·1	44·8		38·3	39·8
	1900	47·2	49·5		42·6	46·9
	1910	52·1	54·3		47·4	51·4
Minden	1861	38·8	36·7	PRUSSIA	37·3	39·2
	1880	40·8	41·7		37·6	40·6
	1900	46·8	48·8		41·6	45·3
	1910	52·2	53·6		47·7	51·1

male expectation of life at birth increased from 37·3 years in 1861 to 41·6 in 1900; female expectation from 39·2 to 45·3. In France the corresponding figures were 40·1 and 45·4 for men in 1861 and 1901 respectively; and for women 41·3 and 48·9. In broad outline, therefore, the picture in the two countries is similar. In each expectation of life for men rose 4–5 years; for women 6–7, reflecting sweeping changes in mortality rates. In detail there were important differences. Expectation of life was higher in France throughout the period, and the favourable margin over Prussia increased for both sexes during the forty-year period. Further examination of these differences will bring out the distinctive patterns of French and Prussian mortality in the late nineteenth century.

Table 24. *Infantile Mortality (per 1,000 live-born)*

FRANCE		1860–2	1880–2	1900–2
Bouches-du-Rhône	m	186	211	172
	f	173	186	146
Seine	m	175	192	151
	f	155	173	135

Finisterre	m	165	188	139
	f	149	163	114
Aisne	m	199	205	164
	f	173	163	138
Somme	m	206	237	185
	f	174	196	152
Nord	m	178	203	188
	f	152	177	156
Pas-de-Calais	m	158	174	156
	f	130	146	131
FRANCE	m	182	184	159
	f	154	155	132

PRUSSIA		1860–2	1879–81	1899–01	1909–11
East Prussia*	m	229	226	244	204
	f	204	198	214	177
Pomerania	m	185	203	260	205
	f	161	179	226	174
Berlin	m	260	313	245	173
	f	227	272	209	145
Hannover	m	—	155	164	137
	f	—	132	140	114
Minden	m	166	152	147	126
	f	142	129	123	105
Münster	m	158	158	186	162
	f	132	133	160	139
Arnsberg	m	153	155	176	147
	f	129	132	147	124
Düsseldorf	m	156	179	194	158
	f	135	150	164	134
Aachen	m	191	209	222	205
	f	165	178	190	165
PRUSSIA	m	213	218	222	181
	f	184	188	189	154

* East and West Prussia combined in 1860–2.

Table 25. *Age Specific Death Rates (per 10,000)*

FRANCE

Region	Year	Sex	0-1	1-4	5-9	10-14	15-19	20-4	25-9	30-4	35-9	40-4	45-9	50-4	55-9	60-4	65-9	70-4	75-9
Bouches-du-Rhône	1861	m	1,863	964	113	86	75	124	91	90	99	128	144	136	145	288	379	501	1,096
		f	1,731	904	105	99	91	95	130	99	100	119	132	114	160	271	278	430	931
	1881	m	2,106	625	96	48	89	107	124	96	115	149	187	218	319	366	562	958	1,554
		f	1,856	640	81	61	70	75	104	106	112	128	152	176	273	325	565	846	1,373
	1901	m	1,718	420	64	46	64	81	76	92	119	143	172	230	343	467	666	952	1,392
		f	1,455	381	73	40	64	78	85	89	89	110	121	184	260	359	554	910	1,490
Seine	1861	m	1,746	723	113	48	97	111	89	95	122	144	183	232	357	462	710	961	1,456
		f	1,550	703	110	58	105	150	134	125	122	125	148	187	264	349	545	854	1,291
	1881	m	1,916	544	101	43	96	126	126	155	165	201	243	307	355	498	687	1,007	1,412
		f	1,732	565	104	60	83	89	127	125	127	139	158	195	253	357	517	767	1,179
	1901	m	1,508	294	68	38	58	84	77	112	149	180	221	292	407	517	754	1,018	1,529
		f	1,347	284	69	40	52	69	75	87	112	122	111	182	237	322	516	750	1,177
Finisterre	1861	m	1,645	475	105	54	81	168	127	154	129	157	195	264	338	483	713	1,077	1,512
		f	1,493	472	140	76	78	100	114	106	139	136	185	248	340	400	594	732	1,126
	1881	m	1,879	727	206	111	107	205	281	113	174	198	217	241	362	434	519	771	807
		f	1,627	749	220	125	122	86	133	161	174	134	151	202	297	441	483	783	1,274
	1901	m	1,391	189	63	40	62	112	117	142	158	174	199	235	297	434	618	965	1,511
		f	1,141	213	67	56	59	86	111	112	139	138	137	168	205	340	514	846	1,230
Aisne	1861	m	1,990	313	62	45	69	80	77	58	76	91	102	169	228	378	542	936	1,269
		f	1,731	276	64	49	69	72	66	82	85	80	96	132	180	293	417	670	1,073
	1881	m	2,951	222	48	44	52	53	95	89	94	123	143	190	233	389	441	819	1,310
		f	1,631	206	46	34	57	65	80	76	75	95	93	122	188	277	396	596	930
	1901	m	1,638	152	41	23	43	73	68	76	99	108	161	213	292	421	624	880	1,156
		f	1,382	145	39	29	50	56	74	57	83	83	99	127	172	279	383	572	1,105
Somme	1861	m	2,059	310	77	46	61	84	68	61	75	81	124	163	232	384	518	796	1,603
		f	1,744	288	83	58	88	85	72	82	80	84	90	133	194	298	406	773	1,247
	1881	m	2,367	247	48	28	79	97	90	76	70	105	114	204	252	355	501	811	1,011
		f	1,961	239	58	32	74	69	87	88	83	91	120	166	184	273	361	627	965
	1901	m	1,846	153	38	26	47	84	73	85	97	106	154	182	218	369	533	798	1,332
		f	1,519	135	41	31	48	68	78	71	86	91	105	138	203	263	422	607	1,016

Region	Year	Sex															
Nord	1861	m	1,777	73	39	63	69	70	61	92	113	112	143	181	286	439	697	1,056
	1861	f	1,515	69	57	77	100	97	105	113	121	143	182	262	332	516	729	826
	1881	m	2,032	56	37	40	87	99	96	98	95	110	196	180	261	368	646	831
	1881	f	1,770	64	35	65	86	113	110	105	100	146	193	243	366	543	825	1,199
	1901	m	1,878	47	25	46	69	69	75	96	116	116	145	190	271	401	608	1,020
	1901	f	1,558	46	31	50	74	80	78	88								
Pas-de-Calais	1861	m	1,579	82	47	55	83	66	72	85	90	117	155	192	332	478	794	1,266
	1861	f	1,298	81	56	78	89	86	91	91	123	105	156	194	308	410	640	977
	1881	m	1,739	67	47	47	63	107	117	130	155	199	280	303	430	603	838	1,607
	1881	f	1,455	68	49	66	89	124	115	127	127	143	168	205	264	357	542	928
	1901	m	1,563	47	27	49	76	85	80	98	130	153	188	246	355	533	811	1,378
	1901	f	1,306	46	30	57	77	81	74	87	95	109	121	178	278	412	617	1,074
FRANCE	1861	m	1,819	85	49	68	104	81	80	87	103	124	169	225	360	487	790	1,227
	1861	f	1,540	88	60	76	88	92	96	95	104	117	156	208	324	476	783	1,190
	1881	m	1,844	69	41	58	96	97	98	106	124	143	190	243	342	513	777	1,112
	1881	f	1,552	71	48	66	70	98	99	99	104	120	152	202	306	450	712	1,039
	1901	m	1,587	48	31	50	81	85	85	105	128	153	198	261	368	552	854	1,382
	1901	f	1,324	49	35	52	69	76	76	86	95	110	140	193	292	460	724	1,207
PRUSSIA East Prussia	1861*	m	2,290	130	62	58	99(81)	116(120)			178(199)			300(318)		544(546)		1,186(1,123)
	1861*	f	2,041	127	60	49	69(62)	115(89)			148(119)			258(221)		500(435)		1,148(1,036)
	1880	m	2,257	100	47	48	77	101	86	141	173	228	282	358	476	663	913	1,504
	1880	f	1,978	95	47	44	58	79	66	99	109	131	181	266	377	529	849	1,357
	1900	m	2,442	79	34	45	58	74	61	101	119	157	203	280	405	611	889	1,460
	1900	f	2,135	87	42	39	44	65	56	76	85	98	141	220	322	537	831	1,312
	1910	m	2,035	49	29	37	46	65	54	76	98	130	164	238	327	515	685	1,084
	1910	f	1,767	44	26	31	39	57	49	61	65	79	106	153	242	369	593	950
Pomerania	1861	m	1,847	84	46	52	95(94)		84(68)			149(144)		271(239)		510(471)		1,145(1,006)
	1861	f	1,608	90	43	43	94(87)		66(62)			128(104)		235(189)		477(400)		1,116(937)
	1880	m	2,033	91	33	48	62	76	85	133	158	201	280	391	590	824	1,299	
	1880	f	1,785	96	42	43	55	69	76	93	116	164	217	347	476	780	1,183	
	1900	m	2,598	54	32	49	65	51	66	109	134	187	273	353	542	879	1,465	
	1900	f	2,257	56	34	37	45	63	73	88	92	135	193	297	512	824	1,330	
	1910	m	2,047	38	26	40	53	49	49	79	111	136	218	283	458	628	1,095	
	1910	f	1,740	36	28	35	41	51	57	69	84	104	161	232	389	616	971	

* East and West Prussia combined in 1861.

Table 25. *Age Specific Death Rates (per 10,000)—continued*

			0–1	1–4	5–9	10–14	15–19	20–4	25–9	30–4	35–9	40–4	45–9	50–4	55–9	60–4	65–9	70–4	75–9
Berlin	1861	m	2,603	456	63	38	61	104(81)	94	122(129)	140	185(193)	210	306(318)	371	599(563)	660	1,286(1,038)	1,397
		f	2,271	476	75	39	59	87(75)	84	111(104)	109	145(118)	125	216(186)	219	422(363)	458	942(846)	1,184
	1880	m	3,134	525	127	39	56	69	94	120	140	181	210	279	371	508	660	826	1,383
		f	2,719	518	116	39	46	66	84	101	109	114	125	159	219	300	458	652	1,184
	1900	m	2,452	280	53	26	34	50	59	76	107	147	206	282	341	461	600	903	1,383
		f	2,086	247	52	23	34	48	56	62	76	82	104	132	196	272	428	705	1,114
	1910	m	1,733	171	46	22	37	45	49	60	81	110	155	213	322	408	601	856	1,230
		f	1,454	154	46	26	32	45	55	65	68	69	97	129	182	253	414	608	980
Hannover	1880	m	1,550	277	67	35	49	70	76	87	110	136	165	217	305	419	603	903	1,349
		f	1,317	270	66	45	46	63	86	96	118	119	137	173	260	390	598	929	1,340
	1900	m	1,643	164	32	25	42	54	52	62	82	102	149	186	277	378	567	868	1,332
		f	1,397	159	37	29	38	51	53	73	79	88	107	149	216	336	549	871	1,313
	1910	m	1,369	127	30	20	35	42	42	48	56	82	108	152	211	319	483	728	1,152
		f	1,140	116	31	21	32	41	47	61	65	69	84	123	177	272	462	699	1,093
Minden	1861	m	1,655	397	92	48	61	91(84)	94	103(120)	130	149(162)	151	268(292)	343	653(556)	681	1,317(1,190)	1,508
		f	1,423	449	132	72	68	93(88)	94	153(137)	153	178(145)	164	298(265)	327	705(533)	651	1,540(1,241)	1,699
	1880	m	1,517	317	80	42	60	76	97	111	130	170	151	244	343	463	681	1,029	1,585
		f	1,293	299	90	55	68	81	56	123	153	129	164	208	327	456	651	990	1,387
	1900	m	1,468	184	38	34	43	57	72	62	82	112	133	232	287	442	654	898	1,208
		f	1,230	166	48	33	45	44	49	71	101	98	108	165	250	379	649	1,070	1,144
	1910	m	1,255	119	23	23	36	45	51	44	51	80	114	164	277	333	524	811	1,208
		f	1,047	113	25	19	31	44	58	65	72	82	94	136	196	340	573	802	1,144
Münster	1861	m	1,580	283	74	59	68	88(85)	92	89(100)	103	133(165)	168	223(277)	313	476(541)	637	1,149(1,142)	1,495
		f	1,317	268	95	78	74	87(86)	97	141(129)	137	152(156)	155	220(263)	305	504(530)	673	1,272(1,190)	1,533
	1880	m	1,579	307	81	46	68	78	92	97	103	163	168	243	313	466	637	952	1,495
		f	1,333	349	97	60	66	78	97	122	137	157	155	225	305	427	673	999	1,533
	1900	m	1,862	275	49	26	56	67	68	79	97	147	177	225	287	386	573	924	1,342
		f	1,600	254	51	36	45	57	66	90	106	98	121	158	243	335	576	931	1,321
	1910	m	1,624	166	31	25	43	55	46	56	70	88	129	172	274	370	493	819	1,220
		f	1,385	166	29	28	37	40	57	69	81	87	92	121	209	331	488	750	1,091

Region	Year	Sex	1	2	3	4	5	6	7	8	9	10	11	12	13	14	15	16	17
Arnsberg	1861	m	1,528	381	90	54	61	98(104)		112(133)		173(193)		308(329)		601(589)		1,363(1,199)	
	1861	f	1,287	408	103	70	60	89(80)		129(135)		152(137)		267(236)		645(512)		1,373(1,167)	
	1880	m	1,549	427	92	46	65	100	107	121	148	177	213	277	391	474	762	1,050	1,480
	1880	f	1,322	429	98	52	60	66	96	127	145	133	142	194	287	404	668	1,043	1,408
	1900	m	1,763	288	51	27	48	71	61	77	99	141	195	271	360	509	679	998	1,476
	1900	f	1,473	272	49	28	40	43	56	72	83	95	119	154	248	363	577	843	1,401
	1910	m	1,469	160	34	20	40	54	49	53	71	96	138	172	291	389	577	861	1,266
	1910	f	1,238	144	33	23	35	42	50	58	65	69	95	118	200	302	499	760	1,163
Düsseldorf	1861	m	1,555	365	69	53	70	108(93)		117(124)		161(189)		258(297)		474(546)		1,204(1,156)	
	1861	f	1,348	370	90	61	60	88(75)		136(113)		141(137)		232(199)		512(446)		1,144(1,032)	
	1880	m	1,787	397	102	40	61	86	99	119	130	170	212	256	345	450	681	990	1,456
	1880	f	1,503	399	97	51	57	65	87	106	121	132	143	166	238	344	586	871	1,315
	1900	m	1,941	272	56	29	43	65	60	70	95	127	174	242	326	435	660	961	1,275
	1900	f	1,635	265	54	29	37	44	57	66	75	88	103	155	227	354	554	826	1,299
	1910	m	1,582	158	30	19	35	49	44	48	62	84	116	169	247	359	484	802	1,103
	1910	f	1,343	155	29	19	29	38	44	52	62	67	81	116	175	289	457	733	1,090
Aachen	1861	m	1,912	387	84	46	54	89(80)		97(84)		144(145)		256(244)		499(443)		1,070(1,082)	
	1861	f	1,652	398	101	64	70	77(72)		122(111)		141(128)		200(201)		505(419)		1,096(1,004)	
	1880	m	2,087	417	91	38	48	70	91	81	87	127	167	221	271	367	549	857	1,486
	1880	f	1,781	416	101	42	58	61	85	103	120	125	132	179	226	338	528	885	1,205
	1900	m	2,223	214	45	22	44	57	54	60	80	102	155	200	288	418	560	940	1,397
	1900	f	1,895	191	36	26	38	41	50	62	68	81	94	140	202	317	542	825	1,321
	1910	m	2,051	160	29	16	27	40	42	43	52	84	127	152	221	343	515	758	1,130
	1910	f	1,650	145	33	17	30	35	41	37	59	69	83	114	176	288	420	666	1,033
PRUSSIA	1861	m	2,128	380	90	48	54	90(79)		101(107)		153(165)		270(278)		530(511)		1,174(1,100)	
	1861	f	1,840	379	95	51	50	72(70)		112(102)		139(122)		239(210)		510(446)		1,199(1,033)	
	1880	m	2,183	369	87	38	51	73	85	96	119	149	183	240	321	433	630	927	1,409
	1880	f	1,879	363	88	43	47	61	80	93	111	114	131	172	252	368	562	867	1,326
	1900	m	2,219	241	48	27	43	58	58	68	92	121	164	217	291	409	605	909	1,404
	1900	f	1,893	232	50	30	38	48	59	69	79	87	103	141	210	326	526	834	1,314
	1910	m	1,814	158	34	22	36	46	47	54	66	91	125	167	249	346	518	759	1,173
	1910	f	1,544	151	35	23	31	41	50	57	64	70	85	118	179	276	441	694	1,085

The figures for 1861 above the age of 20 refer to ten-year periods. Those in brackets are the comparable figures for 1880.

Table 26. Survivors to Certain Ages (of 1,000 live-born)

FRANCE			1	5	10	15	20	25	30	35	40	45	50	55	60	65	70	75	80
Bouches-du-Rhône	1861	m	814	567	535	513	494	464	444	424	404	379	352	329	306	265	219	170	97
		f	827	588	558	531	507	484	453	432	410	387	362	342	316	276	222	179	111
	1881	m	789	621	592	578	553	524	493	470	443	412	375	336	286	238	180	110	49
		f	814	638	612	594	573	552	524	497	470	441	409	374	327	277	209	136	66
	1901	m	828	704	682	666	645	619	596	569	536	499	458	408	344	272	194	120	53
		f	854	737	710	696	674	649	622	595	569	538	507	462	406	339	256	161	74
Seine	1861	m	825	627	592	578	551	521	499	475	447	416	380	338	283	224	157	96	45
		f	845	646	612	594	564	523	489	460	433	406	378	344	275	231	175	114	58
	1881	m	808	656	624	610	582	546	513	475	437	395	350	300	251	196	138	83	40
		f	827	665	632	614	589	563	529	497	466	435	402	364	321	268	207	140	76
	1901	m	849	757	732	718	698	669	644	608	565	516	462	399	325	251	171	102	45
		f	865	774	748	733	715	690	665	636	602	566	536	489	434	370	285	195	106
Finisterre	1861	m	836	695	660	642	617	567	532	493	462	428	388	340	287	225	157	90	41
		f	851	709	661	636	612	582	550	521	487	455	414	366	309	253	187	129	73
	1881	m	812	616	556	526	498	450	391	369	338	306	275	244	203	163	126	85	57
		f	837	630	564	530	499	478	447	412	378	353	328	296	255	205	160	108	56
	1901	m	861	799	774	759	736	696	656	611	565	518	469	417	359	289	211	129	58
		f	886	815	788	766	744	713	674	637	595	555	518	476	430	362	280	182	96
Aisne	1861	m	801	709	687	672	649	624	600	583	561	536	510	468	418	346	263	163	85
		f	827	742	719	701	678	654	633	607	582	559	533	499	456	394	319	228	131
	1881	m	795	728	711	696	678	660	630	602	575	540	503	458	407	335	268	177	90
		f	837	772	754	742	721	698	671	645	622	593	566	532	485	422	346	256	159
	1901	m	836	788	772	763	746	720	697	671	638	607	565	509	444	370	280	188	96
		f	862	814	798	786	767	746	719	699	670	643	612	574	527	458	378	283	161
Somme	1861	m	794	704	677	661	641	615	594	577	555	533	501	462	412	339	262	175	75
		f	826	738	708	687	658	630	608	584	561	538	514	481	436	376	306	207	109
	1881	m	763	693	676	667	641	611	584	562	543	515	487	434	387	324	252	167	100
		f	804	732	711	699	674	651	623	596	572	547	515	474	432	377	314	229	140
	1901	m	815	768	753	744	726	696	671	643	613	581	538	491	441	366	280	187	94
		f	848	804	787	775	757	733											

Nord	1861	m	822	702	[illegible]	[illegible]	[illegible]	[illegible]	[illegible]	[illegible]	[illegible]	[illegible]	[illegible]	[illegible]	[illegible]	[illegible]	[illegible]	[illegible]	[illegible]
		f	848	714	690	670	645	614	585	555	524	496	469	436	398	345	277	195	113
	1881	m	797	700	681	668	655	627	597	569	542	510	475	433	380	322	248	172	111
		f	823	729	706	693	671	643	608	575	545	520	493	447	408	358	298	215	141
	1901	m	812	755	737	728	711	687	664	639	609	577	536	487	431	359	273	180	97
		f	844	791	773	761	742	715	687	661	632	601	568	528	480	419	343	252	150
Pas-de-Calais	1861	m	842	723	694	678	659	632	612	590	566	541	510	472	429	363	286	191	99
		f	870	756	726	706	679	649	622	594	568	534	507	468	425	364	297	215	130
	1881	m	826	720	696	680	665	644	610	576	539	499	452	393	337	272	201	131	56
		f	855	756	731	714	690	660	621	586	550	516	481	442	399	349	292	222	139
	1901	m	844	778	760	749	731	704	675	648	617	579	536	488	431	361	276	183	89
		f	869	800	782	779	749	721	692	667	639	609	577	543	497	432	351	257	148
FRANCE	1861	m	818	699	670	654	632	600	576	553	530	503	471	433	387	323	253	169	90
		f	846	725	693	673	648	620	592	565	538	511	482	446	402	342	269	181	98
	1881	m	816	727	702	688	668	637	607	578	548	515	480	436	386	325	251	170	96
		f	845	753	727	710	687	663	631	601	572	543	511	474	428	367	293	204	120
	1901	m	841	784	766	754	736	707	680	652	618	580	538	487	427	355	269	174	85
		f	868	811	792	778	758	732	705	679	650	620	587	547	497	429	340	236	127
PRUSSIA																			
East Prussia	1861*	m	771	652	611	593	576	—	521	—	464	—	388	—	287	—	164	—	42
		f	796	676	634	616	601	—	561	—	500	—	431	—	333	—	200	—	54
	1880	m	774	653	622	607	593	570	546	519	484	444	396	344	287	226	162	102	46
		f	802	682	651	636	622	604	584	562	534	506	474	433	379	314	240	156	77
	1900	m	756	667	641	630	616	599	581	560	541	510	472	426	370	302	222	141	66
		f	787	698	668	654	642	628	611	590	568	544	518	483	432	368	281	184	93
	1910	m	797	740	723	713	699	684	665	644	620	591	553	510	452	384	296	209	120
		f	823	768	751	742	730	716	699	679	659	638	613	581	539	477	396	294	181
Pomerania	1861	m	815	721	691	676	658	—	605	—	550	—	474	—	361	—	214	—	58
		f	839	741	708	693	678	—	635	—	578	—	508	—	401	—	247	—	84
	1880	m	797	710	678	667	651	631	608	582	553	520	480	434	378	310	231	152	77
		f	821	736	701	687	672	654	631	608	579	552	521	480	431	362	285	192	104
	1900	m	740	675	657	646	631	611	595	576	553	523	490	446	389	326	248	159	74
		f	774	709	689	678	665	650	630	608	584	559	534	499	453	391	302	199	100
	1910	m	795	750	736	726	712	693	677	660	640	615	582	544	488	423	336	246	140
		f	826	784	770	759	746	731	712	692	672	649	622	591	545	485	399	293	178

* East and West Prussia combined in 1861.

Table 26. Survivors to Certain Ages (of 1,000 live-born)—continued

			1	5	10	15	20	25	30	35	40	45	50	55	60	65	70	75	80
Berlin	1861	m	740	620	601	589	572	—	515	—	456	—	379	—	279	—	150	—	80
		f	773	643	619	607	590	—	541	—	484	—	419	—	337	—	219	—	33
	1880	m	687	561	526	516	502	485	463	436	407	371	334	291	241	187	134	88	79
		f	728	596	563	552	539	522	501	476	451	426	400	369	331	285	226	163	42
	1900	m	755	677	659	651	640	624	606	583	553	514	463	402	339	269	199	126	88
		f	791	718	700	692	680	664	646	626	603	579	549	514	466	407	328	230	61
	1910	m	827	773	755	747	733	717	700	679	652	617	571	513	437	356	263	170	130
		f	855	804	786	775	763	746	726	703	679	656	625	586	535	472	383	282	171
Hannover	1880	m	845	758	733	721	703	679	654	626	592	553	510	457	392	318	235	148	73
		f	868	781	757	740	723	700	671	639	603	568	530	486	427	352	260	162	81
	1900	m	836	783	721	762	746	726	707	686	658	626	581	529	460	381	286	184	92
		f	860	808	793	782	767	748	728	702	674	645	612	568	510	431	327	210	106
	1910	m	863	821	809	801	787	771	754	736	716	688	651	604	543	463	363	252	139
		f	886	846	833	824	811	795	776	753	729	704	675	635	581	507	402	283	161
Minden	1861	m	834	715	683	667	647	—	591	—	532	—	459	—	350	—	178	—	37
		f	858	721	675	651	630	—	574	—	492	—	412	—	305	—	146	—	19
	1880	m	848	750	720	705	684	659	629	595	557	512	474	420	354	280	199	117	53
		f	871	775	741	721	697	669	638	599	555	520	480	432	367	292	210	127	51
	1900	m	853	794	778	765	749	728	707	686	659	623	582	519	449	360	259	164	71
		f	877	821	802	789	772	755	728	703	668	636	602	555	489	405	292	169	82
	1910	m	875	834	825	815	801	783	764	748	729	700	662	610	531	449	345	229	123
		f	895	856	845	838	825	807	783	758	731	702	670	626	567	469	352	235	130
Münster	1861	m	842	754	726	705	682	—	625	—	571	—	500	—	400	—	246	—	67
		f	868	782	746	717	691	—	633	—	550	—	472	—	379	—	226	—	50
	1880	m	842	747	717	701	677	651	622	593	563	519	477	422	361	286	207	127	58
		f	867	757	721	699	677	651	620	583	545	503	466	416	357	288	205	123	55
	1900	m	814	731	713	704	685	662	640	615	586	545	498	445	386	318	238	149	74
		f	840	761	741	728	712	692	670	640	607	578	544	503	445	376	282	175	88
	1910	m	838	785	773	763	747	727	710	690	667	638	598	549	478	397	310	205	109

Region	Year	Sex																	
Arnsberg	1861	m	847	731	698	680	659	—	597	—	534	—	449	—	330	—	177	—	34
		f	871	744	706	682	662	—	605	—	532	—	457	—	349	—	179	—	33
	1880	m	845	716	684	669	647	616	584	549	510	467	420	365	300	237	161	94	43
		f	868	735	700	682	661	640	610	572	532	498	464	421	365	298	212	125	60
	1900	m	824	736	717	708	691	667	647	623	593	552	501	437	365	283	201	120	56
		f	853	767	748	738	723	708	688	664	637	607	572	530	468	390	292	190	92
	1910	m	853	801	787	780	764	744	726	707	682	650	607	557	481	396	296	191	99
		f	876	828	814	805	791	775	756	734	711	687	655	617	559	480	374	254	140
Düsseldorf	1861	m	844	733	708	689	666	—	598	—	532	—	453	—	349	—	215	—	54
		f	865	749	716	695	674	—	618	—	539	—	468	—	371	—	220	—	60
	1880	m	821	704	669	656	636	609	580	546	512	470	423	372	313	250	177	107	50
		f	850	728	693	676	657	636	609	578	544	509	474	436	387	326	243	156	79
	1900	m	806	724	704	694	679	658	639	617	588	552	506	448	381	306	219	134	69
		f	837	754	734	723	710	695	675	653	629	602	572	529	472	396	299	197	100
	1910	m	842	791	779	772	758	740	724	707	685	657	620	570	504	421	330	220	125
		f	866	814	802	795	783	768	752	733	710	687	659	623	571	494	392	271	155
Aachen	1861	m	809	696	667	652	635	—	581	—	527	—	456	—	353	—	212	—	64
		f	835	715	680	659	636	—	589	—	521	—	452	—	370	—	221	—	64
	1880	m	791	673	643	631	616	594	567	545	522	490	450	403	352	293	222	144	66
		f	822	699	665	651	633	614	588	559	526	494	463	423	378	319	244	156	84
	1900	m	778	715	699	692	677	658	640	621	597	568	526	476	412	334	252	156	75
		f	811	752	738	729	715	700	683	662	640	615	587	547	494	422	321	211	106
	1910	m	795	746	735	730	720	705	691	676	659	632	593	549	492	414	319	218	122
		f	835	788	775	769	757	744	729	716	695	671	644	608	557	482	391	279	165
PRUSSIA	1861	m	787	679	649	634	617	—	564	—	509	—	437	—	333	—	193	—	50
		f	816	704	672	655	638	—	594	—	531	—	462	—	364	—	216	—	54
	1880	m	782	677	648	636	620	598	573	546	515	478	436	387	329	265	193	120	58
		f	812	705	675	660	645	626	602	574	543	513	481	441	389	323	244	157	79
	1900	m	778	708	691	682	668	648	630	609	581	547	504	452	391	319	235	148	71
		f	811	740	722	711	698	681	662	639	614	588	559	521	469	398	305	200	101
	1910	m	819	769	756	748	735	718	701	683	661	631	593	545	482	405	312	213	116
		f	846	797	783	774	762	746	728	708	685	662	634	598	547	476	382	269	154

Perhaps the most remarkable general feature of Prussian mortality was that expectation of life at birth improved by ten years for men and twelve years for women between 1861 and 1910 while infantile mortality hardly fell at all. Indeed between 1861 and 1900 while expectation of life rose by four and six years respectively for men and women, it actually rose slightly. The greatest proportionate falls in mortality were in the age-groups 1–4 and 5–9 in each of which the death-rate had fallen by 1910 to only about 40 per cent of its 1861 level. There were striking improvements also in all the age-groups between ten and forty, and smaller but clearly marked improvements after forty: in general, however, the falls were smaller as a proportion of the initial rate, and later in inception, with each successive age-group. Between 1880 and 1900, for example, there was a marked improvement in the age-groups between twenty and forty, while age-specific death-rates above sixty fell only very slightly, though in the following decade there was a noticeable fall at all ages. The greater fall in mortality in the earlier rather than the later age-groups meant, of course, a much bigger impact on expectation of life, net reproduction rates, and numbers passing through the economically productive years of life than would have been the case if the main reduction in mortality had been in the higher age-groups. In 1861, out of 1,000 new-born male babies, 617 reached the age of twenty; by 1910 this figure had risen to 735, even though infantile mortality had improved very little in the interim. In 1861 out of the original 1,000 male babies 213 died in their first year of life, and a further 170 before reaching the age of twenty: in 1910 the first figure was still as high as 181 while the second had fallen to only 84 (in 1900 the two figures were 222 and 110). The drastic changes in age-specific death-rates between the ages of one and twenty are of greater importance than the changes in any other of the age-specific rates in improving the expectation of life and for most other demographic, economic and sociological considerations.

Improvement in expectation of life gathered momentum between each successive census date. Male expectation of life grew more between 1900 and 1910 than in the preceding forty years, and female almost as much. The gap between male and female expectation of life steadily widened: in 1861 the gap was only 1·9 years; in 1910 3·4 years. It is interesting in this connexion to note that while male expectation of life grew only by about three months between 1861 and 1880, female expectation grew by more than one and a half years. Throughout the period female mortality rates were always higher than male in the age-groups 5–14; and intermittently higher than male rates in the age-groups 25–34. At all other ages the male mortality rates were higher than the female.

The French national picture is substantially different. Infantile mortality was throughout the period considerably lower in France than in Prussia: moreover, the infantile death-rate showed a substantial fall in France between 1881 and 1901 at a time when it was still rising slightly in Prussia. In the years between one and twenty French experience was similar to Prussian with especially big falls in the death-rate in the 1–4 age group, but marked falls in the three next age-groups also. In all these age-groups there was a clear fall between 1861 and 1881, and a further clear fall between 1881 and 1901. The next age-group, 20–4, also shows a regular fall for both sexes from one census date to the next; but thereafter there are marked divergences from the pattern found in Prussia. Above the age of twenty-five there was in France a sharp rise in male age-specific death-rates between 1861 and 1881 in almost all age-groups. In 1901 the rates were lower up to the age of forty than they had been in 1881; though often still higher than they had been in 1861. Above the age of forty in every male age-group there was a further rise between 1881 and 1901, so that rates were in every instance above, often substantially above, the rates obtaining in 1861. In view of the very great improvements of mortality in other male age-groups, and the contemporary improvements in public health and medical science, this is rather surprising. It forms a strong contrast with Prussian experience, for in Prussia in 1900, although male age-specific death-rates above forty showed no very dramatic improvement over 1861, yet in every case they were lower. The position is different for female rates, which approximate much more closely to the typical Prussian pattern. Between 1861 and 1881 there were slight rises in mortality in some age-groups above the age of twenty-five, but by 1901 the rates were in all cases lower than in 1861.

Absolute age-specific death-rates were lower in France than Prussia for the age-groups 1–9 (except for the 1–4 age-group in 1861), but were then above Prussian rates for both sexes and in all age-groups 10–34. Thereafter French rates were again in general lower, though there are exceptions to this rule (e.g. in the female age-groups 35–54 in 1901).

In France still more than in Prussia any improvement in expectation of life stemmed from changes in age-specific death-rates in the age-groups 1–24, and especially in the earlier among these age-groups. In 1861 out of 1,000 new-born male French babies 632 reached the age of twenty: in 1901, 736 (Prussia 617 and 668): 182 of the initial 1,000 died in their first year in France in 1861, and a further 186 before reaching twenty (Prussia 213 and 170): in 1901 the figures were 159 and 105 (Prussia 222 and 110).[1]

---

[1] Note that after 1861 Prussian figures always refer to the year before the French 1880 and 1881 etc.). For brevity's sake this is not always explicitly stated when

In France the difference between male and female expectation of life in 1861 was 1·3 years; and in 1901 3·6 years: a development very like contemporary Prussian changes. In France, as in Prussia, female mortality was higher in the age-groups 5–14, but in France this characteristic extended into the next five-year age-group also at each census date. As in Prussia, female rates were also higher in the age-groups 25–34 (except in the 30–4 age-group in 1901): and almost invariably lower in all other age-groups.

Any discussion of the differences in the pattern of mortality between Prussia and France, and speculation about possible causes is best left to a later stage in the chapter after the comparison of similar areas inside each country, since it is always possible that 'national' differences are only statistical abstractions obtained by averaging. A country in which three-quarters of the population is agricultural and only a quarter industrial or urban may show a very different mortality pattern from a country in which the proportions are reversed even though mortality patterns are similar in similar areas. In such a case 'national' differences are like differences between two cost-of-living indices which show conflicting trends only because their components have been weighted in a different fashion

TEXTILE INDUSTRIAL AREAS: AACHEN, DÜSSELDORF AND NORD

There was very little difference in expectation of life in these three areas. Nord was at each comparable date slightly in advance of the two Prussian areas, but whereas Nord was usually at or a little below the French national average, Aachen and Düsseldorf were normally a little above the Prussian national average, so that the difference between the three areas was slight.

Infantile mortality was always higher in Aachen than in the other two areas, and usually higher in Nord than in Düsseldorf, but there is a similarity in the order of magnitude of infantile mortality in the three areas, and the trends in all three were rather similar. In each there was a much bigger rise between 1861 and 1880 than in the national rates. In Aachen and Düsseldorf a further strong rise occurred in the next period to 1900, and though in Nord the level fell absolutely it continued to rise if expressed as an index figure to which the national rate stood as 100. In infantile mortality, in short, as in expectation of life, the three areas appear more like each other than they are like the national wholes of which each was a part.

The pattern found in death-rates above the age of one in Nord is rela-

French and Prussian figures for similar years are quoted together, but the difference should be borne in mind.

tively clear-cut. As with infantile mortality, death-rates in the 1–4 age-group were above the national average, but from 5–19 death-rates were below the national average. From 20–44 there is a very significant difference between the sexes, when contrasted with national averages, since male death-rates are either at, or more usually below, the national rates at all three census dates, whereas female rates are usually above the national average. Indeed between the ages of ten and forty female rates in Nord are well above the male rates; once more a strong contrast with the national position. In the higher age-groups male rates are much like the national average, while female rates are normally less than in the country at large.

It has sometimes been asserted that industrial work in textile establishments was unhealthy and that this was reflected in unwontedly high female death-rates at ages when women were most commonly employed in the factories, that is between fifteen and forty. These might be expected to be relatively high when compared with men in the same age-groups or with women of the same age in the country as a whole. The evidence of Nord suggests that this assertion may be justified.

In Aachen in 1861 and 1880 the Nord pattern is apparent with female rates generally higher than the national average in the age-groups 5–39 and male rates normally less than the national average. In 1900 and 1910 at all ages and in both sexes death-rates were below the Prussian average. If, therefore, the Nord situation is in any sense typical of textile industrial areas at some stage of their industrial development, then this stage had been passed in Aachen by the end of the century (it is perhaps worth noting that in Nord the extent by which female death-rates 20–44 exceeded the national average was greatly reduced in 1900, suggesting a development parallel to that in Aachen). The death-rate in the youngest age-group, 1–4, in Aachen as in Nord was above the national average in 1861 and 1880, though in 1900 a very rapid fall in the death-rate in this age-group in Aachen had taken it below the Prussian average (there was a parallel but less pronounced development in Nord). In the upper age-groups, above the age of forty, death-rates in Aachen were at all times near to, if usually a little less than, the national average.

The Düsseldorf situation was more complicated. In so far as female mortality rates are concerned Düsseldorf bears a strong resemblance to Aachen. In 1880 in every age-group 1–49 death-rates were higher than the national average, and above fifty very close to it. By 1900 the very great fall in female death-rates visible in Aachen is to be found also in Düsseldorf. In that year at every age above ten and below forty death-rates were less than in Prussia as a whole: in 1910 at every age between one and sixty.

However, male death-rates, which in Aachen were less than the national average in almost all age-groups at the several census dates, and in Nord were not only less than the French average, but also commonly less absolutely than the female rates, in Düsseldorf were not only high above the female rates, but also above the Prussian average except at the last date, 1910, by which time death-rates were less than the national average for both sexes and at most ages. This is true of men at all ages in 1880 and 1900: only in 1910 was there a sudden dramatic improvement in the local position compared with the general Prussian average.

When viewed as an isolated group, therefore, the three textile industrial areas show a considerable degree of uniformity in female mortality experience, and conform to the view that such areas were relatively unhealthy for women at least during the early years of a developing textile industry based on the factory rather than the home. On the argument that occupation and mortality are closely connected, the anomalous behaviour of male death-rates in Düsseldorf might perhaps be explained as due to the greater relative importance in this area of heavy metal and coal-mining industries which tended to raise male mortality during the working life, just as textile employment raised female mortality. For these arguments to be justified, however, it is necessary to prove not only that there are explicable differences between mortality patterns in textile areas and in the country as a whole, but also that in industrial areas of different occupational types mortality experience was different: in other words, to show that in heavy industrial and coal-mining areas where there was very little employment available for women, female death-rates were less high than in textile areas. Some similar comparative test is needed for the male death-rates in Düsseldorf. As it turns out, support for the argument from occupational structure is slender and conflicting. Other coalfield industrial areas with very different occupational structures display very similar mortality patterns.

COAL-MINING AND HEAVY INDUSTRIAL AREAS: ARNSBERG, MÜNSTER AND PAS-DE-CALAIS

These areas form a complete contrast with the preceding group in occupational structure. Arnsberg rapidly developed a very big iron and steel industry during the later nineteenth century, and much coal was mined there. Industrial towns like Dortmund, Hörde, Bochum, Gelsenkirchen and Hagen grew apace. Münster and Pas-de-Calais became important industrial areas with the spread of coal-mining into them from the older industrial areas (in the 1880s in Münster; twenty years earlier in Pas-de-

Calais). Both remained largely without manufacturing industry even after their coal-mining populations had grown to a great size.

It is perhaps most convenient to compare each area initially with a neighbouring area already considered: Arnsberg and Münster with Düsseldorf; Pas-de-Calais with Nord. Expectation of life in Arnsberg was less at each census date than in Düsseldorf (there is one exception to this; female expectation of life was slightly greater in Arnsberg in 1900): but the differences between the two areas were never large, in spite of the fact that age-specific death-rates were almost without exception higher in Arnsberg. The vital exception to this generalization is that infantile mortality was consistently less in Arnsberg, a fact which counterbalanced the high death-rates in other age-groups. In Arnsberg age-specific female death-rates were as commonly above the Düsseldorf rates as were male rates; and this was true for the 15–39 age-groups as well as for other ages. The difference in expectation of life between the sexes was actually less in Arnsberg than in Düsseldorf in 1861 and 1880 (i.e. female mortality was relatively higher), though higher in 1900 and 1910. As in Düsseldorf, age-specific death-rates, with the exception of the infantile mortality rates, were above the national average, but the gap between local and national rates tended to lessen with each successive census date. By 1900 there were already some ages (5–14 and 20–9) at which local rates were below national averages for women. In 1910 there were also a few ages at which male rates had fallen below the Prussian average. Allied to the much more favourable infantile mortality rates in Arnsberg, this improvement relative to national trends meant that in 1910 expectation of life was a year greater for men in Arnsberg than in Prussia as a whole and almost one and a half years better for women, whereas in 1880 male life expectancy was almost exactly at the national average and female life expectancy several months less than the average.

In Münster in 1880 the extension of the Ruhr coal-mining areas into Recklinghausen was still a thing of the future, and a comparison of the mortality experience of a primarily agricultural area such as it then was with Arnsberg is interesting. Infantile mortality was almost identical in the two areas. In the next age-group 1–4 the rates in Münster were much less than in Arnsberg, but above the age of five there is very little difference between the two areas in female mortality rates, although male rates are usually higher, and occasionally much higher, in Arnsberg (the difference is so pronounced that, whereas female life expectancy was only five months greater in Münster than in Arnsberg, male expectancy was more than three years greater). By 1900 male rates in Münster had risen to about the Arnsberg level with female rates remaining higher, and Münster had largely lost its earlier advantage in the 1–4 age-group. In 1910 this had gone entirely: by this date, in fact, male life expectancy and death-rates at most ages were very like those of Arnsberg, while female expectation of life was less good. The relative healthiness of male life in Münster, which in 1861 and 1880 gave men a greater expectation of life than women (a rare phenomenon in Europe by this date), faded later on with the vast growth in the number of coal miners in Recklinghausen. The evidence of Düsseldorf, Arnsberg and Münster suggests that female mortality rates were little affected by industrialization, whether or not they were themselves industrially employed, but that male rates might be affected quite strongly by entry into heavy industrial employment.

Pas-de-Calais in 1861, like Münster in 1880, was still unaffected by the great increases of industrial population which were later to take place there with the development of coal-mining. The occupational structure was what it had been for many decades past, yet the differences in mortality rates between Pas-de-Calais and Nord, where there were already scores of thousands employed in textile mills, coal mines, blast furnaces and metal shops, was very slight. Expectation of life, it is true, was about two years higher for men and more than two and a half years higher for women in Pas-de-Calais; but this was largely due to the better infantile mortality figures there. Death-rates at other ages were only slightly less in Pas-de-Calais, and occasionally in both sexes they were higher. Twenty years later in 1881 expectation of life in Pas-de-Calais was considerably less than in 1861 for men and slightly less for women. Male rates at almost every age above one were now higher in Pas-de-Calais than in Nord: female rates 1–49 were also higher than in Nord. Any argument dependent upon occupational structure for an explanation of changes in mortality rates is in difficulty here since only men were involved directly in the economic changes between 1861 and 1881: female employment in the coal mines was negligible. In 1901 mortality experience in both sexes was very similar in the two departments, and the difference of expectation of life between the two was largely a function of the lower infantile mortality in Pas-de-Calais.

Though there were considerable differences between French and Prussian industrial areas connected with the national differences between the two countries (for example, the marked 'plateau' effect in French mortality rates in the age-groups 20–39, which changed little during these two decades of life whereas Prussian rates rose steadily), it is reasonable to describe the mortality patterns and expectation of life in all the coalfield industrial areas of France and Prussia as broadly similar. In all areas infantile mortality was of the same order of magnitude. In all areas death-rates in the 1–4 age-group tended to be high. Experience in the older age-groups varied rather more, though it is true in general that death-rates tended to be above national averages in the earlier years, but to fall below the national level at the later census dates. If the rates had not fallen below the national averages by the end of the century, then they were almost invariably falling more quickly than national rates. There is, however, very little solid ground for claiming that industrial areas of different occupational types experienced mortality patterns which are significantly different from one another. Some evidence can be gathered to support the view that occupational structure affected both male and female mortality rates, but the evidence for either on balance is rather inconclusive. It is true that if it were possible to construct a detailed picture of the demography of smaller areas which were occupationally 'pure' differences might emerge; but it is also true that it is their inability to dominate trends in a large agglomeration of industrial population which is of greater importance from many points of view.

When the coalfield industrial areas are compared with other types of area, further aspects of their mortality experience in the late nineteenth century can conveniently be examined. The next step, therefore, towards placing these industrial areas in a general demographic perspective will be to compare them with immediately adjacent, but non-industrial, areas in each country, in order to judge how far the coalfield industrial areas have diverged from the normal regional pattern in their neighbourhoods.

ADJACENT AGRICULTURAL AREAS:
MINDEN, HANNOVER, AISNE AND SOMME

Expectation of life was always higher in Aisne than in Nord, and with one exception (male 1881) was also higher in Somme, two French departments which adjoin the Austrasian field industrial areas of northern France. They had, indeed, a higher life expectancy than any other of the French areas studied. Since infantile mortality was higher in both Aisne and Somme than in Nord except in 1901 (and well above the national average), it is obvious that age-specific death-rates were usually less in these departments above the age of one. The expectation of life figures also reveal another characteristic of the agricultural areas surrounding the French coalfield area: that there was a much higher differential in favour of women in these areas.

Age-specific death-rates were always much lower in Aisne than in Nord in the age-groups 1–4 and 5–9. Above the age of ten and up to the

I

age of forty rates were again usually lower in Aisne, but the differences were much more pronounced for women than for men: male rates in these age-groups were always near to the Nord level and occasionally above it, whereas female rates were usually much below the Nord level. Above the age of forty Aisne's advantage was slight at the beginning of the period in 1861 and had quite disappeared at the time of the later censuses. What is true of Aisne is also normally true of Somme. In 1861 and 1901 the slightly lower expectation of life of Somme was principally due to its poorer infantile mortality figures. In 1881 there was a larger hiatus than usual between infantile mortality in Somme and Aisne, and a correspondingly greater gap in the expectation of life.

Mortality experience became more uniform between the industrial and agricultural departments as the half-century passed. Infantile mortality improved less fast in Nord between 1881 and 1901 than in Somme and Aisne, but mortality at other ages improved faster. In 1901, for the first time, infantile mortality in Nord was higher than in Aisne and Somme, but mortality at other ages improved so rapidly that expectation of life improved as fast in Nord as in the other two departments.

Hannover and Minden, the two Prussian agricultural areas close to the Austrasian field, resemble Aisne and Somme in one vital respect; that in these areas expectation of life was better than in the coalfield industrial areas or elsewhere in Prussia (Minden in 1861 is the only exception to this generalization), but differ in two others; that infantile mortality in Hannover and Minden was normally lower than on the Austrasian field, and that the difference between male and female life expectancy was less in Minden and Hannover than on the coalfield, a reversal of the French case.

Minden, unlike the two other *Regierungs-bezirke* in Westphalia (Münster and Arnsberg), had a singularly regular and steadily improving mortality pattern throughout the half-century before the First World War. It is the only Prussian area studied in which infantile mortality fell regularly from census to census. Mortality indeed fell regularly at every age-group for both sexes for each census date between 1861 and 1910. The only exceptions are that female mortality 15–19 was fractionally higher in 1880 than in 1861, and that female mortality 70–4 was slightly higher in 1900 than in 1880. Otherwise the picture is one of uninterrupted, steady improvement throughout the entire period, a most remarkable instance of stable advance over a long period of time. The mortality history of Minden presents an interesting contrast with that of Arnsberg. In 1861 death-rates in the younger age-groups, below twenty, were higher in Minden than in Arnsberg, and, combined with a higher infantile mortality in Minden, this led to a lower expectation of life in Minden, especially for women. By 1880 Minden had become much healthier for men than Arnsberg except at a very great age, though for women Minden's advantage was either slight or negative except for the 1–4 age-group. Infantile mortality was by now slightly less in Minden than in Arnsberg. Expectation of life for men was much higher in Minden, but for women only slightly so. In 1900 and 1910 the position remained much the same. Male mortality rates were, except at advanced ages, noticeably less in Minden, but female rates were often higher. The slight advantage in life expectancy enjoyed by women in Minden sprang from the much lower infantile mortality and the lower death-rate 1–4.

The case of Hannover is very similar to that of Minden, except that life expectancy for both sexes was a little higher in Minden at each census (except male 1910). The slight difference between male and female expectation of life was as strongly marked in Hannover as in Minden.

A table of the mean deviation in life expectancy for men and women in Aachen, Düsseldorf, Arnsberg, Münster, Minden and Hannover considered together as a group reveals the interesting fact that male expectation of life varied more than female: 1861 is an exception to this rule, but at that early date the absolute numbers involved in the new industrial areas was not very great and may not have made itself felt in the population of the administrative areas used in the table. The mean deviation of female life expectancy hardly changed down to 1910 in spite of the enormous increase of industrial population in some areas, whereas the mean deviation for men grew very substantially until 1900. It would appear, in other words, that the change from rural to industrial living made relatively little difference to the life expectancy of women; that life in the new industrial areas was neither much more, nor much less healthy for them than for the women in the surrounding country areas, but that the men in the new industrial areas were adversely affected by the typical mortality patterns of the industrial areas and suffered a marked deterioration in life expectancy compared with near-by rural areas. Expectation of life was

Table 27. *Mean Deviation in Life Expectancy (in years)*
(*Aachen, Düsseldorf, Arnsberg, Münster, Minden and Hannover*)

	Male	Female
1861*	1·06	1·34
1880	1·90	1·25
1900	2·18	1·33
1910	1·66	1·02

* Without Hannover.

generally higher in the surrounding country areas, but the female advantage in this respect was much less clear-cut than the male: hence the difference in mean deviation of life expectancy for the two sexes.

The same method, however, produces an exactly opposite conclusion in the French areas. When Nord, Pas-de-Calais, Aisne and Somme are grouped together and mean deviations in expectation of life calculated, the result shows bigger deviations for women than for men. Here the agricultural areas also have in general a better expectation of life, but the margin of advantage for men is less great than that for women. It might

Table 28. *Mean Deviation in Life Expectancy (in years)*
(*Nord, Pas-de-Calais, Aisne and Somme*)

	Male	Female
1861	0·58	1·06
1881	0·88	1·53
1901	0·57	0·80

be argued that the heavy employment of women in textile industries in Nord produced high female mortality there, and so increased the female deviation, but the inadequacy of this argument has already been shown when comparing Nord and Pas-de-Calais. Moreover, there was a strong contrast between the French and Prussian agricultural areas quite apart from any differences in occupational structure in the industrial areas, since in Prussian rural areas close to the Austrasian field the difference between male and female life expectancy was always rather small, while in comparable French areas it was rather large. The agricultural areas near to the Austrasian field in France and Prussia, in short, not only present a considerable contrast with the near-by industrial areas, but also with each other, except in so far as all enjoyed better expectation of life than the industrial areas.

A little further light may be thrown on the mortality characteristics of the Austrasian coalfield and surrounding areas by studying crude death-rates, since these are available for smaller areas than the more refined measures of mortality used hitherto.

In France the distinction between rural and urban population used in the censuses (i.e. urban *communes* are those in which the *population agglomérée* was 2,000 or more) was observed also in the publication of vital statistics, so that it is possible to construct crude death-rates for the urban and rural parts of each department. The crude rates do strongly

Table 29. *Crude Death-Rates* (*per* 1,000)
birth-rates in brackets

Urban	1872–3	1880–2	1890–2	1900–2
Nord	25·6 (41·4)	25·9 (36·6)	26·1 (33·6)	19·8 (27·4)
Pas-de-Calais	22·1 (32·7)	28·6 (36·4)	24·4 (32·9)	20·2 (31·8)
Aisne	26·7 (28·2)	24·0 (24·9)	23·9 (23·6)	21·9 (23·2)
Somme	23·4 (25·9)	23·5 (23·7)	23·5 (22·3)	21·4 (19·1)
Rural				
Nord	16·2 (24·8)	16·3 (23·1)	15·8 (19·9)	18·6 (26·6)
Pas-de-Calais	21·3 (29·9)	19·7 (26·7)	20·7 (26·8)	19·0 (28·9)
Aisne	18·9 (21·2)	21·3 (22·8)	23·4 (21·3)	20·8 (22·2)
Somme	21·9 (23·6)	23·4 (23·2)	24·3 (21·4)	22·0 (21·2)

There are slight inaccuracies in the figures for 1880–2, 1890–2 and 1900–2 because the communes classified as urban and rural changed slightly at the censuses of 1881, 1891 and 1901.

suggest that life was healthier in the countryside than in the towns, though there is little indication that the urban areas of Nord were more unhealthy than the urban *communes* in the surrounding departments. Only in Somme were crude death-rates in rural areas as high as in urban areas. The explanation of the wide discrepancy in rates may lie in part in the insanitary conditions of urban life; but appears also to be closely related to the

Table 30. *Crude Death-Rates* (*per* 1,000)
birth-rates in brackets

Nord	1890–2	1900–2
Lille	24·8 (31·4)	20·9 (28·7)
Avesnes	18·3 (22·9)	16·9 (22·1)
Cambrai	19·8 (25·0)	17·7 (22·8)
Douai	20·5 (26·9)	18·2 (26·9)
Dunkerque	25·4 (33·9)	21·1 (31·9)
Hazebrouck	22·8 (29·1)	20·7 (27·1)
Valenciennes	20·4 (27·1)	17·4 (27·3)
Pas-de-Calais		
Arras	21·5 (24·4)	18·8 (24·8)
Béthune	22·0 (36·2)	19·9 (37·0)
Boulogne	23·2 (31·0)	20·1 (29·9)
Montreuil	22·6 (27·0)	20·2 (27·3)
St Omer	22·2 (27·1)	18·8 (26·3)
St Pol	20·9 (23·0)	18·8 (24·1)

higher crude birth-rates in the urban areas. In Nord, for example, in 1872–3, 1880–2 and 1890–2 the crude urban birth-rate was about 70 per cent higher than the rural rate. Since between 25 and 30 per cent of total deaths in Nord were deaths under one it was natural that the crude death-rate should be much higher in areas where the birth-rate was also high. In 1901 when the urban crude birth-rate fell almost to the level of the rural crude birth-rate in Nord, the difference in the death-rates also became negligible.

The same point emerges from a consideration of the crude death-rates for the several *arrondissements* in 1891 and 1901. The crude death-rate in industrial Lille was high, but so also was the birth-rate, and the only non-industrial *arrondissement* with a high crude death-rate, Dunkerque, also had a high crude birth-rate.

In the Ruhr a rather similar result appears when crude death-rates are taken into consideration. In 1895 it is possible to construct crude death-rates for the industrial *Kreise* and the non-industrial *Kreise* within each *Regierungs-bezirk* (for a definition of the industrial *Kreise* see pp. 62–4). In

Table 31. *Crude Death-Rates (per 1,000)*
birth-rates in brackets

	1894–6
Industrial Arnsberg	20·6 (44·4)
Rest of Arnsberg	19·6 (35·5)
Total Arnsberg	20·4 (42·7)
Industrial Düsseldorf	20·3 (40·2)
Rest of Düsseldorf	20·6 (34·8)
Total Düsseldorf	20·3 (39·1)
Industrial Aachen	22·2 (38·3)
Rest of Aachen	21·8 (32·9)
Total Aachen	22·0 (35·9)
Industrial Münster	22·1 (51·3)
Rest of Münster	21·7 (34·7)
Total Münster	21·8 (38·1)

general the differences in crude death-rates between the industrial and other areas were very small. The age-structure of the population in industrial areas may have favoured low death-rates, but on the other hand crude birth-rates were much higher in the industrial *Kreise* and infantile deaths a high proportion of the total, which counts in an opposite sense, so that there is no reason to suppose that if more refined measures of mortality were available they would show that the industrial *Kreise* viewed as a whole experienced less favourable mortality patterns than the non-industrial areas. It is highly probable that in the larger cities like Essen and Düsseldorf, mortality was high, but there is no evidence to suggest that the coalfield industrial development as a whole caused a rise in mortality, or else it had disappeared by this comparatively late date.

GREAT CITIES: BERLIN, PARIS AND MARSEILLES

The great capital cities and seaports form another type of area with which it seems profitable to compare the coalfield industrial areas, since these cities were a second type of urban area which grew very fast in the later nineteenth century. In Prussia Berlin, and in France Seine and Bouches-du-Rhône, have been used as controls.

Expectation of life in all three cities[1] was very much lower than in the industrial areas of the Austrasian field and than the national averages. In all three the expectation of life was in the lower thirties both in 1861 and 1881, but rose very substantially to around or a little over forty in 1900. The reasons for a low expectation of life, however, were not the same in Berlin as in the two French cities. That this must be so is suggested by the infantile mortality rates, for whereas Berlin except in 1910 had infantile mortality rates well above the high Prussian average (more than three children in every ten in Berlin died in their first year of life in 1880), in Seine and Bouches-du-Rhône infantile mortality was at a much more modest level. In Seine except in 1881 infantile mortality was below the national average, and less than two-thirds the Berlin rate, and in Bouches-du-Rhône only a little above the French average. Since expectation of life was about the same in all three cities, it follows that age-specific death-rates at ages above one must have been much higher in the two French cities than in Berlin. The differences are well brought out by a comparison between the cities and an industrial area in each country.

Age-specific death-rates in Berlin in 1861 and 1880 were very similar to those in Düsseldorf at the same dates apart from infantile mortality and mortality in the age-group 1-4, where the Berlin rates were much higher. Above the age of ten death-rates for men were often lower in Berlin, and for women almost always so. In 1900 even in the 1-4 age-group Berlin was down to the Düsseldorf level: at higher ages the advantage was usually with Düsseldorf for men, but with Berlin for women. By 1910 the one remaining weakness of Berlin mortality rates, its high infantile

[1] Seine and Bouches-du-Rhône included, of course, some population which was outside Paris or Marseilles, but it was a small and declining fraction of the total.

mortality, had largely disappeared, and expectation of life for women was almost as high as in Düsseldorf, while for men it was not far behind, though at most ages death-rates were still a little higher in Berlin.

Seine presents quite another picture, when compared with Nord. At all three census dates a greater proportion of babies survived their first year in Seine than in Nord, but above the age of one died at a greater rate than in the corresponding Nord age-groups. Although age-specific death-rates fell fairly steadily in Seine, the gap between rates in Seine and rates in Nord showed only a slight tendency to close. When in 1900 Berlin had virtually caught up with Düsseldorf in age-specific death-rates above the age of one, Seine had still some little way to go to come abreast of Nord. If a direct comparison of rates in Berlin and Seine is made the same impression results: that progress in reducing mortality was less in Seine than in Berlin. Both in 1880 and 1900 with very few exceptions age-specific death-rates were higher in Seine than in Berlin in both sexes. In Bouches-du-Rhône death-rates were normally less high than in the corresponding Seine age-groups, but both infantile mortality and mortality in the very important 1–4 age-group were much higher even than in Seine so that expectation of life was actually less than in Seine. There is, however, a strong family resemblance between Seine and Bouches-du-Rhône in their mortality patterns.

The usefulness of comparing Seine with Nord, or Berlin with Düsseldorf may be questioned on the ground that the great cities were almost 'pure' urban populations, while the industrial areas were less 'pure' because of the large non-industrial population in both Nord and Düsseldorf. It is assumed on this argument that any unfavourable age-specific death-rates in the industrial areas would be dampened out to some extent by the inclusion of considerable agricultural populations. The extent of the dampening out, however, is unlikely to have been very great either in Nord or Düsseldorf both because industrial populations were a large fraction of the total (in later years a very large majority) in the two areas, and because rates in the near-by agricultural areas were similar to those on the coalfield.

It has sometimes been argued that death-rates show a tendency to rise as the size of the town or city increases, reaching a peak in the biggest cities. There is certainly plenty of literary evidence to support this contention; suggesting, for example, that death-rates in Lille were higher than in the smaller textile towns elsewhere in Nord. Yet in some contexts this would be an observation without great significance. If it were true, for example, that coalfield industrial development habitually centred on relatively small towns, whereas the major administrative and commercial cities were normally much larger, then it would still be important to distinguish between the mortality characteristics of the new industrial populations, and those of urban agglomerations of a different type. The totals of population involved were no smaller in the former than the latter case. Moreover, the example of Berlin casts doubt upon any generalization about a correlation between the size of the city and the height of the death-rates, since even in 1861 and 1880 and more clearly at later dates, Berlin compares well in age-specific mortality rates with the Ruhr industrial areas except in infantile mortality and mortality in the 1–4 age-group. Above the age of five it would be difficult to show Berlin to be decisively less healthy than a wide range of other Prussian industrial or agricultural areas, while the example of Seine prevents any generalization about a correlation between infantile mortality and the size of cities.

REMOTE AGRICULTURAL AREAS:
EAST PRUSSIA, POMERANIA AND FINISTERRE

Finisterre forms the western extremity of the Breton peninsula, an area of population pressure and generally low living standards during the later nineteenth century. Like East Prussia it was an area without great agricultural wealth. These two areas together with Pomerania will serve to carry a step further the attempt to distinguish between national and local demographic characteristics.

Expectation of life in Finisterre was much lower than the national French average at each census date (in 1881, indeed, it was lower than in Seine and Bouches-du-Rhône), and far less, therefore, than in Nord. This was so in spite of the rather surprising fact that infantile mortality was less in Finisterre than in Nord, and below the national average except in 1881, when it was fractionally higher. Mortality was so high in Finisterre in 1881 that expectation of life was only 28·5 years for men, and 30·8 years for women.[1] Only exceptionally high mortality rates above the age of one could produce such a situation.[2] In fact in 1861 and 1881 rates in Finisterre

[1] Heckscher gives the average expectation of life for both sexes together as 35·2 years during the period 1751–1800 in Sweden, at a time when, in his view, mortality experience closely reflected agricultural conditions because so many people lived close to the margin of subsistence (this view is not shared by Utterström, however). E. F. Heckscher, 'Swedish Population Trends before the Industrial Revolution', *Economic History Review*, 2nd series, vol. II (1950), p. 273.

[2] In this instance the danger of relying on one year's mortality experience is clear for 1881 in Finisterre was a year of unusually high mortality. If the mortality experience of a three-year period 1880–2 is taken instead, male expectation of life rises to 31·1 years and female to 33·0 years; still low figures, but substantially higher than those given above. The distortion involved in basing tables on one year's experience

at all ages were far higher than those in, for example, Nord, but preeminently so in the younger age-groups 1–19. These were the age-groups in which dramatic improvements or deteriorations in mortality rates most commonly occurred in all areas throughout the half-century (above the age of forty differences and fluctuations were very much less). It was very largely the great increases in mortality rates in the age-groups 1–19 which caused the great worsening of expectation of life in Finisterre between 1861 and 1881. Equally it was an enormous drop in the death-rates in these years which produced an increase in life expectancy of fourteen years for men and fifteen years for women between 1881 and 1901. At the latter date rates in these age-groups were still higher than in Nord or in France as a whole, but now the differences were relatively slight, seldom more than 50 per cent above the national rate and often much less, where twenty years earlier they had been between two and three times as high as the national average. Throughout the entire period rates in most ages in Finisterre were steadily and substantially above those in Nord or France, but by 1901 the gap had been reduced substantially. The tendency for mortality rates all over the country to grow more uniform was exemplified in Seine and Bouches-du-Rhône for the great cities, and is further exemplified by Finisterre for the rural slums.[1]

As in the mortality patterns in the great cities of Prussia and France, so in the remote agricultural areas, there is a marked difference between French and Prussian experience. In the remote agricultural areas as in the big cities expectation of life is less than the national average in both countries, but again as in the big cities, in France in the agricultural areas the low expectation of life is largely a result of very high death-rates above the age of one, whereas in Prussia a high infantile mortality is the most prominent feature of the situation. It is almost as if low life expectancy in Prussia found its expression in heavy mortality soon after birth, while in France the heavy mortality was reserved to a greater age. Comparison of East Prussia with Düsseldorf brings out this feature, just as comparison of Finisterre and Nord brought out French characteristics. Infantile mortality

is normally much less. To use a three-year base for Nord or for France as a whole at the same date, for example, lowers male expectation of life by only about two months in each case. Visual inspection suggests that the distortion involved in using only one year's experience is usually only of this order of magnitude. Finisterre in 1881 is a most exceptional case.

[1] A direct comparison of Seine and Finisterre, two of the most unhealthy departments, is interesting. Mortality was normally much higher in Finisterre than in Seine in the 20–39 age-groups, very similar in both areas above the age of forty, whilst in the sensitive under twenty age-groups the balance swung between the two, Finisterre being healthier in 1861 and 1901, but Seine in 1881. Infantile mortality was in each year slightly lower in Finisterre.

in East Prussia was about fifty per 1,000 higher than in Düsseldorf throughout the period, whereas in Finisterre it was always substantially less than in Nord. Above the age of one, however, the position was very different. East Prussian death-rates in the 1–4 age-group were at each census date a little higher than in Düsseldorf: death-rates were also commonly higher in the 5–19 age-groups: but above the age of twenty rates were broadly similar in the two areas, with rates often higher in Düsseldorf (for example for both sexes 20–39 in 1880). There was no enormous difference between the two areas in death-rates in the early and middle years of life such as existed between Finisterre and Nord. A direct comparison of East Prussia and Finisterre reveals higher rates as a rule at most ages in Finisterre (though there are exceptions: in 1900 rates were much lower in Finisterre in the 1–9 age-groups; and in 1861 there was little to choose between the two areas in male rates 1–19). The difference between the two areas was, of course, at its greatest in 1880 when the age-groups 1–44 seemed in Finisterre to be gripped by a Malthusian spasm which did not touch East Prussia. In infantile mortality, however, the boot was on the other foot. The rate in East Prussia was always substantially higher, though by a variable amount. In 1880 it was fifty per 1,000 higher; in 1900 the difference was as large as a hundred per 1,000, a very large margin indeed.

Pomerania, an agricultural area geographically in between Hannover and East Prussia, was between the same two in most respects in its mortality patterns. Expectation of life was at each census date midway between Hannover and East Prussia. Infantile mortality rates were also in a midway position, except in 1900 when the rates rose suddenly in Pomerania to exceed that of any other Prussian area considered. An oddity in Pomerania's demographic history is that expectation of life was almost exactly the same in 1861, 1880 and 1900, in spite of a most regular improvement in death-rates at all ages above one. Infantile mortality, however, rose steadily during this period (from 185 per thousand in 1861 to 260 in 1900 for men; and from 161 to 226 for women), and cancelled out the gain from changes in mortality at other ages. Mortality rates in Pomerania were similar to those in East Prussia, though normally somewhat lower. They were considerably less than the rates in Düsseldorf in 1880. In 1900 Pomerania and Düsseldorf were close to one another in the age-groups 1–39, but rates in Pomerania were lower in the above forty age-groups: in 1910 the advantage lay with Düsseldorf below forty, but above forty still with Pomerania, though not by any great margin.

Certain general reflexions suggest themselves when considering the mortality of the group of areas in Prussia and France whose mortality has been studied. It is striking how similar expectation of life was in areas in France and Prussia which were of a similar economic and sociological constitution. Nord in France, Düsseldorf in Prussia: Aisne and Somme, Hannover and Minden: Seine and Bouches-du-Rhône in France, Berlin in Prussia: Pas-de-Calais in the former, Münster in the latter: Finisterre in the one country, East Prussia in the other; in all these groups expectation of life was very similar. This is true in spite of the fact that national expectation of life was considerably higher at each comparable date in France than in Prussia. These coincidences, however, conceal very wide differences in several of the groups in age-specific death-rates which are worth examining further.

Infantile mortality in Prussia was much higher than in France, but the average level of infantile mortality in the nine Prussian and seven French areas studied was almost exactly the same in 1861 and 1880, though in 1900 there was a steep fall in the French areas at a time when the rate was still rising in the Prussian areas. Such an average is, of course, almost meaningless in itself (though interesting as suggesting similarities which national figures conceal): what, however, is very significant is that the mean deviation from this average in the nine Prussian areas is almost double that of the seven French in 1861 and more than double it in 1880 and 1900.

Table 32. *Mean Deviation in Infantile Mortality Rates*
(per 1,000 live-born)

Prussian areas					French areas				
	Average		Mean Dev.			Average		Mean Dev.	
	M	F	M	F		M	F	M	F
1861*	187	162	30	28	1861	181	158	16	15
1880	194	167	38	35	1881	201	172	14	13
1900	204	175	34	31	1901	165	139	14	10
1910	168	141	25	21					

* Excluding Hannover.

Fluctuations in infantile mortality were relatively unimportant in French areas in controlling expectation of life: in Prussian areas infantile mortality was of far greater significance. In Prussia an area of high infantile mortality was normally an area of low expectation of life: in France there was no such correlation. Furthermore, comparable areas in the two countries deviated from their respective means in opposite directions. Thus in France Somme and Aisne had high infantile mortality rates, while their opposite numbers in Prussia, Minden and Hannover, experienced low death-rates in the first year of life. Again infantile mortality in Berlin was very high indeed, while in Paris and Marseilles (Seine and Bouches-du-Rhône) it was only about the average of the French areas studied. In France, Finisterre, though apparently in earlier decades of the period in a Malthusian situation, had an infantile mortality rate less than the average, whereas East Prussia's rate was high. Only indeed in the industrial areas of the two countries was infantile mortality experience similar on both sides of the frontier (with the exception of Aachen, where rates were rather high —the chief reason for the rather low expectation of life in Aachen compared with other industrial areas).

Examination of the infantile mortality figures also casts doubt on a generalization frequently advanced in the past, 'that when mortality rates rise or fall, they generally do so at all ages together'.[1] The balance of evidence in the French and Prussian areas studied suggests rather an inverse relation between infantile and other mortality rates. Berlin, East Prussia, Aachen, Aisne and Somme all had rather high infantile mortality and relatively low mortality at other ages: while Seine, Bouches-du-Rhône and Finisterre enjoyed relatively favourable infantile mortality rates, but experienced heavy mortality in the later years of life.[2] Even apart from the infantile mortality rates there are many exceptions to the rule that mortality rates tend to fluctuate in unison. The widespread rise in male mortality in the middle years of life in France took place at a time when mortality rates in the younger age-groups were falling rapidly.

In the age-groups 1–19 there were no clear national patterns distinguishing France from Prussia. These were the age-groups in which the greatest proportionate falls in death-rates took place in both countries: changes in them largely account for the great increase in expectation of life in this half-century. On the whole it seems true that rates in the vital 1–4 age-group were lower in the French areas than in comparable Prussian ones. In this age-group there was a general fall in France between 1861 and 1881 which is not always paralleled in Prussia, and a further steep fall in the following twenty years which kept French rates generally below the Prussian. There are, however, sufficient exceptions to most observations about these age-groups to inhibit generalization.

The pattern of age-specific death-rates above the age of twenty was characteristically very different in French and Prussian areas. In the age-groups 20–39 French rates were normally higher than the Prussian rates

---

[1] A. R. Burn, 'Hic Breve Vivitur', *Past and Present*, No. 4 (1953), p. 14.

[2] This conforms to the view that a high infantile mortality weeds out the weaklings and reduces mortality in later age-groups, and vice versa. Cohort analysis, where possible, would help to throw more light on this question.

in comparable areas. The French rates during these four five-year age-groups, however, show little tendency to rise with age, and frequently decline, whereas in Prussian areas what might be called the mortality gradient was steep. The death-rate for the 35–9 age-group in Prussian areas was much higher (often double) the rate in the 20–4 age-group. This steep rise in death-rates with increasing age in Prussian areas continues into the later age-groups, so that in comparable areas Prussian rates in the age-groups 40–59, and indeed 60–79, are usually higher than the French rates, which rise much more sluggishly.

If the group of areas considered in each country was representative of conditions in general in the two countries, it seems fair to assert that expectation of life during this half-century was, on the whole, highest in the prosperous agricultural areas; that the next best areas from this point of view were the Austrasian field industrial areas (even after any reasonable allowance has been made for the fact that a proportion of the population in the political units chosen was not industrially employed); and that the worst areas were the great administrative and maritime cities, and the remote agricultural areas. A fuller regional study, however, might well reveal important exceptions to these observations.

After 1880 the differences in expectation of life in the several areas in each country showed a tendency to diminish, which is reflected in the mean deviations from average life expectancy in the seven French and nine Prussian areas.

Table 33. *Mean Deviation in Life Expectancy (in years)*

Prussian areas			French areas		
	M	F		M	F
1861*	2·2	1·9	1861	3·8	4·1
1880	2·8	1·8	1881	4·5	5·0
1900	2·2	1·8	1901	2·3	2·4
1910	1·8	1·2			

* Excluding Hannover.

Demographic conditions in general were becoming more uniform after 1880 (fertility as well as mortality shared this characteristic). Whether the converse is true: that before, say, 1861 differences in mortality patterns in the areas studied were greater than at a later period is more difficult to decide. Perhaps they were not much different from the 1861 position. Between 1861 and 1880 there were no great overall changes, and general considerations (especially the relative steadiness in life expectancy over a long period before 1861) make it unlikely that swift or radical changes in mortality took place in the generation or so before 1861. The great advances in expectation of life, and the major falls in age-specific death-rates occurred after 1880.

It is possible by the study of regional variations in age-specific mortality rates to call in question many widely held beliefs about the effect, for example, of urban life in raising death-rates; about the healthiness of rural areas; or about the tendency of age-specific death-rates at all ages to fluctuate in unison. It is also possible to distinguish more accurately between the elements in French and Prussian national mortality statistics which reflect general national conditions, and those which are the result simply of a different numerical balance between different types of area. It is not, however, possible by the use of statistics alone to arrive at an understanding of the sociological conditions which underlie them. Many interesting hares can be started—how to explain the remarkable contrast between the mortality gradient of men between twenty and forty in France and that of men of the same age in Prussia; how to understand the strong contrast in mortality experience of Paris and Berlin; how to account for the rise in Prussian infantile mortality between 1861 and 1900; and so on —but relatively few have so far been caught. Perhaps fuller information about demographic history will expose some of these problems as spurious or mis-stated: but there appears to be a hard core of questions of the greatest interest whose existence can be detected, but whose solution requires a much more detailed historical study than the scope of the present inquiry permits. Regional analysis can, however, isolate a range of important problems, and can take the important, if negative, first step of exposing the limitations of some stock answers to them.

VII. FERTILITY

Just as some aspects of French and Prussian national and local mortality are conveniently examined by regional analysis, so their fertility history invites the same procedure. The half-century before the First World War experienced changes in fertility as sweeping as those in mortality, and equally striking national and local contrasts; some of them difficult to understand, others which can with confidence be related to particular sociological circumstances. As might be expected comparable areas in the two countries normally displayed similar fertility patterns, measured by their deviation from national averages, although the very great national differences in fertility rates between France and Prussia meant that there were much larger percentage differences in fertility between comparable areas than in mortality.

MARITAL FERTILITY

It is convenient to begin by taking marital fertility.[1]

The national fertility pictures are simple. In Prussia marital fertility remained unchanged between 1871 and 1880 at 314 per 1,000; then fell somewhat in 1900 to 290, and very steeply in 1910 to 239.[2] In France the rate even in 1851 was only about two-thirds of the early Prussian figures. Fertility declined gently between 1851 and 1861, and again between 1861 and 1881 at a period when the Prussian rates were steady; and between 1881 and 1901, while Prussian rates had turned down only slightly, in France the fall was already steep.[3] Viewed as a group the French areas studied afford a great contrast with the Prussian not merely in the absolute levels of marital fertility, but also in the fact that the mean deviation in marital fertility rates was far higher in France than in Prussia, especially in

[1] Marital fertility has been calculated by relating the average number of legitimate live-born children born in a three-year period centred on a census date to the number of married women 15–44 living at that date. The figures given are the number of children born per annum per 1,000 women at risk. In the Prussian census of 1871 there is no division of the number of married women between forty and fifty years of age: here an approximation to the numbers 40–4 has been made by dividing the larger group in the same ratio as it was divided in the 1880 census when a fuller breakdown is available for each area.

[2] For simplicity a single year only is quoted, but each census year figure given throughout this chapter actually represents a three-year average centred round that year.

[3] It is interesting to note that infantile mortality rates had begun to fall steeply in France during this same twenty-year period, whereas in Prussia they rose slightly.

Table 34. *Marital Fertility*

FRANCE	1850–2	1860–2	1880–2	1900–2
Bouches-du-Rhône	263	280	201	150
Seine	152	165	150	114
Finisterre	311	309	310	286
Aisne	173	165	167	153
Somme	189	169	169	144
Nord	297	284	280	196
Pas-de-Calais	249	246	264	236
FRANCE	216	205	196	159

PRUSSSIA	1870–2	1879–81	1899–1901	1909–11
East Prussia	333	331	322	293
Pomerania	312	313	288	235
Berlin	270	255	169	127
Hannover	273	275	260	218
Minden	328	332	355	263
Münster	331	347	380	350
Arnsberg	352	351	346	277
Düsseldorf	363	358	325	243
Aachen	379	381	373	307
Hamburg	300	271	202	146
PRUSSIA	314	314	290	239

Table 35. *Mean Deviations in Marital Fertility*

Prussian areas	A	B	C
1870–2	324	28	8·6
1879–81	322	34	10·6
1899–01	302	58	19·2
1909–11	246	52	21·1
French areas	A	B	C
1850–2	233	53	22·7
1860–2	231	56	24·2
1880–2	220	55	25·0
1900–2	183	49	26·8

A average marital fertility rates
B mean deviation
C B as a percentage of A

the earlier part of the period. Prussia 1871 seems to be a country in which little was done to prevent conception inside marriage; or if anything was done, it was done uniformly: whereas in France the range of different

K

customs found was substantial. Thus it was that some areas which were comparable in occupational structure in the two countries had radically different marital fertility rates, while in others the difference was far less, though it always existed.

Coalfield industrial areas

In Arnsberg, Düsseldorf, Aachen and Münster marital fertility was always above the Prussian average. In 1871 and 1880 the rate in Aachen was the highest of the Prussian areas studied: at the two later censuses Münster took the lead. A rate between 325 and 375 was normal for all four areas in 1871, 1880 and 1900. With one exception there is no evidence before 1900 of any decline in marital fertility in the coalfield industrial areas (the exception is that there was a moderate fall, from 358 to 325, in Düsseldorf between 1880 and 1900). In Arnsberg and Aachen rates were steady near 350 and 375 respectively, while in Münster there was a substantial rise between 1880 and 1900, the period during which coal-mining spread north into the area. In these areas, therefore, if Düsseldorf is excepted, the national tendency to decline between 1880 and 1900 is absent. All the four, however, experienced marked and substantial falls in marital fertility in the last decade of the period. The fall was greatest in Düsseldorf, where it had first begun, but was of the same order of magnitude in both Aachen and Arnsberg. It was much less in Münster, now in a period of very rapid change in the occupational constitution of its population. The 1910 rate in Münster was, in fact, higher than the rate in 1871.

In Nord and Pas-de-Calais the absolute level of marital fertility was less than in the comparable Prussian areas, but the difference was much less than the national differences between the two countries. In the French coalfield industrial areas rates were far above the French average. Nord escaped for a time the steady fall which was typical of much of France. Between 1851 and 1881 marital fertility was on a high plateau in the department, on each occasion above 280. In Pas-de-Calais there was even a considerable rise between 1861 and 1881, coincident with the beginning of large-scale coal-mining.[1] Between 1881 and 1901, however, there were falls in both areas, slight in Pas-de-Calais, very steep in Nord. As in the case of infantile mortality French experience anticipates the Prussian by a decade or so. It may be, indeed, that the falls in marital fertility and infantile mortality are related to each other. The history of the French areas

[1] For an interesting study of the demography of the coal-mining area of Pas-de-Calais, see P. Ariès, *Histoire des populations françaises et de leurs attitudes devant la vie depuis le XVIIIe siècle* (Paris, 1948), esp. pp. 202–67.

lends some support to this conclusion, although there are many instances between 1861 and 1881 of areas in which infantile mortality was still rising after marital fertility had begun to fall.

It is possible that marital fertility in the French industrial populations of Nord and Pas-de-Calais was in fact nearer to the comparable Prussian areas than this analysis would suggest, because there is little doubt that in the French departments such of the population as was non-industrial had a much lower marital fertility, whereas in the German areas this was probably not so (compare rates in Minden and Arnsberg, for example). The following table of crude birth-rates may be rather misleading, since the French census definition of urban and rural is not the same as an occupational distinction between industrial and non-industrial. Moreover, crude birth-rates are, of course, liable to deceive because of the influence of the age-structure of the population on them. Nevertheless there are points of interest.

Table 36. *Crude Birth-Rates (per 1,000)*

FRANCE

Urban	1872–3	1880–2	1890–2	1900–2
Nord	41·4	36·6	33·6	27·4
Pas-de-Calais	32·7	36·4	32·9	31·8
Aisne	28·2	24·9	23·6	23·2
Somme	25·9	23·7	22·3	19·1
Rural				
Nord	24·8	23·1	19·9	26·6
Pas-de-Calais	29·9	26·7	26·8	28·9
Aisne	21·2	22·8	21·3	22·2
Somme	23·6	23·2	21·4	21·2

In Aisne and Somme birth-rates in rural and urban areas were much the same: in Nord there was a very wide gap between the two during the years before the great end-of-century changes. Pas-de-Calais is in an intermediate position; but this might be expected in such an area since many coal-miners lived in small villages, and would be accounted rural by the French census authorities. It seems fair to conclude that the admixture of any considerable rural populations must have depressed marital fertility rates in Nord and Pas-de-Calais somewhat, since the differential between the urban and rural rates is too large to be accounted for by differences in the age distribution of the populations or in the proportions married in the child-bearing age-groups.

For purposes of comparison it is perhaps interesting to see the differ-

ences in crude birth-rates between those *Kreise* of the four Prussian industrial *Regierungs-bezirke* which have been counted as industrial and the
remaining *Kreise* in each *Regierungs-bezirk*. The figures refer to the years
1894–6, the first years for which such material is readily available. It can

Table 37. *Crude Birth-Rates (per 1,000)*

PRUSSIA	1894–6
Industrial Arnsberg	44·4
Rest of Arnsberg	35·5
Total Arnsberg	42·7
Industrial Düsseldorf	40·2
Rest of Düsseldorf	34·8
Total Düsseldorf	39·1
Industrial Aachen	38·3
Rest of Aachen	32·9
Total Aachen	35·9
Industrial Münster	51·3
Rest of Münster	34·7
Total Münster	38·1

be seen that the differences are considerable, especially in Münster, but are
less than in Nord. For what they are worth, therefore, the crude birth-
rate figures support the view that the marital fertility figures for larger
units, such as have been used, over-state the difference in marital fertility
between French and Prussian Austrasian coalfield areas. Before the great
fall in fertility in the French departments at the end of the century, it is
possible that a better measure of the marital fertility of the industrial areas
would reveal a tolerably close similarity between them.

Adjacent agricultural areas: Minden, Hannover, Aisne and Somme

In these areas the differences between French and Prussian experience
reached an extreme, for rates in Aisne and Somme were sometimes less
than half the rates in Minden and much below those of Hannover. In
Aisne and Somme there was a steady decline in rates throughout the
period, in strong contrast with the near-by industrial departments where
the rates held up firmly for a time, only to drop sharply at the end of the
century. Aisne and Somme experienced neither the earlier plateau, nor
the subsequent, sudden descent. Marital fertility in these two departments
must have been controlled from an early date reaching back into the first
half of the century (the crude birth-rate in Aisne in the decade 1811–20

was 35 per 1,000, and higher than in Nord, but fell steeply between 1820 and 1850, while in Nord the decline was comparatively slight). During most of the second half of the century their rates were less than two-thirds

Table 38. *Crude Birth-Rates (per 1,000)*

FRANCE	1801–10	1811–20	1821–30	1831–40	1841–50	1851–60	1861–70	1871–80	1881–90	1891–1900
Bouches-du-Rhône	36·0	35·0	34·0	31·0	32·1	31·0	29·4	27·3	26·6	24·5
Seine	34·0	34·0	38·0	33·0	31·1	30·6	29·2	26·9	26·1	22·8
Finisterre	37·0	37·0	38·0	35·0	33·2	33·0	33·9	35·0	33·5	31·7
Aisne	31·0	35·0	33·0	28·0	25·9	25·0	23·9	23·7	22·5	22·4
Somme	31·0	31·0	28·0	26·0	25·6	24·8	23·6	23·1	22·6	21·7
Nord	35·0	34·0	35·0	33·0	30·9	32·6	32·3	32·4	30·2	28·3
Pas-de-Calais	32·0	31·0	30·0	29·0	27·6	28·5	29·3	30·0	29·9	30·0
FRANCE	32·0	31·0	31·0	29·0	27·4	25·5	25·8	25·4	23·9	22·1

of the Nord rate, and were falling gently. They had no part in the sudden and violent changes in marital fertility which characterized the industrial areas of Nord towards the end of the century, and those of the Ruhr a little later.

With this picture Minden forms a complete contrast, for here marital fertility was high and rising in the period up to 1900, being almost identical with the rates of its industrial neighbour, Arnsberg. As in the Ruhr areas, so in Minden the decade 1901–10 was a period of rapidly falling marital fertility, during which presumably methods of controlling conception began to be practised throughout the whole of Westphalia (though less in Münster, which was Catholic, than in Minden and Arnsberg which were largely Protestant). In broad outline the course of events in Hannover was similar to that in Minden, but there were two important differences. The fertility rates in Hannover were about 50 per 1,000 lower than in Minden, and the first clear fall in marital fertility occurred between 1880 and 1900, although it was not of great size, at a period when fertility was still rising in Minden.

Great cities: Berlin, Hamburg, Paris and Marseilles

Berlin and Hamburg displayed similar trends in marital fertility, although at any given date the rate in Hamburg was the higher by about 25 per 1,000. In 1871 the rate in Berlin was, at 270, less than the national average and considerably less than in the coalfield industrial areas, but it was absolutely a high rate and not very much lower than in some other areas (Hannover, for example). Thereafter, however, and in strong contrast with the general Prussian experience, it fell steadily: after 1880 the falls became substantial. The 'plateau' effect, so common in most of Prussia, was absent here. Control of conception was presumably spreading in the great cities sooner than elsewhere. By 1910 the Berlin rate was barely half the national average. Hamburg's history conforms to the same pattern at a slightly higher absolute level.

Seine and Bouches-du-Rhône, like Berlin and Hamburg, showed similar trends in fertility—a small rise between 1851 and 1861, followed by falls to 1881 and 1901—but between the two French areas there was a large difference in the absolute levels of marital fertility. In Seine, even in 1851, the rate was very low at 152; so that although in 1901 the rate was still lower (114) there was no great percentage fall. In Bouches-du-Rhône, on the other hand, the rate at the first two census dates was high by French standards (280 in 1861), being a long way above the national average. Even after the severe fall between 1861 and 1881 the rate was still a little higher than in the country as a whole. In Marseilles, it would seem, the control of conception had gone much less far than in Paris until 1861, though the gap closed rapidly thereafter.

The great cities in the two countries were, in general, the areas where marital fertility fell earliest, most steeply, and ultimately to the lowest levels. In France in some of the agricultural departments marital fertility was also very low in 1851, but these areas did not experience large subsequent falls after the fashion of the great cities.

Remote agricultural areas: East Prussia, Pomerania and Finisterre

Of the French areas considered, Finisterre is alone in exceeding 300 per 1,000 in its marital fertility rate. From 1851 to 1881 marital fertility in this department was steady at 310 per 1,000, or very near to the Prussian national average for the period. Here also the 'plateau' effect is visible, as in the French industrial areas, and generally in Prussia. Moreover, although the rate fell between 1881 and 1901, the fall was more moderate than in other French areas which had high marital fertility rates in the early part of the period. 'Malthusian' Finisterre had a fertility appropriate to an area in which mortality was so high and expectation of life, except at the last census date, so brief. The fertility history of the Breton departments was probably unmatched by any agricultural area of comparable size in France in the second half of the nineteenth century.

East Prussia and Pomerania show very similar traits to those of Finis-terre. The absolute marital fertility rates in Pomerania were almost exactly the same as those in Finisterre at the same dates. The parallel extended to the fall between 1880 and 1900, which in Pomerania as in Finisterre was moderate. In East Prussia the trend was exactly as in the other two, but the absolute rates were a little higher, and the fall between 1880 and 1900 a little less marked.

It seems proper to conclude of marital fertility rates in general in the two countries that the differentials between similar French and Prussian areas varied very greatly according to the occupational and sociological nature of the areas.

In most Prussian areas other than the great cities marital fertility was high and stable until the last years of the century. The statistics suggest that little family limitation was practised except in the great cities. In the French areas there was far greater variety. There were areas of France in which also marital fertility was high and stable for several decades,[1] notably in the Austrasian field industrial departments and the remote Breton department of Finisterre, though such areas were not common. The explanation of the great difference of marital fertility levels in France and Prussia as a whole cannot be found in areas like Nord and Finisterre. Nor can it be found in the great cities, which have tolerably similar his-tories, although the decline in marital fertility began earlier in Paris than elsewhere and continued further. Berlin and Hamburg were alone amongst the Prussian areas in showing considerable falls in marital fertility well before the end of the century: they slipped off the 'plateau' at a much earlier date than other Prussian areas. If all Prussia and France had been made up of areas of these three types, Prussian marital fertility would have been greater than French, but not greatly so. The evidence of the limited group of areas considered suggests that if Aisne and Somme are repre-sentative of the bulk of agricultural France, it is to this sociological type that one must turn for the explanation of the low average national fertility, for in these two departments even in 1851 there was effective and rela-tively drastic family limitation, whereas in comparable Prussian areas marital fertility remained high. A study on a much larger scale than this would be necessary to establish the point, because sociologically agricul-

---

[1] Bertillon's suggestions about the reasons for the absence of family limitation in the areas of factory industry and in a scatter of agricultural communes in France may be only partially correct, but his recognition of the existence of areas in France where marital fertility was little checked by artificial means seems just. The areas in question may have been much larger than he supposed. See J. Bertillon, *La Dépopulation de la France* (Paris, 1911), esp. pp. 110–11 and 319–25.

tural France was far from uniform, but once again the tendency of national averages to cloak important regional variations is clear.

For many purposes marital fertility statistics are of less use than those of general fertility.[1] Striking differences may exist between the ranking of an area in marital fertility and its ranking in general fertility; and the study of these differences is illuminating. Aachen, for example, had the highest marital fertility rate of any Prussian area studied in 1871 and 1880, but came amongst the lowest in general fertility at these two dates. The explanation of this contrast, which appears to be related to the marriage habits typical of a Catholic area, shows what is important demographically in the sociology of the area.

The chief reason for contrast between marital and general fertility ranking is, of course, differences in the proportion of women married in the child-bearing age-groups, though the frequency of illegitimate births may also affect matters slightly. Since the proportion of women married in the child-bearing age-groups is much influenced by economic and sociological circumstances, this proportion varied widely within the groups of areas previously considered in France and Prussia. Consideration of marriage and general fertility forms the next step in an outline of the economic and sociological differences between the several groups of areas which are reflected in their demographic patterns.

As with mortality, so in marriage patterns there were some characteristic differences between France and Prussia. In the younger age-groups 15–29 more women were married in France than in Prussia, while for the 30–44 age-groups the figures were higher in Prussia. In 1880 in Prussia, for example, the number of women ever married per 1,000 total female population was 17, 262 and 649 for successive five-year age-groups 15–29: for France in 1881 the figures were 61, 398 and 681. On the other hand, for the next three age-groups 30–44 the figures in Prussia were 820, 875 and 891; while in France they were 776, 824 and 847. Since the fertility of married women falls as they grow older, these figures suggest that general

---

[1] General fertility has been calculated by relating the average number of live-born children born in a three-year period centring on a census date to the total number of women 15–44 in the population at that date. The figures given are the number of children born per annum per thousand women at risk. Some approximation was necessary to derive a rate for the Prussian areas in 1861. It was assumed that half of the women in the age-group 14–16 were over 15. The age group 40–9 was divided up into 40–4 and 45–9 age-groups in the same ratio as obtained between these two age-groups in each area at the census of 1871 when fuller figures were given.

Table 39. *General Fertility*

FRANCE	1850–2	1860–2	1880–2	1900–2	
Bouches-du-Rhône	146	152	101	93	
Seine	112	111	99	76	
Finisterre	145	142	150	144	
Aisne	110	114	112	106	
Somme	113	106	107	99	
Nord	147	148	147	116	
Pas-de-Calais	124	137	143	145	
FRANCE	116	115	112	97	
PRUSSIA	1860–2	1870–2	1879–81	1899–1901	1909–11
East Prussia*	185	175	170	172	150
Pomerania	167	167	172	165	135
Berlin	134	135	138	93	77
Hamburg	—	145	146	114	88
Hannover	—	147	151	147	125
Minden	158	160	167	159	133
Münster	127	137	155	187	185
Arnsberg	174	195	204	204	168
Düsseldorf	162	175	181	171	136
Aachen	147	160	166	160	137
PRUSSIA	165	164	168	160	134

* East and West Prussia combined in 1861.

fertility in France benefited from this position. If the marriage patterns of the two countries were interchanged the differences between French and Prussian marital and general fertility rates would have been still greater.[1] The same point can be made by expressing Prussian marital and general fertility as percentages of the French figures. In 1880, for example, Prussian marital fertility was 160 to the French 100, while general fertility was only 151: in 1900 the figures were 182 and 166. Although in both countries the proportion ever married in the earlier age-groups showed a tendency to rise as time passed, the characteristic national differences remained and are reflected in most regional comparisons (it is interesting, incidentally, to note that just the same pattern emerges with the male age-groups 15–44; there was a higher percentage of French men ever married in the first three age-groups, but a lower percentage in the later three). There were considerable variations in the percentages of women ever married in the

[1] It would be of great interest in the study of marital fertility to be able to present age-specific marital fertility rates. Unfortunately, however, the absence of information about age of mother at the time of the birth of the child makes this impossible until a rather late date in the period under study.

several age-groups in different areas within each country, but they were not so great as to obscure the large national differences. Comparison of similar areas in the two countries, therefore, will tend to be comparison of deviations from national patterns, rather than a direct comparison.

Table 40. *Numbers per 1,000 Total Population Ever Married*

FRANCE			15–19	20–4	25–9	30–4	35–9	40–4
Bouches-du-Rhône	1861	m	3	81	374	608	716	738
		f	30	253	595	712	816	807
	1881	m	6	149	409	611	709	725
		f	71	301	624	719	746	793
	1901	m	16	135	482	689	769	817
		f	106	424	676	779	829	842
	1911	m	6	152	549	726	800	827
		f	82	439	696	796	840	855
Seine	1861	m	1	83	341	620	750	807
		f	64	393	621	748	806	841
	1881	m	4	104	449	637	731	777
		f	75	413	617	711	768	799
	1901	m	14	132	442	730	801	837
		f	115	410	638	746	800	830
	1911	m	7	66	564	757	825	856
		f	95	447	680	773	811	832
Finisterre	1861	m	1	97	432	672	732	799
		f	57	269	516	726	783	797
	1881	m	1	69	573	682	693	832
		f	46	394	655	764	787	751
	1901	m	8	102	523	773	850	884
		f	75	379	693	812	851	861
	1911	m	1	96	531	770	855	887
		f	54	397	714	828	863	872
Aisne	1861	m	3	237	621	842	892	918
		f	83	506	787	875	891	891
	1881	m	1	151	644	818	863	888
		f	69	503	815	870	887	893
	1901	m	16	140	661	837	869	893
		f	109	543	794	870	891	927
	1911	m	3	154	692	836	875	895
		f	144	606	823	883	897	909

			15–19	20–4	25–9	30–4	35–9	40–4
Somme	1861	m	3	169	543	797	867	896
		f	36	369	694	820	871	888
	1881	m	3	147	571	787	857	887
		f	51	410	728	827	858	866
	1901	m	4	162	660	829	863	888
		f	92	488	768	851	882	894
	1911	m	4	189	682	825	871	893
		f	73	514	799	863	878	892
Nord	1861	m	3	117	412	658	774	814
		f	22	261	584	740	809	841
	1881	m	3	122	481	697	780	811
		f	27	298	641	745	804	827
	1901	m	9	147	593	784	839	878
		f	67	371	690	798	841	862
	1911	m	4	170	639	818	856	876
		f	54	415	726	828	856	865
Pas-de-Calais	1861	m	2	136	448	700	796	826
		f	23	289	608	764	827	832
	1881	m	2	119	560	734	818	847
		f	26	351	694	778	822	845
	1901	m	7	149	620	805	853	869
		f	67	431	749	837	866	876
	1911	m	3	180	663	823	868	891
		f	60	488	795	871	889	892
France	1861	m	3	127	441	699	811	857
		f	54	349	626	760	823	852
	1881	m	2	123	514	750	798	844
		f	61	398	681	776	824	847
	1901	m	10	110	523	766	838	873
		f	95	427	707	814	855	872
	1911	m	3	117	590	772	843	874
		f	77	460	736	827	860	874
Prussia								
East Prussia	1880	m	2	97	529	817	894	919
		f	19	220	596	794	869	889
	1900	m	2	80	534	788	886	919
		f	16	251	604	775	843	871
	1910	m	1	75	509	781	878	910
		f	15	259	623	783	840	861

Table 40—*continued*

			15–19	20–4	25–9	30–4	35–9	40–4
Pomerania	1880	m	1	81	512	801	887	920
		f	15	258	643	822	879	904
	1900	m	1	106	564	806	885	909
		f	16	299	674	821	869	892
	1910	m	1	95	543	808	892	918
		f	14	298	682	832	881	891
Berlin	1880	m	1	53	425	733	845	882
		f	16	224	571	765	836	862
	1900	m	0	80	461	747	846	883
		f	17	255	573	741	806	840
	1910	m	0	71	440	724	834	883
		f	17	250	581	747	816	845
Hannover	1880	m	2	73	439	733	850	894
		f	15	268	669	840	892	906
	1900	m	1	85	485	765	865	897
		f	17	302	686	846	890	903
	1910	m	1	75	477	770	864	898
		f	15	303	708	850	889	906
Minden	1880	m	2	85	487	770	874	903
		f	13	243	661	836	876	892
	1900	m	2	94	498	766	866	899
		f	12	258	659	827	868	886
	1910	m	1	99	480	773	864	900
		f	7	237	660	829	863	886
Münster	1880	m	1	42	302	608	765	824
		f	8	170	533	740	814	824
	1900	m	1	70	411	692	802	842
		f	20	269	629	795	843	865
	1910	m	1	78	456	738	835	866
		f	24	321	684	841	869	876
Arnsberg	1880	m	1	91	486	763	861	893
		f	22	373	781	900	922	924
	1900	m	2	114	535	790	868	893
		f	24	421	775	887	915	929
	1910	m	1	101	529	797	876	900
		f	28	408	781	890	916	925
Düsseldorf	1880	m	2	82	452	736	831	867
		f	13	250	637	811	863	879
	1900	m	1	100	496	767	844	871
		f	20	310	676	826	864	878
	1910	m	1	89	494	776	858	887
		f	18	314	702	841	877	891

			15–19	20–4	25–9	30–4	35–9	40–4
Aachen	1880	m	1	43	315	610	741	796
		f	7	153	507	708	789	814
	1900	m	1	59	369	657	770	813
		f	6	167	508	709	775	809
	1910	m	1	61	374	674	787	823
		f	7	173	534	736	789	806
PRUSSIA	1880	m	2	80	486	772	871	903
		f	17	262	649	820	875	891
	1900	m	1	97	525	788	873	901
		f	19	298	663	816	863	884
	1910	m	1	88	513	787	873	905
		f	16	299	678	820	866	883

Coalfield industrial areas

A striking feature of this group is that general fertility in the areas with large textile industries compared unfavourably with their marital fertility, when each is expressed as a percentage of the national level, as the following table shows for the year 1880.

Table 41. *Marital and General Fertility Expressed as Percentages of National Averages*

	Marital fertility	General fertility
Nord	143	132
Aachen	122	98
Düsseldorf	114	107

Women in textile areas did not marry so young or so generally as in the other coalfield industrial areas. It has been argued that the independence gained by a woman who was able to support herself induced women in the textile areas to delay marriage to a later date than women in, say, iron and steel or coal-mining areas, and encouraged a great proportion not to marry at all. Employment opportunities, however, appear to have operated indirectly through the sex-ratios in textile areas rather than directly in the manner suggested. It is significant that there was frequently either an absolute majority of women in textile areas in the age-groups when most marriages occur, or a smaller minority than in other industrial areas. Assuming that men in textile areas had marriage patterns similar to male patterns elsewhere, this fact alone would necessarily reduce the percentages of women married in the child-bearing age-groups, since there would be a greater surplus left over after each man who wished to marry had made his choice. A comparison of Arnsberg with Düsseldorf illustrates this point. In 1880 and 1900 the proportions of men married in each age-group 15–44 was less in Düsseldorf than in Arnsberg, but only by a small margin. The differences in the female figures, on the other hand, were very great (with important consequences for the general fertility rate, which was much more in Arnsberg's favour than the marital fertility rate). A glance at the table giving the numbers of men per 1,000 women in each age-group suggests the reason for this contrast, since Arnsberg had at all ages a higher figure than Düsseldorf.[1]

Table 42. *Sex Ratios (men per 1,000 women)*

FRANCE		15–19	20–4	25–9	30–4	35–9	40–4
Bouches-du-Rhône	1861	1,120	1,185	1,287	1,089	1,257	1,115
	1881	961	898	856	1,011	1,203	1,076
	1901	1,023	1,000	1,000	1,033	1,063	1,062
	1911	995	918	975	1,004	1,008	1,047
Seine	1861	1,004	1,062	1,068	1,130	1,134	1,134
	1881	1,026	849	1,029	1,047	1,037	1,066
	1901	952	788	957	931	947	959
	1911	931	680	955	959	976	935
Finisterre	1861	939	1,006	912	951	1,061	1,051
	1881	1,009	788	636	1,197	1,039	909
	1901	1,037	980	995	990	980	986
	1911	1,024	922	967	987	989	975
Aisne	1861	1,015	959	1,013	1,039	1,059	1,036
	1881	1,013	1,048	1,192	1,048	1,044	1,044
	1901	991	1,024	1,017	1,008	1,016	1,024
	1911	925	906	988	968	968	949
Somme	1861	1,015	897	950	1,067	1,011	980
	1881	973	945	998	1,007	1,013	1,038
	1901	997	874	986	982	980	991
	1911	994	877	997	994	983	964
Nord	1861	1,046	1,084	1,100	1,089	1,128	1,094
	1881	1,013	992	969	1,085	1,082	1,115
	1901	987	883	994	988	1,008	1,007
	1911	982	882	1,002	988	1,013	985

[1] A table of men per thousand women in each age-group is, of course, rather misleading since the average age of marriage was considerably higher for men than for women. It might be more realistic to compare the numbers in one female age-group with the number in the next older male age-group: but each alternative method involves difficulties, and it is perhaps better to ignore the difficulty than to attempt an unsatisfactory solution. Its existence must, however, be noted.

		15–19	20–4	25–9	30–4	35–9	40–4
Pas-de-Calais	1861	1,022	1,030	1,047	1,027	1,017	1,032
	1881	962	1,304	1,025	1,073	1,002	996
	1901	1,074	954	1,090	1,068	1,087	1,063
	1911	1,056	898	1,063	1,083	1,054	1,013
FRANCE	1861	1,009	951	991	1,020	1,021	1,021
	1881	1,011	934	1,032	1,018	1,022	1,013
	1901	996	968	993	981	992	990
	1911	998	978	981	989	996	976
PRUSSIA							
East Prussia	1880	977	852	903	884	907	886
	1900	981	1,018	891	881	878	889
	1910	1,008	1,095	965	936	932	894
Pomerania	1880	1,011	989	960	934	918	903
	1900	1,027	905	963	964	962	941
	1910	1,055	946	965	956	975	968
Berlin	1880	871	990	921	993	1,004	989
	1900	871	1,004	987	963	949	856
	1910	862	1,028	1,010	980	970	945
Hannover	1880	1,030	1,031	1,011	1,006	986	962
	1900	1,044	1,007	1,011	1,015	1,009	1,008
	1910	1,058	1,074	1,044	1,031	1,025	1,011
Minden	1880	1,002	897	942	945	963	927
	1900	997	930	997	965	987	979
	1910	1,003	915	965	986	1,031	973
Münster	1880	1,007	977	1,034	1,010	1,013	1,015
	1900	1,105	1,067	1,167	1,124	1,103	1,100
	1910	1,082	1,024	1,129	1,063	1,165	1,118
Arnsberg	1880	1,119	998	1,162	1,143	1,141	1,097
	1900	1,258	1,108	1,285	1,222	1,194	1,165
	1910	1,165	1,043	1,184	1,176	1,183	1,145
Düsseldorf	1880	1,025	929	1,041	1,036	1,047	1,044
	1900	1,095	1,008	1,150	1,124	1,104	1,061
	1910	1,050	979	1,122	1,124	1,118	1,101
Aachen	1880	1,060	932	1,021	999	1,012	1,031
	1900	1,040	870	961	956	993	975
	1910	1,036	885	1,012	1,004	994	978
PRUSSIA	1880	996	949	962	941	958	943
	1900	1,015	970	991	983	979	957
	1910	1,012	989	1,005	1,000	1,000	979

A similar conclusion may be drawn from a comparison of Nord and Pas-de-Calais in France. In 1861 the proportions ever married amongst both men and women were lower in Nord than in Pas-de-Calais in spite of the fact that there were more men per 1,000 women in each age-group in the former than in the latter. This, therefore, presumably reflects a difference in general sociological conditions in the two departments which led to a greater reluctance to marry amongst women in Nord. In this instance the sex-ratio cannot be invoked to explain the situation. In 1881 and 1901, however, there were fewer men per thousand women in the 15–44 age-groups in Nord than in Pas-de-Calais as coal-mining developed in the latter. This made little difference to the proportions of men ever married in each age-group in Nord compared with its fellow in Pas-de-Calais: the proportions in Nord remained lower, but only a little lower, whereas the difference between the two areas in comparable female figures grew considerably, until in 1901 it was much greater than it had been in 1861. The changes between 1861 and 1901 seem closely connected with the changes in sex-ratios in Pas-de-Calais in the period, which would tend to magnify in the proportions of women ever married any differences in the male rates.

It might be supposed that Aachen illustrated the tendency of women in textile areas to marry little and late better than either Düsseldorf or Nord, for the proportion married, especially in the younger age-groups, was very low and made Aachen into an area of low general fertility in spite of having an exceptionally high marital fertility. Since Aachen was also an area in which the number of men per thousand women was lower than in Düsseldorf (and *a fortiori* than in Arnsberg), Aachen can be represented as merely an extreme case of the general tendencies discussed above. Such a representation, however, would certainly be inadequate and misleading because it ignores the question of religious adherence. To understand the importance of religion it is necessary to turn to Münster and Minden since they very neatly show the significance of religious adherence in determining marriage habits and patterns.

Aachen and Münster were both Catholic areas with insignificant Protestant minorities. Minden, on the other hand, was more than 60 per cent Protestant; while Arnsberg and Düsseldorf had populations of mixed religious adherence, the former having a slight Protestant majority, the latter a rather stronger Catholic majority. An examination of the marriage patterns in 1880 shows a strong resemblance between Münster and Aachen on the one hand and Minden and Arnsberg on the other, with Düsseldorf in between the two groups. Comparison of Münster and Minden is particularly illuminating in this connexion because this was a date before the

Table 43. *Religious Adherence* (*per 1,000 either Protestant or Catholic*)

	1880		1900	
	Prot.	Cath.	Prot.	Cath.
Aachen	37	963	41	959
Münster	103	897	152	848
Düsseldorf	408	592	419	581
Arnsberg	562	438	557	443
Minden	620	380	658	342

spread of coal-mining north into Münster with its disrupting influence on demographic patterns. In 1880 both Münster and Minden were still largely agricultural areas. In that year marital fertility was very similar (347 per 1,000 in Münster, 332 in Minden), but general fertility was only 155 in Münster compared to 167 in Minden. Twenty years earlier in 1861 the difference was still greater, for the figures then were 127 and 158. The chief cause of the difference between the marital and general fertility pictures was that in Protestant Minden men and women married younger than in Catholic Münster.[1] The correspondence in the proportions of men married in each age-group between Münster and Aachen, which were both Catholic areas, is, on the other hand, remarkably close; and for women the correspondence is only slightly less exact. In view of the very different occupational structure of the populations in Aachen and Münster, and the close similarity of the occupational structure between Münster and Minden it is difficult not to conclude that religion played an important part in determining general fertility rates, though the nature of the mechanism connecting religious adherence and marriage habits remains, of course, obscure. By 1900 circumstances had changed considerably in Münster which was at that time in the middle of the great expansion of coal-mining which took place there at the end of the century. The proportions of men married in each age-group had risen considerably and were somewhat above the Aachen level, though they were still lower than the rates

[1] A subsidiary cause of some importance, however, was that the number of illegitimate births was a much higher proportion of the total in the Protestant than in the Catholic area, and this helped to raise its general fertility. This was so in spite of the fact that the proportion of unmarried women in Minden was less than in Münster. The figures in brackets are percentages.

	1860–2		1879–81	
	Total	Illeg.	Total	Illeg.
Münster	12,467	329 (2·64)	15,676	372 (2·37)
Minden	16,139	800 (4·96)	18,422	691 (3·75)

	1899–1901		1909–11	
	Total	Illeg.	Total	Illeg.
Münster	27,959	540 (1·93)	39,278	828 (2·11)
Minden	22,541	910 (4·04)	22,105	834 (3·77)

in the same age-groups in Minden, which had remained agricultural, and much lower than in Arnsberg. For women the differences between Münster and Aachen were larger than for men because at this date Münster had a large surplus of men and Aachen of women in the marriageable age-groups.

Both the importance of religious adherence in determining marriage patterns, and the importance of the sex-ratios in governing the proportion of women who married in the younger age-groups are well illustrated by Arnsberg. In contrast with the textile areas, general fertility in Arnsberg was higher above the national average than marital fertility. In 1880 general fertility was 121 per cent of the Prussian average: marital fertility only 112 per cent. In that year general fertility in Arnsberg was substantially higher than in its neighbour Düsseldorf (204 per 1,000 to 181) even though marital fertility was slightly less (351 per 1,000 to 358). Religion and the sex-ratios serve to explain the anomaly. In Düsseldorf, where the ratio of Protestant to Catholics was roughly the reverse of the ratio in Arnsberg, it was to be expected, if the contrast between Münster and Minden is any guide, that the proportions married in the younger age-groups would be lower than in Arnsberg which had a much higher percentage of Protestants: and this expectation is upheld by the statistics. The proportions of men married in each age-group was lower in Düsseldorf at all three census dates, and the difference for women was once more much greater because the ratio between the sexes was less unbalanced in Düsseldorf than in Arnsberg. With a higher proportion of men married and a bigger majority of men over women it was natural that many more women should be married in Arnsberg than in Düsseldorf and that the general fertility rate should be relatively much higher than the marital fertility rate.

A comparison of Arnsberg and Minden is as interesting as the comparison with Düsseldorf, and supports the same conclusions. The proportions of men married in each age-group in Arnsberg in 1880 hardly differed from those in Minden where the proportion of Protestants was similar even though the occupational structure of the population was very different. For women the figures were very different, largely because the sex-ratios of men per 1,000 women were in each age-group very much higher in Arnsberg, where men were in a considerable majority, than in Minden, where they were in a minority. In 1900 the position had changed slightly since by that date more men were married in the younger age-groups in Arnsberg than in Minden, although the difference was still small. The difference for women had grown still larger, but so had the imbalance in numbers between the sexes.

Pas-de-Calais provides a final illustration of the importance of sex-ratios in governing the proportions of women married in the younger age-groups, and thus influencing general fertility. Changes in Pas-de-Calais were much like those in Münster. As coal-mining developed, a strong majority of men in the young adult age-groups became characteristic of the department. As a result of this, the proportion of women married in the younger age-groups rose sharply. It is interesting to note that there was very little change in the relative positions of Nord and Pas-de-Calais between 1861 and 1901 as far as the proportions of men married in each age-group are concerned. At both dates (and in 1881) there were rather more men married in Pas-de-Calais than in Nord, but in spite of the vast growth of coal-mining in the former in these forty years the tendency among men to marry younger did not accelerate more in Pas-de-Calais than it did in Nord. The differences between the two areas in the comparable female statistics, however, became much greater during the forty years. Both this and the Prussian evidence suggest that marriage habits among the male population did not change very much even though the occupational structure of the area might change greatly, nor were they greatly different in neighbouring industrial areas with contrasting occupational structures (except where religious differences also occurred); but that women were much more sensitive to changes in sex-ratios than men, and that the proportions married in the three younger age-groups might vary quite rapidly and widely as the sex-ratios altered. Male rates were 'sticky' where female rates were commonly quite fluid (see below pp. 155-7 for a fuller treatment of this point).

Adjacent agricultural areas

Both in Aisne and Somme marriage normally came early and covered a very high proportion of the population at risk, so that general fertility figures in these two departments were very close to the national French average even though their marital fertility was well below the average. Thus in 1881 in Aisne marital fertility was only 85 per cent of the national average, whereas general fertility was 101 per cent: in Somme the comparable figures were 86 and 96 per cent. These were characteristics of long standing. In 1851 marital fertility in Aisne was 80 per cent of the French national level; general fertility 95 per cent of it (in Somme 87 and 98 per cent respectively). In 1861 the proportions ever married both in the male and female age-groups were higher in Aisne than in any other French area, and in the younger age-groups very much higher. In 1881 the same position obtained although the differences were growing less great; and again in 1901 the same characteristics can be traced, but they were by this time much less strongly pronounced. In Aisne, as elsewhere, a closer approximation to the national average was typical of the last decades of the century.

In Prussia the case of Minden has already been discussed. Hannover had a markedly lower general fertility rate because marital fertility was lower than in other Prussian areas except for the great cities. The comparison of Hannover and Minden re-emphasizes the importance of sex-ratios in determining the proportion of people married in either sex. Both in 1880 and in 1900 the proportions of men married in each age-group were lower in Hannover than in Minden, but since there were relatively more men than women in Hannover, a higher proportion of women was married in each age-group in Hannover.[1]

Great cities

In 1880 Berlin's marital fertility rate was 81 per cent of the Prussian average and her general fertility rate 82 per cent: in 1900 both stood at 58. At first sight this is surprising since the proportions of women married in Berlin were at both dates well below the national levels. The explanation lies in the relatively high percentage of illegitimate births occurring in Berlin, which raised the general fertility rate appreciably.[2] Marriage rates per 1,000 in each age-group were higher in Berlin than in the purely Catholic areas studied, but lower than was usual in a Protestant area (Berlin was overwhelmingly a Protestant city throughout the period). Since there was a female majority in the marriageable age-groups in Berlin, female rates tended to lag further behind the male, though the differences were not pronounced. The great cities in Prussia were the first areas to show the effects of a very rapid decline in fertility, a decline so abrupt that general fertility in Berlin fell from 82 per cent of the national level to 57 per cent in a period of thirty years to 1910. The absolute rate fell to barely a half of its former level.

In Paris the position was different in several respects. Marital fertility fell no quicker in Paris between 1851 and 1901 than it fell in the country

---

[1] It is possible that the lower male marriage figures in Hannover are a hangover from the days when there were restrictions upon free marriage imposed by a government moved by Malthusian considerations. Such restrictions had disappeared in Hannover a decade before the 1880 census.

[2] In Berlin 14·7 per cent of total live births were illegitimate in 1860–2: 13·2 per cent in 1879–81: 14·8 per cent in 1899–1901: 20·7 per cent in 1909–11. For Prussia as a whole the corresponding figures were 8·1 per cent: 7·7 per cent: 7·3 per cent: and 7·8 per cent.

at large, being just over 70 per cent of the national level at both dates. General fertility, on the other hand, which was almost as high as in France as a whole in 1851 fell steadily as a percentage of the national figure during the following fifty years (from 97 to 79 per cent of the average). The reason for the much better showing of general than marital fertility in Paris is partly that, in the early decades at least, the proportions married per 1,000 women in the child-bearing age-groups was higher than the national average, but mainly that in the Seine department illegitimate births formed such a high proportion of the total live-born.[1] General fertility rates were naturally in these circumstances much higher relatively than marital fertility rates. In Paris, unlike Berlin, there was a majority of men in the age-groups 15–44, a fact contributing to the relatively high percentage of women married in Paris, just as the converse contributed to an opposite situation in Berlin. In Marseilles (Bouches-du-Rhône) there was a much higher marital fertility rate than in Paris, but fewer women in the child-bearing age-groups were married, and there was a much lower percentage of illegitimate births, so that marital and general fertility rates differed from the national averages in a broadly similar fashion—in short, a position much more like that of Berlin than that of Paris. The position in Hamburg was much the same as in Berlin, except that fertility (both general and marital) was at a higher level in Hamburg in the early decades and fell away less quickly until the last decade before the First World War.

Remote agricultural areas

Marital fertility in Finisterre was much higher than the French average: general fertility was higher also, but by a smaller margin (in 1851, 1881 and 1901 marital fertility was 144, 158 and 179 per cent respectively of the national average: general fertility was 125, 134 and 149 per cent at these dates). The reasons for the percentage differences lie partly in the fact that fewer women of child-bearing age were married in Finisterre than in France as a whole, and partly in the very low proportion of illegitimate to total births.[2] While there were usually fewer men and women married in the age-groups 15–44 in Finisterre than in France, Finisterre was not very far behind national averages in most years and age-groups. The very unfavourable living conditions reflected in the mortality statistics and life

---

[1] In Seine 26·2 per cent of total live births were illegitimate in 1860–2: 23·9 per cent in 1880–2: 24·5 per cent in 1900–2. For the whole of France the corresponding figures were 7·4 per cent: 7·5 per cent: and 8·8 per cent.

[2] 3·6 per cent in 1860–2: 2·3 per cent in 1880–2: 2·4 per cent in 1900–2.

expectation figures in 1861 and 1881 do not seem to have caused marriage to take place later or less frequently. Upon the whole (for there were a few exceptional age-groups) more men were married in Finisterre at all three dates than in Seine and about as many as in Nord (except in the early age-groups in 1901), though many fewer were married than in Aisne. The position of women was very similar to Nord. The sex-ratios in Finisterre call for little comment except in 1881 when a very large proportion of Finisterre men 20–9 were apparently living outside the department, per-haps as a result of the severe economic and social conditions which pro-duced such exceptionally high mortality at that time.

In East Prussia general fertility was relatively slightly less than marital fertility in 1880 and 1900, when each is compared with the national averages by the method used above, but the difference was slight. More men were married in each age-group in East Prussia in 1880 than in any other Prussian area studied: and in 1900 only Pomerania and Arnsberg were higher. On the other hand at both dates fewer women were married than in any but the purely Catholic areas. The explanation for this curiosity must lie chiefly in the unusual sex-ratios in East Prussia for at both dates there was a heavy surplus of women in the province. The great poverty of East Prussia did not dissuade men from marrying: more men married in East Prussia than in comparable Protestant agricultural areas in the west, such as Hannover and Minden, where, however, the prevalence of small farms rather than large estates may, perhaps, have influenced the marriage decisions of the local farming community. But the differences were slight between East Prussia and the Protestant agricultural areas far-ther west: far less than the differences which appear to be associated with religious adherence. In Pomerania general fertility was a little lower than in East Prussia: the imbalance in numbers between the sexes was much less pronounced: the proportions of women married in the age-groups 20–44 was normally higher, but the proportions of men lower (at least until the end of the century). In short, in general fertility, marriage habits and sex-ratios, as in so many other demographic characteristics, Pomerania came part-way between East Prussia to the east and Hannover to the west.

Some general conclusions may tentatively be drawn from this section on general fertility and marriage. The section on marital fertility showed that rates were normally higher in industrial than in neighbouring agri-cultural areas.[1] General fertility was also commonly higher in the coalfield

[1] Marital fertility was higher in Nord and Pas-de-Calais than in Aisne or Somme; and was higher in Aachen, Arnsberg and Düsseldorf than in Minden, Hannover, or even East Prussia, though in Prussia the differences were less and tended to fade away about the turn of the century.

industrial areas. This was to be expected in view of the marital fertility rates, but in some areas the hiatus between the two types of area was magnified by the higher percentages of married women in the child-bearing age-groups. This feature appears to be connected more with the sex-ratios in such areas than with, for example, a willingness to marry young amongst men who reached their maximum earning power in early manhood. There is little evidence in this period to support the view that the proportions of men married in each age-group was higher in coalfield industrial areas than in near-by agricultural areas (compare Nord or Pas-de-Calais with Aisne or Somme, or indeed Finisterre: or Arnsberg and Düsseldorf with Minden, Hannover or Pomerania). Nor is there much evidence of substantial differences between different types of industrial area in this respect. There is no clear evidence, for example, that in textile areas men married later or less than in coal-mining or heavy industrial areas[1] (Nord compared with Pas-de-Calais points mainly one way: Düsseldorf compared with Arnsberg points slightly the other, but here religion enters strongly into the picture, as, of course, it does far more in Aachen). If there were local peculiarities in marriage patterns in textile towns, they were not sufficiently weighty to affect the general trends in any of the units considered. On the other hand, the proportions of women married might vary much more between coalfield areas and near-by agricultural areas, or between heavy industrial areas and textile areas

---

[1] There is, of course, *some* evidence that this was so. In Germany in 1895, for example, the percentages of all male workers between twenty and thirty years of age who were married was as follows for several industries:

	Percentage
Coal mining and associated industries	46·5
Iron manufacture	42·5
Metal working (smithying, etc.)	31·4
Spinning and ancillary textile industries	41·4
Weaving	38·3
Brewing	31·4
Shoemaking	33·6
Building (masons)	35·2
Farming and forestry	27·8

(*Statistik des Deutschen Reichs*, Neue Folge, Bd. 103, Tab. 7, 'Familienstand und Beruf der Bevölkerung des Reichs').

The percentage married in coal mining was slightly higher than in textiles, but since the figures refer to the whole of Germany they are uncertain evidence of the position in any one area. Moreover the great range in marriage patterns in other industries which were also numerically important would blur the pattern from area to area. Only in Münster do the marriage statistics of Table 40 suggest that occupational changes strongly affected male marriage rates. There the great influx of miners into Recklinghausen substantially increased the proportions of men married in the younger age-groups (but even in 1910 men were still marrying later and less in Catholic Münster than in Protestant Minden which was without mines).

(being in each case higher in the first one of the pair), apparently because sex-ratios were radically different. The proportions of men married in each age-group were far more 'sticky' than the proportions of women. There might seem no *a priori* reason why a large surplus of women should not result in a very high proportion of men marrying rather than a very low proportion of women, but in practice the second is the normal case.[1] The following table may serve to illustrate the point. In Protestant areas the 'stickiness' of male marriage statistics is more clear-cut than in all areas

Table 44. *Mean Deviations in Numbers Married per 1,000 Total Population*

A average number ever married per 1,000 total population
B mean deviation from A
C B as a percentage of A

1880—All Areas*

Men	A	B	C	Women	A	B	C
20–4	72	17	24·1		240	43	17·8
25–9	438	55	12·5		622	63	10·1
30–4	730	54	7·4		802	44	5·5

Protestant Areas Only†

Men	A	B	C		A	B	C
20–4	80	10	12·3	Women	262	33	12·7
25–9	476	32	6·7		651	57	8·7
30–4	765	27	3·5		824	30	3·6

1900—All Areas*

Men	A	B	C	Women	A	B	C
20–4	87	14	16·3		281	46	16·4
25–9	484	37	9·7		643	57	8·9
30–4	753	36	4·8		803	43	5·3

Protestant Areas Only†

Men	A	B	C	Women	A	B	C
20–4	94	11	11·3		299	39	14·3
25–9	510	29	5·7		664	46	6·9
30–4	775	17	2·1		818	34	4·2

* East Prussia, Pomerania, Berlin, Hannover, Minden, Münster, Arnsberg, Düsseldorf and Aachen.
† Same without Münster and Aachen.

Average rates and mean deviations have been rounded to nearest whole number. Percentages are therefore sometimes apparently inaccurate.

[1] See in this connexion the *Report of the Royal Commission on Population*, Cmd. 7695, p. 249, para. 25 which speculates that this is true also of England in recent decades.

taken together, because the inclusion of Catholic areas introduces wide variations from the mean in both sexes, but the same pattern appears in both tables. In both sexes mean deviations fall steadily as the proportions married rise, but amongst men it is always lower at a point when any given proportion is married than at the point where the same proportion of women is married. The 'stickiness' is visible also in France (for example, in the comparison of Nord and Pas-de-Calais). There is strong evidence in Prussia that religious adherence had a very marked effect on the proportions married in each age-group, and that this largely accounts for the un-favourable showing of Catholic areas in general fertility, a feature which was not at all apparent when considering marital fertility. Until a plausible mechanism to connect religious persuasion and marriage habits has been suggested the correlation can only be noted, and its importance in modi-fying fertility rates in Catholic areas examined. Regional analysis suggests, however, that this is a demographic conundrum well worth solving. In the great cities, where marital fertility was low and falling, the proportions married in each male age-group were normally low when compared with the national average or with coalfield industrial areas, but general fertility was supported by the large number of illegitimate births, so that it was rarely a smaller percentage of the national average than was the com-parable percentage for marital fertility. Men living in agricultural areas where economic conditions were unfavourable (e.g. East Prussia and especially Finisterre), do not appear to have been induced by this to marry less or later as a result: women follow the same pattern, though strongly modified by the large surplus of women in some areas.[1] In general there seems good ground for believing that regional variations were growing less pronounced as the century wore on, and many that were marked in 1850 had disappeared by 1910.

NET REPRODUCTION RATES

So far mortality and fertility patterns have been treated in isolation from one another; but in any existing population they interact with one another constantly, and it is desirable to have some single measure of population change which combines the two in a single statement where this is possible. The best known and most useful single measure of this type is the female

[1] Such a situation is, of course, perfectly reconcilable with a fluctuation of mar-riage rates in conformity with the business cycle (see in this connexion, for example, D. S. Thomas, *Social Aspects of the Business Cycle* [London, 1925], ch. 3), since it reflects general marriage propensities rather than short-term fluctuations, except in the case of the age-group 15–19 and 20–4 in which most married persons had been married only a very short time.

net reproduction rate, in which some elements at least of female mortality are combined with the general fertility position to give a measure of the increase which will obtain in each generation assuming constant conditions of fertility and mortality.[1]

In order to calculate female net reproduction rates it is necessary to know births by age of mother as well as to have female life tables and to know the total number of female live-births.[2] Births by age of mother were not given by French and Prussian statistics until late in the century; and often later for political divisions within the country than for the country as a whole. If, therefore, a net reproduction rate is to be calculated throughout the period certain assumptions must be made about the age-specific fertility of women in the six five-year age-groups 15–44. Inevitably this must mean some distortion. None of the net reproduction rates cited below, therefore, can be taken as perfectly accurate. Their usefulness, however, does not lie in the absolute rates, but in the opportunity they afford for comparing different areas. This is feasible because the largest distortions which appear likely to result from the method used are much less than the differences between different areas.

The method used is to split the total female live-births into six divisions to correspond with the six five-year age-groups 15–44, and to derive a fertility rate for each by relating these to the number of women in each age-group. The use of female mortality tables then allows the number of years lived per 1,000 women to be calculated for each age-group, and a net reproduction rate to be derived. For French areas the ratio used in dividing up the female live births was 50 : 250 : 300 : 225 : 125 : 50. For Prussia the ratio was 25 : 200 : 300 : 233 : 167 : 75. These ratios are typical of those found in the two countries at the time when information about age of mother first became available in the 1890s. It is true, of course, that

---

[1] These assumptions are, of course, unrealistic in two senses. Firstly, because there were secular changes in both fertility and mortality during the period, so that no one figure gives an accurate measure of the performance of a cohort over a period of years: and secondly, because within any secular trends there are fluctuations in fertility and mortality rates in sympathy with economic circumstances. Since the mortality tables used are the product of only one year's mortality experience, and the fertility tables of only three years' experience, the absolute levels of the net reproduction rates derived should be viewed with caution. These difficulties, however, are not so serious in the present study as they would be in some, since the absolute level of the reproduction rates is of much less interest than the differences between different areas, which are less exposed to criticism on these scores. In this chapter the rates are used as a sort of convenient shorthand expression of a large variety of fertility and mortality characteristics. See in this connexion the *Report of the Royal Commission on Population*, Cmd. 7695, Appendix 3, especially paras. 15–17.

[2] The method of calculating the female net reproduction rates used here is that described by Kuczynski, *The Measurement of Population Growth*, pp. 205–9. Births have been related only to the female age-groups 15–44.

the ratios had in all probability been changing in the thirty years before this time and that they changed a little in the next two decades; but the inaccuracy which results from this is not serious. More serious is the inaccuracy involved in distributing births in the same way in areas which differed very markedly in relative numbers of women in the six age-groups and in marriage habits. Even if age-specific fertility were the same all over the country, the fact that in some areas the numbers of women in each successive age-group changed little while in others it fluctuated greatly would reduce the accuracy of the arbitrary distribution. But age-specific fertility was not uniform, if only because of the very different percentages married in the younger age-groups in the several areas, which compounds inaccuracy. Nevertheless experiment shows that the degree of possible distortion involved is much less than might be feared.[1] If two actual but very extreme distributions of births between the six age-groups are taken and applied to populations selected to test the range of inaccuracy possible, upper limits can be set to the degree of distortion which is likely to occur.

The populations should clearly be those in which distortion is likely to be greatest. Two French areas, Seine and Finisterre, and one Prussian, Minden, have been chosen for this purpose. In Prussia in some areas the number of women 40–4 was only a little more than half the number 15–19, and here if anywhere large differences might be expected to show themselves in the rates derived from different assumptions. In Minden in 1880, for example, the numbers of women 15–19 was 24,823, but fell with successive age-groups until the number in the 40–4 age-group was only 14,002. In France, on the other hand, in theory possible differences should be small because the number of women in successive age-groups did not fall quickly. The numbers did, however, fluctuate greatly in some departments, and Seine and Finisterre in 1881 have been chosen with this in mind. If the numbers in the 15–19 age-group in Seine are taken to be 100, then the successive age-groups 15–44 varied as follows: 100, 145, 109, 108, 100, 88. In Finisterre the corresponding figures were 100: 116: 69: 74: 68: 73. Assuming distribution of births in the ratios given above, net reproduction rates for these three areas were:

1880	Minden	1·6224
1881	Seine	0·7448
1881	Finisterre	1·0221

The next step is to derive net reproduction rates for the three areas with

[1] See in this connexion the discussion of a similar problem by D. V. Glass, 'Changes in Fertility in England and Wales, 1851 to 1931', in *Political Arithmetic*, ed. L. Hogben (London, 1938), esp. pp. 161–5.

births distributed in ways designed to test the degree of possible distortion. One of the most extreme historical divergences in the distribution of live births of which there is record is that between Sweden in 1871–5 and Bulgaria in 1921–6.[1] Births were distributed in the following manner between the six age-groups.

Sweden 1871–5   19 : 145 : 250 : 264 : 203 : 119
Bulgaria 1921–6   50 : 300 : 275 : 177 : 125 : 73

It is now possible to compare three net reproduction rates for each of the three areas: (*a*) the rate on the assumptions given above, (*b*) the rate with births distributed as in Sweden in 1871–5, and (*c*) the rate with births distributed as in Bulgaria in 1921–6.

1880	(*a*) 1·6224	1881	(*a*) 0·7448	1881	(*a*) 1·0221
Minden	(*b*) 1·6521	Seine	(*b*) 0·7540	Finisterre	(*b*) 1·0391
	(*c*) 1·5753		(*c*) 0·7390		(*c*) 1·0002

The following table illustrates the percentage differences on the several assumptions.

A is the percentage by which (*b*) is greater than (*c*)
B is the percentage by which (*b*) is greater than (*a*)
C is the percentage by which (*c*) is less than (*a*)

Minden:	A is 4·88%	Seine:	A is 2·03%	Finisterre:	A is 3·89%
	B is 1·83%		B is 1·24%		B is 1·66%
	C is 2·90%		C is 0·78%		C is 2·14%

The maximum variation is found in Minden, but is less than 5 per cent. This, however, is between the two extreme assumptions. The maximum deviation from the rate derived from the general assumptions about France and Prussia, also in Minden, is less than 3 per cent. It is most unlikely that any deviation as large as this has in fact occurred in calculating net reproduction rates for the French and Prussian areas, and it seems reasonable, therefore, to use them for comparison of regional variations in net reproduction rates.

The net reproduction rate in France as a whole was remarkably steady over the forty-year period, standing at unity or very near to it. Falls in fertility and improvements in mortality broadly counter-balanced one another in generation replacement. In Prussia, on the other hand, the rate rose slowly between 1861 and 1900 from about 1·45 to about 1·55; but in spite of the tremendous improvement in mortality in the last decade before the war, fertility was falling still faster, so that during the decade between

---

[1] See Kuczynski, *The Measurement of Population Growth*, pp. 243–4.

Table 45. *Female Net Reproduction Rates*

	PRUSSIA					FRANCE		
	1861[1]	1880	1900	1910		1861	1881	1901
East Prussia	1·53	1·53	1·62	1·67	Bouches-du-			
Pomerania	1·58	1·65	1·74	1·47	Rhône	1·03	0·75	0·83
Berlin	1·03	0·96	0·85	0·79	Seine	0·76	0·74	0·71
Hannover	—	1·50	1·58	1·44	Finisterre	1·12	1·02	1·45
Minden	1·35	1·62	1·76	1·58	Aisne	1·06	1·14	1·13
Münster	1·14	1·43	1·87	1·99	Somme	0·94	0·99	1·04
Arnsberg	1·54	1·82	2·07	1·90	Nord	1·26	1·34	1·16
Düsseldorf	1·49	1·62	1·72	1·50	Pas-de-Calais	1·25	1·36	1·48
Aachen	1·29	1·44	1·65	1·50	FRANCE	0·99	1·05	0·99
PRUSSIA	1·44	1·51	1·56	1·45				

1900 and 1910 the net reproduction rate fell sharply back to the level of 1861.

In both countries net reproduction rates tended to be higher in the industrial areas than anywhere else. Rates were sometimes extremely high, Arnsberg just exceeding two at one date.[2] Rates rose up to the turn of the century because fertility was roughly constant while mortality fell steadily, especially in the age-groups which are most influential in the calculation of a net reproduction rate. In Aachen the influence of religious adherence shows as strongly in the net reproduction rates as in those of general fertility. Münster in 1861 and 1880 also showed the influence of Catholic marriage patterns, and its net reproduction rate was much lower than that of Minden as a result. Later the influx of coal miners and the rapid alteration of sex-ratios, and hence of marriage patterns, led to a very rapid rise in the reproduction rate, until in 1910 it was higher here than in any other Prussian area. The same type of economic development and consequent change in sex-ratios is reflected also in the net reproduction rates in Pas-de-

[1] Prussian women are grouped decennially above the age of twenty in the 1861 census. For this table each ten-year group has been divided into five-year groups in the ratios which existed at the time of the 1880 census.

[2] A more serious objection to these net reproduction rates than those considered above is that they are very sensitive to sex-ratios. Marital fertility and mortality might be the same in two areas with quite different net reproduction rates because many more women were married in the one area than the other due to a great male surplus in the marriageable age-groups. Male net reproduction rates might show quite a different picture. They would be relatively lower than the female rates in the coal-mining and heavy industrial areas, but relatively higher in the textile areas. This should be borne in mind in considering the female rates for Arnsberg, and for Münster and Pas-de-Calais in the later decades.

The same reservations are necessary about accepting the female net reproduction rates in other areas where the sex-ratios were unusual.

Calais whose economic history was very similar to that of Münster, although the changes occurred a little earlier in time.

There was greater uniformity in the net reproduction rates of the agricultural areas within each country than in either mortality or fertility rates, which often showed wide variations, because differences in mortality and fertility tended to cancel each other out in the net reproduction rates. Rates were rising gently up to 1900 in all the Prussian agricultural areas, East Prussia, Pomerania, Hannover and Minden, and were usually slightly above the national average. It is interesting to note that net reproduction rates in Pomerania were higher than in East Prussia in spite of the higher general fertility of the latter, an evidence of the better mortality position in Pomerania. Hannover and Minden combined fertility and mortality in such a way as to produce rather similar net reproduction rates, though Minden's rate was the higher. Rates in all three French agricultural departments were similar except in 1901 because Finisterre's crippling mortality concealed her very high fertility. Mortality in Aisne and Somme, by contrast, was so good and improved so much that rates rose slightly during the period and finished above unity in both areas in spite of the very low fertility of these two departments.

The net reproduction rates in the great cities were low, as was to be expected in view of their high mortality and low fertility. In 1861 the population of Paris was far from replacing itself, while Berlin and Marseilles were barely doing so. Thereafter rates fell steeply in both Berlin and Marseilles to approach the very low Parisian level. Paris remained lower than either, but experienced very little further decline after 1861 because mortality was improving as rapidly as fertility fell.

The types of area at the extremes of the range of net reproduction rates were the two types of rapidly growing urban area; the great commercial and administrative cities on the one hand, and the large coalfield industrial areas on the other. The population of Berlin rose from 548,000 in 1861 to 2,071,000 in 1910: that of Hamburg from 267,000 to 1,015,000. Over the same period the population of the Ruhr industrial area rose from 1,348,000 to 5,448,000: for Aachen the figures were 199,000 and 410,000.[1] In France the population of Seine rose from 1,954,000 in 1861 to 4,090,000 in 1911; that of Bouches-du-Rhône from 262,000 to 808,000: while the increase in the industrial areas of Nord and Pas-de-Calais was from 1,052,000 to

[1] These figures are intended as a rough guide only: they are not an accurate measure of the rise in urban or industrial population in the four areas. The population of the city area of Berlin, for example, ceased to grow about 1900 because new additions to the population went to live in suburbs which for census purposes counted as part of Brandenburg province. The difficulties involved in measuring such populations precisely are discussed above in Chapter V.

1,902,000. In both countries the increase of population in the great cities and the coalfield industrial areas formed a very substantial fraction of the total increase taking place during the half-century. Increase of population was very rapid in both types of area, but the sources of the upsurge were largely internal in the one case, external in the other. The net reproduction rates emphasize how very different the demography of the industrial areas was from that of the great cities. An isolated population with the demography of Berlin during this period would fall to less than four-fifths of its original level over the course of two generations: an isolated population with Arnsberg's demography would increase to more than three times the original over the same period.[1] A similar comparison of Seine and Nord would give populations of about 55 and 150 per cent of the original.

A comparison of the natural increase of population with the total increase in each area confirms what the net reproduction rates suggest: that most of the population increase in the coalfield industrial areas was from

Table 46. *Gross Increase and Total Natural Increase of Population* (*in* '000s)

	(a) gross increase				(b) total natural increase			
	PRUSSIA							
	Rheinland		Westphalia		Berlin		Hamburg	
	(a)	(b)	(a)	(b)	(a)	(b)	(a)	(b)
1861–70	391	387	168	178	268	52	70	22
1871–80	495	504	268	261	296	103	115	43
1881–90	636	606	386	348	457	139	169	56
1891–1900	1,051	853	759	547	310	166	145	90
1901–10	1,361	1,153	938	810	182*	164	247	91

	FRANCE							
	Nord		Pas-de-Calais		Seine		Bouches-du Rhône	
	(a)	(b)	(a)	(b)	(a)	(b)	(a)	(b)
1861–70	145	124	37	48	266	9	48	2
1871–80	155	139	58	57	599	72	34	0
1881–90	133	146	51	68	315	46	44	−14
1891–1900	131	138	85	87	456	49	101	−4
1901–10	95	125	113	109	484	30	72	−4

* Main city growth increasingly outside city boundaries.

[1] This assumes an appropriate age-structure in the population, which, however, did not exist in the actual populations of Berlin and Arnsberg in 1861, and would only have been attained over a number of generations if their actual populations had been isolated.

local natural increase, whereas most of the increase in the great cities came from immigration. It is true that the figures of natural increase for the industrial departments and provinces are unsatisfactory because they include considerable non-industrial populations. Some of the natural increase occurred in the non-industrial populations and could be transferred to the industrial areas by short-distance migration while still appearing in the table as local natural increase. Yet industrial population was such a large fraction of the whole in these areas that most of the natural increase must have occurred within the industrial population itself. The differences between the two types of area are much too striking to be explained away as products of the idiosyncrasies of national census accounting.

In this connexion it is useful to point to the danger in accepting at its face value some of the information printed by the census in tables dividing present population into those born inside the census unit and those coming from outside. It is dangerous to assume that because there are large numbers born outside a given area the population has grown only because of immigration. Often there is as great or nearly as great a movement outwards: in this case a large proportion recorded by the census as born outside the census unit simply reflects the greater propensity to migrate which often exists in areas of rapid change and growth. Moreover, whereas the existence within an industrial area of a high percentage of people born outside their area of present residence is often taken as evidence of the importance of immigration to the growth of population in that area, the fact that equally high percentages may be found in rural areas with stationary populations is sometimes overlooked. In 1881 in Nord, for example, 63·7 per cent of the total population was born in its *commune* of present residence. This was higher than the national average (60·7 per cent); and well above the figures in Aisne (57·9 per cent), though Nord was in the middle of a period of rapid industrial growth with a rising population, while the population of Aisne was stationary. A different picture is obtained if the percentages of population born inside the department are taken. These are 82·5: 86·7: and 82·9 per cent respectively for Nord, Aisne and France; and it now appears that Nord owes more than either Aisne or France as a whole to immigrants from outside its borders. The very fact that the two sets of percentages suggest opposite conclusions is an indication of the frailty of arguments based upon this type of census material unsupported by other data. The probable explanation of the discrepancies is quite simple. A high proportion of the population of Nord was concentrated in a small knot of textile towns near Lille which are close to the border of the department. Assuming a uniform pattern of short-range population movements in both Aisne and Nord, a much

Table 47. *Migration (in 'ooos)*

PRUSSIA 1900   A Total population   B Birth population
C Of B those still resident
D Immigration   E Emigration

		A	B	C	D	E
Berlin	0–16	516	516	418	98	98
	16–30	568	286	199	370	87
	30–50	547	174	109	437	64
	50–70	221	61	39	181	22
	70+	37	11	7	29	4
	TOTAL	1,889	1,048	773	1,116	275
Hamburg	0–16	250	242	212	37	30
	16–30	201	121	93	108	29
	30–50	212	75	59	153	17
	50–70	89	36	30	60	6
	70+	16	8	7	10	2
	TOTAL	768	483	400	369	83
Westphalia	0–16	1,298	1,241	1,189	109	52
	16–30	821	702	585	236	117
	30–50	697	583	487	210	97
	50–70	315	294	252	63	42
	70+	57	56	49	8	7
	TOTAL	3,188	2,877	2,562	625	315
Rheinland	0–16	2,183	2,132	2,072	111	60
	16–30	1,479	1,318	1,190	290	128
	30–50	1,320	1,174	1,066	254	108
	50–70	653	605	563	90	42
	70+	125	117	111	14	6
	TOTAL	5,760	5,346	5,001	758	344
Hannover	0–16	958	954	901	56	52
	16–30	619	613	487	133	126
	30–50	603	601	479	124	122
	50–70	333	341	287	45	54
	70+	78	81	71	7	10
	TOTAL	2,591	2,591	2,226	365	365

Figures rounded to nearest thousand: hence the totals sometimes appear slightly inexact.

M

higher proportion of these will appear as cross-boundary movements in Nord than in Aisne because the population is evenly spread in the latter but very eccentrically distributed in the former. This means that the statistics of population born outside the department will suggest more immigration into Nord than Aisne, but the statistics of population born outside the *commune* of residence will bear no trace of this. As it happens the Nord border near Lille is also the national frontier so that a high percentage of those born outside the department are Belgian by birth, not Frenchmen from other departments. The high proportion of Belgians in the Nord population has long been remarked, but it appears unnecessary to invoke exceptional circumstances in Nord to explain their presence, since when added to all others born outside the department they form a percentage of the total Nord population little greater than the comparable figure in Aisne (17·5 and 13·3 per cent respectively). Moreover, the difference between these two figures seems explicable on the ground of the eccentricity of the population distribution in Nord.

A further illustration of the same point comes from the imperial German census of 1900. In that year the census published a table showing present population, birth population (i.e. the people born in a given area but living anywhere in Germany), the number of the birth population still living in the area, immigration and emigration. The populations were divided into several broad age categories (Table 47). Unfortunately the same analysis was not made of the *Regierungs-bezirke* inside each province, and this makes impossible any precise picture of the position in the purely industrial areas, yet the extent of the contrast between the coalfield industrial areas and the great cities is apparent; and the danger of equating the presence of immigrants with an insufficiency in local natural population increase again emphasized. The table makes it clear by how wide a margin the birth population of the great cities fell short of the present population: the great bulk of the adult population was and had to be an immigrant population. In Rheinland and Westphalia, on the other hand, the birth population was not greatly smaller than the present population in any age-group. Moreover, Tables 46 and 48 show that it was not until the 1890s that birth population began to fall short of present population: before then the net movement of population was very small. Even after 1890 the bulk of the total increase of population was covered by local natural increase. Any large percentage of immigrants in the population is a result of social habit, of a high propensity to migrate, rather than an evidence of the insufficiency of local increase. A final illustration of the importance of the propensity to migrate in determining census residence figures may be drawn from Table 47. The significant pair in this context are Rheinland

Table 48. *Net Exchange of Populations (in '000s)*

	Berlin		Hamburg		Westphalia		Rheinland		Hannover	
	1890	1900	1890	1900	1890	1900	1890	1900	1890	1900
East Prussia	69	88	8	12	36	99	28	63	12	18
West Prussia	55	69	5	6	14	30	9	20	4	6
Berlin	—	—	1	neg.	6	6	9	9	8	9
Brandenburg	203	150	9	10	neg.	neg.	2	1	2	neg.
Pomerania	96	111	8	10	2	5	neg.	7	5	7
Posen	73	91	3	4	13	52	6	26	8	13
Silesia	116	128	7	9	19	40	13	25	7	11
Saxony	69	69	11	14	7	18	10	21	17	28
Schleswig-Holstein	3	3	*77*	*77*	*1*	*1*	*1*	*1*	*11*	*12*
Hannover	8	9	39	37	1	11	5	12	—	—
Westphalia	6	6	2	2	—	—	46	61	1	11
Hessen-Nassau	4	5	3	3	33	43	27	36	6	7
Rheinland	9	9	3	3	*46*	*61*	—	—	5	12
Hohenzollern	neg.	neg.	neg.	neg.	neg.	neg.	1	1	neg.	neg.
PRUSSIA	712	738	175	187	70	230	140	265	36	46
GERMANY	762	801	247	267	79	260	139	292	*34*	20

Figures in italics represent net losses.

and Hannover. In the former the birth population in the two age-groups 16–30 and 30–50 was only 89 per cent of the present population, whereas in Hannover the birth and present populations were almost identical. Yet the proportion of the population born and still resident in Hannover in the two age-groups was smaller than in Rheinland, a paradoxical situation, and one which shows again the danger of using material of this type to corroborate an argument about the importance of immigration to population growth in the coalfield industrial areas.

Many nineteenth-century writers considered that the most fundamental of all the possible demographic divisions of a population was that between the urban and the rural: and some writers of the past fifty years have shared this view. Discussions of both mortality and fertility commonly assumed that the differences between urban and rural populations were great and that other differences were smaller. The implicit assumption was that the demographic extremes were to be found in the deeply rural areas and the largest of the cities. The demographic characteristics of other areas were to be found somewhere in between these two. It was further commonly assumed that mortality was highest in the cities and fertility greatest in the countryside. The draining away of healthy, vital population from the country into the city therefore caused great concern, both because of its effect on the physical and moral health of the individual and because it destroyed old values and loyalties, encouraged political unrest, and impaired the soldierly virtues associated with a peasant life. Assumptions of this sort not only coloured the literature of the day, but are reflected in the way in which census information was treated by the bureaux of census. The French census, for example, made great play with the division of the population into rural and urban halves. Many of the main census tables contain a breakdown into rural and urban population, making possible an analysis of the returns in these terms as well as by age, sex, department, etc. Similarly the annual vital statistics are divided into rural and urban births and deaths, as well as in the other standard ways. It even happened occasionally that a man intent upon the primacy of the rural-urban division would present evidence which cast doubt upon the validity of his contention without appearing to grasp its significance. An example of this is the long article of Nicolai.[1] As the title suggests Nicolai was concerned at the declining proportion of Belgians living in the countryside. He vigorously denounced the vices of urban life, 'la débauche dorée qui y pavane son luxe arrogant',[2] and the bad sanitary conditions which prevailed there. Yet, in his anxiety to give precise statistical illustration to his fears, he paradoxically threw doubt upon his whole argument. He divided all Belgian *communes* into three types: urban, industrial and rural. The first class included all *communes* with a population of 20,000 or more and all *chefs-lieux d'arrondissement*; the second and third were divided from one another by occupation: the former being all *communes* in which a majority of the work force was industrial, the latter including all others. For these three groups he calculated crude birth- and death-rates in each *arrondissement*. The crude rates are, of course, likely to be misleading, but in so far as they can be trusted they show that the industrial *communes* in the coalfield industrial areas were perhaps the most distinctive group, with higher birth-rates than the other two in most areas, and low death-rates.[3] This is imperfect evidence: but it is clearly against the contemporary view of the normal situation.

A regional treatment of material and the use of more refined demographic techniques suggests a very different picture. The contrast between rural areas, for example, can be shown to be as great as their similarities,

[1] E. Nicolai, 'La dépopulation des campagnes', *Bulletin de la Commission Centrale de Statistique*, tome XXI, vol. I (Brussels, 1921), pp. 1–160.

[2] Nicolai, *Bull. de la Comm. Cent. de Stat.*, p. 97.

[3] For example, in 1891–1900 in *arr.* Charleroi crude birth-rates in urban, industrial and rural *communes* were 25·71: 26·17: and 21·34 respectively. Death-rates were 17·13: 15·61: and 16·06. In Liège the figures were 25·20: 29·32: 23·93 and 18·89: 17·25: and 16·17 (Nicolai, *Bull. de la Comm. Cent. de Stat.*, pp. 57–9, 61–3 and 68–70).

so that no generalization about their fertility or mortality can be more than a very rough guide. In France the contrast in fertility, mortality and marriage patterns between Aisne and Finisterre was probably greater than the contrast between any two great cities, or even between the great cities and the industrial areas; and as great possibly as the differences between the great cities and the countryside. In Prussia also there were wide differences between different rural areas. Marital fertility and mortality were substantially different in Hannover and East Prussia, for example: while the Protestant areas as a group differed so markedly from the Catholic in the proportions married in the younger age-groups that there were marked differences between them in general fertility, even though marital fertility was almost uniform. And if it was true that there was no uniformity of demographic experience in rural areas, it was true equally in the urban areas. The great administrative and trading cities were typically places of low fertility and high mortality, whereas the coalfield industrial areas experienced high marital and general fertility rates, and a much more moderate mortality than the great cities.

Regional analysis emphasizes certain characteristic national differences between France and Prussia. Marital fertility in Prussia varied little in the early decades (except in the great cities) so that any large differences in general fertility are connected with age of marriage, and this in turn above all with religion, but also with sex-ratios and possibly occupational structure. In France, on the other hand, there were from the start of the period very wide variations in marital fertility (the mean deviation in marital fertility rates did not greatly change during the half-century). As a result the age and universality of marriage was not of such importance in governing general fertility as in Prussia (for example, marriage came early and generally in Aisne for both sexes, but general fertility was low; a phenomenon unknown in Prussia at that period). While there were national differences, however, there were also regional similarities. The coalfield industrial areas on both sides of the border, for example, were areas of high marital fertility; and within them sex-ratios were similar in areas of comparable occupational structure. As a group the coalfield industrial areas in both countries form a strong contrast with the great cities, and so on.

Since population forms so large a part of the general economic history of the nineteenth century, it is unfortunate that it is so commonly discussed only globally for each country as a whole. Economic histories which reach great heights of sophistication in their treatment of other aspects of economic growth, such as interest rates, banking practice, technical innovation, structural adjustment between industries, home and overseas investment and so on, are often forced to dismiss the question of population rather summarily, even when its importance is recognized, because only the national situation as a whole is known. The only aspects of population history which appear to have received extensive detailed treatment, both historically and from a theoretical viewpoint, are internal and external migration. The fruitfulness of some of the studies which have been done on migration suggest that regional studies of demographic material of other types might also yield very interesting results. The tools which are now available for such work are so much better than those with which three generations ago Levasseur was able to produce such remarkable results, that the opportunities seem very great, especially as some of the most common assertions about demographic history are among the most open to question. It is clear, for example, that the alleged close correlation between high infantile mortality rates and high death-rates at other ages is not true of France and Prussia in the nineteenth century. It seems doubtful whether there is any close connexion between reaching maximum earning power at an early age and early marriage; doubtful whether in textile areas there is any marked tendency for women to marry at a later age because of their financial independence; doubtful whether the conventional rural-urban division serves any useful purpose in studies of fertility and mortality at this period: clear, on the other hand, that in Prussia religious adherence made a profound difference to marriage habits, and, in the years before any widespread artificial limitation of births, to general fertility; clear also that the sex-ratio in most areas had a considerable effect on marriage patterns; probable that male marriage rates were relatively 'sticky', female rates more fluid; and so on. Some of the differences between France and Prussia emerge as truly national differences—for example the very great differences in the 'mortality gradient' in the middle years of life between twenty and sixty which seems to be characteristic of all French as opposed to all Prussian areas. Sometimes a regional analysis reveals differences which might otherwise not be expected—for example the mortality patterns in Paris and Berlin were strikingly different even though the crude death-rates and the expectation of life at birth were similar. On the other hand, some of the differences which appear important in national averages disappear when similar regions are compared—for example infantile mortality rates in all the coalfield industrial areas of the Austrasian field are rather similar to one another and their trends over the half-century show much greater resemblance to each other than to national trends. A better knowledge of regional demographic characteristics may suggest modifications to the accepted view of the relationship between demographic and economic or sociological circumstances.

The search for general causes of economic growth or of demographic trends, and for a framework which links them together is one which will, perhaps, never cease to attract historians and demographers; but it is a hazardous search. Great care is necessary where some attempt at causal explanation is made to select a cause which is appropriate to its result. In historical and social studies there is no built-in corrective to false selection such as frequently obtains in the physical sciences. The result of this is that categories of explanation which have once been shown to be appropriate tend to continue to be used when new interests develop. The existence of the state is the fundamental fact of political history and the national unit the natural one to work with. Familiarity with older forms of history and the convenience of the national unit for studies involving statistical treatment has overbalanced economic and demographic history toward the study of national development, and brought into favour explanations which depend upon national trends. These are sometimes appropriate; but not so frequently as is assumed. Regions within national areas or overlapping them are sometimes better units of study. Most of those who use statistics are well aware of the danger of producing causal rabbits out of correlation top-hats: most recognize, that is to say, that while the existence of a correlation may put out of court one explanation it cannot of itself establish another. An equally serious danger in marshalling statistical evidence—that of its nature it tends to deal with average conditions, and that these averages may conceal very wide variations within the universe in question—is less generally observed. This is the reason why preoccupation with national units is so liable to lead to unsatisfactory explanations, and here regional analysis is peculiarly helpful since it will, where it is possible, help to make clear how uniformly a feature which appears in a national average is common to the country as a whole and how far it is restricted to certain smaller areas. International comparisons of similar regions are equally important in supplying a corrective.

The main theme of this book has been the examination of some aspects of industrial growth and demographic history on the Austrasian coalfield in the light of these ideas. How far it is possible or desirable to apply them to other periods and places is a matter for argument. Most new cases begin by being over-stated: but if intellectual history is dialectical, perhaps this exaggeration may prove useful.

NOTE ON STATISTICAL SOURCES

Where the statistical material used in this book was taken directly either from a government publication or from a secondary source, its origin is usually given in a footnote in the text. Many of the tables, however, embody material taken either from several different government statistical publications, or else from corresponding sources in a number of publications within the same series. The following is a list by country of the main sources. Each is given a reference number to simplify the subsequent discussion of the sources used in each table in the text.

GERMANY

G 1 *Preussische Statistik*, Königlichen statistischen Bureau (Berlin)
    Population censuses: 1861 vol. v
                        1871   XXX
                        1880   LXVI
                        1890   121
                        1900   177
                        1910   234

G 2 *Statistisches Handbuch für den Preussischen Staat*, Königlichen statistischen Bureau (Berlin, 1888–1903)

G 3 *Statistisches Jahrbuch für den Preussischen Staat*, Königlich preussischen statistischen Landesamt (Berlin, 1903–)

G 4 *Statistik des Deutschen Reichs*, Kaiserlichen statistischen Amt (Berlin)
    Erste Reihe, I–LXIII (1873–83)
    Neue Folge, 1–149 (1884–1903)
    without prefix, 150– (1903–)
    Population censuses: 1871 E.R. II and XIV
                        1880 E.R. LVII
                        1890 N.F. 68
                        1900 150 and 151
                        1910 240
    Industrial and occupational censuses:

Gewerbezählung, 1875	E.R.	XXXIV and XXXV
Berufs– und Gewerbezählung, 1882	N.F.	2–7
Berufs– und Gewerbezählung, 1895	N.F.	102–19
Berufs– und Betriebszählung, 1907		202–22

G 5 *Statistisches Jahrbuch für das Deutsche Reich*, Kaiserlichen statistischen Amt (Berlin, 1880–)

G 6 *Monatshefte zur Statistik des Deutschen Reichs*, Kaiserlichen statistischen Amt (Berlin, 1884–91), continued as: *Vierteljahrshefte zur Statistik des Deutschen Reichs*, Kaiserlichen statistischen Amt (Berlin, 1892–)

FRANCE

F 1 *Dénombrement de la Population,* Ministère de l'Intérieur (Paris) (published in each census year: see F 2 and F 3)

F 2 *Statistique de la France* (Paris)
Deuxième série, I–XXI
Nouvelle série, 1871–   (Statistique Annuelle)
Population censuses: 1851   D.S.   I and II
                      1861   D.S.   XIII
                      1872   D.S.   XXI
Industrial censuses:
Industrie, 1847 (4 vols.)
Enquête industrielle de 1861–5   D.S.   XIX

F 3 *Résultats statistiques du Recensement Général de la Population,* Ministère du Commerce, de l'Industrie, des Postes et des Télégraphes (Paris) 1881, 1891, 1901, 1911 (title varies slightly)

F 4 *Statistique de l'Industrie Minérale,* Ministère des Travaux Publics (Paris)

F 5 *Annuaire Statistique de la France,* Ministère du Commerce, de l'Industrie, et des Colonies (Paris, 1878–   )

BELGIUM

B 1 *Annuaire Statistique de la Belgique,* Ministère de l'Intérieur (Brussels)

B 2 *Exposé de la Situation du Royaume,* Ministère de l'Intérieur (Brussels)

B 3 *Population: Recensement Général,* Ministère de l'Intérieur (Brussels). 1846, 1856, 1866, 1876, 1880, 1890, 1900, 1910

B 4 *Annales des mines de Belgique,* Ministère de l'Industrie et du Travail (Brussels)

B 5 *Industrie: Recensement Général* (1846), Ministère de l' Intérieur (Brussels)
Industrie: Recensement de 1880, Ministère de l'Intérieur et de l'Instruction Publique (Brussels, 1887)
Recensement Général des Industries et des Métiers (1896), Ministère de l' Industrie et du Travail (Brussels)
Recensement de l'Industrie et du Commerce (1910), Ministère de l'Industrie et du Travail (Brussels)

Table 1
Belgian figures: B 2, 1851–60, vol. III, p. 83
French figures: E. Vuillemin, *Le bassin houiller du Pas-de-Calais* (Lille, 1880), vol. III, p. 343
German figures:
Aachen: Benaerts, *Les Origines de la grande industrie allemande,* p. 416
Ruhr: Baumont, *La Grosse industrie allemande et le charbon,* p. 49
Table 2
Calculated from: F 3, 1911, vol. I, pt. I, tab. I,
    Population par département aux divers recensements: accroissements ou diminutions de la population de 1801 à 1911

Table 3

Calculated from: G 4, E.R. xxxvii (July), Ubersicht 1,
> *Bevölkerung der Deutschen Staaten und ihrer grösseren Verwaltungsbezirke in der Begrenzung zur Zeit der jedesmaligen Volkszählung seit 1816*
> E.R. lvii (1880 census)

Table 4

Calculated from:

Belgian figures: B 2
> 1851–60
> 1861–75
> 1876–1900

French figures: F 4, *Tableau de la production des combustibles minéraux par département*

German figures: *Die Produktion der Bergwerke, Salinen und Hütten im Deutschen Reich und in Luxembourg*
> G 4 1871 (ii 2), 1872 (viii 3), 1873 (xiv 2), 1874 (xx 2), 1875 (xxv 2), 1876 (xxx 2), 1877 (xxx 10), 1878 (xxxvii 10), 1879 (xlii 10), 1880 (xlviii 10), 1881 (liii 10), 1882 (lxix 10)
> G 6 1883–90 (1884 x–1891 x)
> 1891–1911 (1892 iv–1912 iv)

Table 5

See Table 1 and Table 4 above

Table 6

See Table 1 and Table 4 above

Table 7

Calculated from Table 6

Table 8

Belgian figures: Calculated from B 1
French figures: See Table 4 above
German figures: See Table 4 above

Table 9

Source dealt with in text

Table 10

Source dealt with in text

Table 11

Source dealt with in text

Table 12

Source dealt with in text

Table 13

See list of censuses under G 1 and G 4

Table 14

See list of censuses under B 3

Table 15
   See F 1

Table 16
   See list of censuses under F 2 and F 3

Table 17
   See Tables 6, 13, 14 and 16 above

Table 18
   Calculated from Table 17

Table 19
   See below Table 21

Table 20
   See below Table 22

Table 21
   Calculated from G 4, N.F. 117, *Gewerbliche Betriebsstatistik der kleineren
   Verwaltungsbezirke*
        218, *Die gewerblichen Betriebe der kleineren Verwaltungsbezirke*

Table 22
   Calculated from:
        B 3, 1890, vol II, pt. 2, sect. 2, *Répartition des habitants d'après les profes-
        sions, fonctions et positions*
           1900, vol. II, pt. 7, sect. B, *Répartition des habitants d'après les professions,
           fonctions et positions*
           1910, vol V, pt. 11, sect. D, *Recensement des professions*

Table 23
   Vital statistics:
        F 2   D.S. XI, *Mouvement de la population* (1858–60)
               D.S. XVIII, *Mouvement de la population* (1861–5)
               N.S. *Statistique Annuelle: mouvement de la population* (1879–82 and
                     1899–1902)
        G 1 vol. V (1859–61), X (1862–4), 11 (1878), LVI (1879), LXI (1880),
               LXVIII (1881), *Bewegung der Bevölkerung;* 160 (1898), 164 (1899),
               169 (1900), 178 (1901), 220 (1908), 224 (1909), 229 (1910), 233
               (1911), *Die Geburten, Eheschliessungen und Sterbefälle*
   Census material:
        F 2   1861, tab. 16, *Population par état civil suivant les âges*
        F 4   1881, tab. 5, *Population par âge et par état civil*
               1901, tab. VII, *Population présente totale suivant le sexe, l'état de famille
               et l'âge, par départment*
        G 1   1861, I. A. 2, *Alter und Geschlecht*
               1910, A. IX, *Die ortsanwesende Bevölkerung nach Alter, Geschlecht und
               Familienstand*

G 4 1880, pt. 2. B, Ubersicht VIII, *Die ortsanwesende Bevölkerung nach*
Geschlecht und Familienstand in fünfjährigen Altersklassen
1900, tab. VII, *Alter und Familienstand der Bevölkerung*

Table 24
See Table 23 above

Table 25
See Table 23 above

Table 26
See Table 23 above

Table 27
Calculated from Table 23 above

Table 28
Calculated from Table 23 above

Table 29
See Table 23 above for the vital statistics used in calculating this Table. Births
1872–3 and 1890–2 are also from relevant years of F 2 N.S. *Statistique*
Annuelle: mouvement de la population (résultats par arrondissement)
For *arrondissement* population totals see list of censuses under F 2 and F 3

Table 30
See Table 23 and Table 29 above

Table 31
Calculated from G 6, 1899, I, *Die Geburtenhäufigkeit im Deutschen Reich nach*
kleineren Verwaltungsbezirken im Durchshnitt 1894–6
1901, I, tab. VI, *Sterblichkeit und Geburten-Ueberschuss in den Jahren* 1894
bis 1896

Table 32
Calculated from Table 24 above

Table 33
Calculated from Table 23 above

Table 34
See Table 23 above for vital statistics. In addition:
F 2 D.S. II and III, *Mouvement de la population*
G I vol. XIX, *Die Geburten, Trauungen und Sterbefälle*
See Table 23 above also for census material. In addition:
F 2 1851, tab. 41, *Population suivant les âges par départements*
G 4 1871, A. III, *Die ortsanwesende Bevölkerung nach Geschlecht, zehnjährigen*
Geburtszeiten und Familienstand

Table 35
Calculated from Table 34 above

Table 36
> See Table 29 above

Table 37
> See Table 31 above

Table 38
> F 2   N.S., xxxi, 1901, pp. cxxii–cxxiii, *Rapport du nombre des naissances au chiffre de la population—de 1801–1900*

Table 39
> See Table 34 above

Table 40
> See Table 23 above

Table 41
> Calculated from Table 34 and 39 above

Table 42
> See Table 23 above

Table 43
> G 4   1880, E.R. lvii, D, Ubersicht x, *Die ortsanwesende Bevölkerung nach dem Religionsbekenntniss,* and 1900, vol. 150, p. 109*, *Die evangelische und römisch-katholische Bevölkerung in den kleineren Verwaltungsbezirken*

Table 44
> Calculated from Table 40

Table 45
> Years lived in child-bearing age-groups calculated from Table 26. Fertility data same as those used in Table 39

Table 46
> See Table 23 above for vital statistics material. For census population totals see G 1, G 4, F 2, and F 3

Table 47
> G 4   1900, vol. 150, tab. 47, p. 165*, *Gerbürtigkeit und Altersgliederung*

Table 48
> G 4   N.F. 68, p. 67*, *Gewinn oder Verlust der einzelnen deutschen Staaten beim Austausch ihrer Geburtsbevölkerung mit der Geburtsbevölkerung anderer Bundesstaaten,* and vol. 150, p. 145*, *Gewinn oder Verlust der einzelnen Bundesstaaten beim Austausch ihrer Geburtsbevölkerung mit der Geburtsbevölkerung anderer Bundesstaaten*

INDEX

Aachen
  Belgian influence in, 18–19, 26, 27, 92
  brass industry in, 27
  chemical industry in, 71
  coal: industry in, 63; industry, pro-
    ductivity in, 38, 39, 40, 43; prices
    in, 44, 49; production in, 12, 26, 41,
    42, 43, 70–2
  coalfield, geology of, 31, 32, 33, 35, 37
  coke-fired blast furnaces at, 19
  connections with Liège, 19, 27
  copper industry in, 27
  engineering industry in, 71
  expectation of life in, 100
  fertility: general, 122–3, 136, 140, 141,
    145–51; marital, 133, 134–6, 140
  French occupation of, 18–19, 26–7,
    27
  glass industry in, 63
  industrial development in, 25–8
  industrial employment in, 80–4
  iron production in, 12, 63, 71
  lead industry in, 27
  marriage patterns, 145, 148, 149, 150
  mortality, 101, 105, 109, 112–14, 119–
    20, 122–3, 129
  net reproduction rates, 161
  population of, 26; growth in 25, 64,
    70
  putative industrial population of, 70,
    72, 77 n., 78–9, 80, 81
  religious adherence of, 148–50
  Ruhr: competition with, 48–9, 54;
    lead over, 18–20, 26, 27–8; rail link
    to, 29; relation to, 54
  sex-ratios, 145, 147, 148, 150
  steam: drainage in, 27; power in, 12
  textile industry in, 27, 71, 75
  unit population/coal ratios, 70, 71, 72,
    75, 82, 83–4
  woollen industry in, 63
  see also Coal; Fertility; Mortality;
    Rheinland
Aachener Walz- und Hammerwerk, 19
Age-specific: fertility, 158, 159; mortality, see Mortality
Agricultural populations
  and fertility, 134–6, 136–7, 138–9, 140,
    145–57 passim

and mortality, 117–23 passim, 125,
  130, 131
and net reproduction rates, 162
slow growth in, 60–1, 67–8
Aisne
  coal prices in, 49, 50
  expectation of life in, 99, 128
  fertility: general, 121, 135, 136–7, 141,
    151–2; marital, 133, 136–7, 139
  marriage patterns, 142, 151, 169
  migration in, 164, 166
  mortality, 101, 102, 106, 117–19, 120,
    121, 128, 129
  net reproduction rates, 161–2
  sex-ratios, 146
A. G. Altenberg, 19
A. G. für Bergbau, Blei- und Zinkfabrikation, 19
Alsace, cotton industry of, 22
Altena, coal consumption of, 29
Anthracitic coals, 33, 34, 35
Anzin
  canal built to, 48
  discovery of coal at, 17
  metal workers at, 23
Ardennes
  Belgian, iron industry in, 15–16
  coal prices in, 49, 50
  French and Belgian, iron ore in, 22
  geology of, 31
  iron industry of, 22
  Massif, 32
Ariès, P., 134 n.
Armentières
  population growth at, 10, 18
  successful linen industry of, 10, 18
Arnsberg
  coal: industry, productivity in, 38–9,
    43; prices in, 44; production in, 41,
    42, 43, 70–1, 73
  expectation of life in, 100, 128
  fertility: general, 122–3, 136, 141,
    145–51; marital, 133, 134–6, 137
  industrial employment in, 80–4
  iron and steel industry in, 74
  marriage patterns, 144, 146, 150
  mortality, 101, 105, 109, 114–17,
    119–20, 122–3
  net reproduction rates, 161

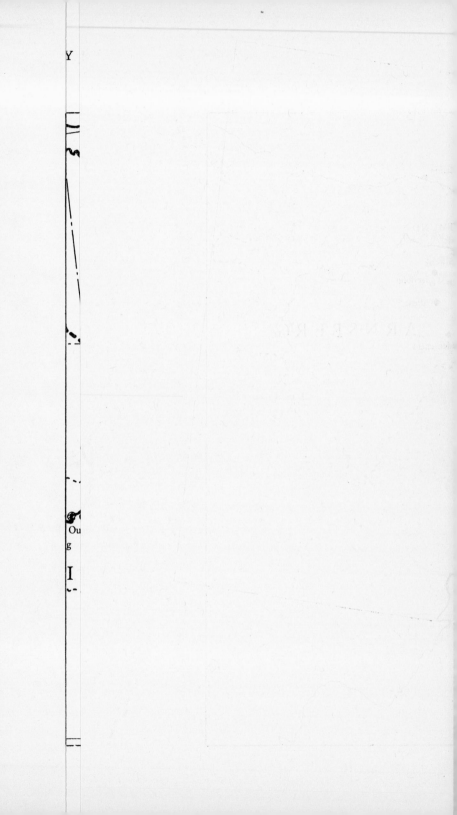

THE AUSTRASIAN FIELD: WESTERN WING

Administrative Divisions

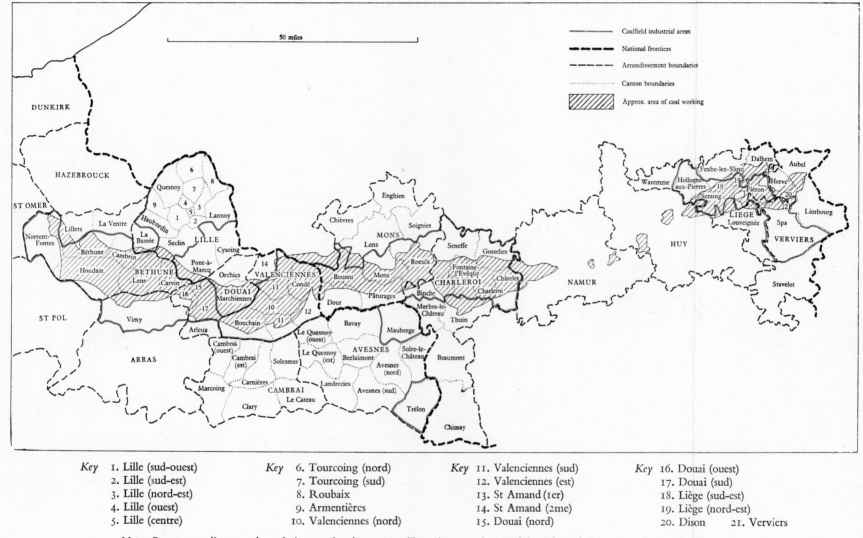

Legend:
- ———— Coalfield industrial areas
- – – – National frontiers
- – – – Arrondissement boundaries
- ········· Canton boundaries
- ░░░ Approx. area of coal working

50 miles

Key	*Key*	*Key*	*Key*
1. Lille (sud-ouest)	6. Tourcoing (nord)	11. Valenciennes (sud)	16. Douai (ouest)
2. Lille (sud-est)	7. Tourcoing (sud)	12. Valenciennes (est)	17. Douai (sud)
3. Lille (nord-est)	8. Roubaix	13. St Amand (1er)	18. Liège (sud-est)
4. Lille (ouest)	9. Armentières	14. St Amand (2me)	19. Liège (nord-est)
5. Lille (centre)	10. Valenciennes (nord)	15. Douai (nord)	20. Dison 21. Verviers

Note: Some arrondissement boundaries are also department (France) or province (Belgium) boundaries, as may be seen by comparison with the Key Map.

THE AUSTRASIAN FIELD: EASTERN WING

Administrative Divisions

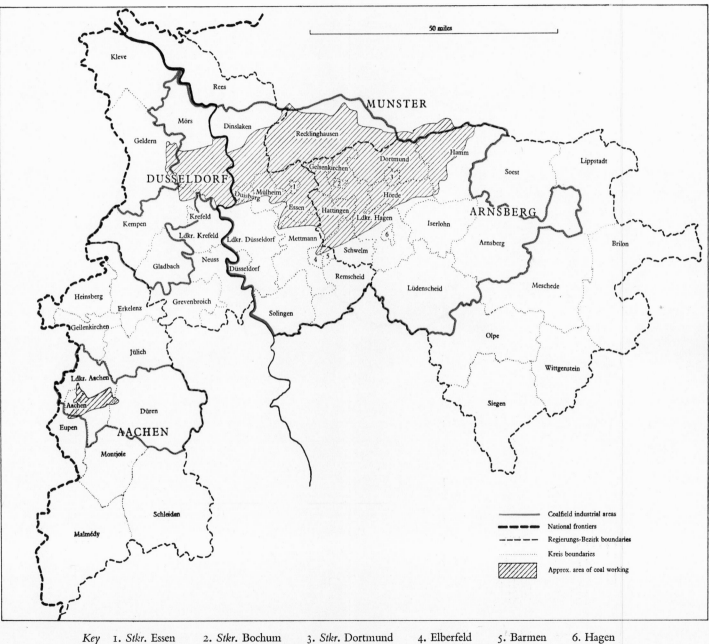

50 miles

Kleve

Rees

MUNSTER

Mörs

Dinslaken

Geldern

Recklinghausen

DUSSELDORF

Gelsenkirchen

Dortmund

Hamm

Soest

Lippstadt

Duisburg

Mülheim

1

2

Hörde

3

Krefeld

Essen

Hattingen

Ldkr. Hagen

ARNSBERG

Kempen

Ldkr. Krefeld

Ldkr. Düsseldorf

Mettmann

6

Iserlohn

Brilon

Gladbach

Neuss

4 5

Schwelm

Arnsberg

Düsseldorf

Remscheid

Meschede

Heinsberg

Grevenbroich

Lüdenscheid

Erkelenz

Solingen

Geilenkirchen

Olpe

Jülich

Wittgenstein

Ldkr. Aachen

Aachen

Düren

Eupen

AACHEN

Siegen

Montjoie

Schleiden

Malmédy

—————— Coalfield industrial areas

– – – – National frontiers

– – – Regierungs-Bezirk boundaries

·········· Kreis boundaries

/// Approx. area of coal working

Key   1. *Stkr.* Essen   2. *Stkr.* Bochum   3. *Stkr.* Dortmund   4. Elberfeld   5. Barmen   6. Hagen